Reflective Teaching: A Bridge to Learning

Selected Papers Presented at the Thirty-First
National LOEX Library Instruction Conference
held in Madison, Wisconsin
8 to 10 May 2003

edited by
Deb Biggs Thomas, Director
LOEX Clearinghouse
Halle Library
Eastern Michigan University

Rosina Tammany
Randal Baier
Eric Owen
Heidi Mercado
Halle Library
Eastern Michigan University

Published for the University Library
Eastern Michigan University
by
Pierian Press
Ann Arbor, Michigan
2004

ISBN 0-87650-370-9
Copyright ©2004, The Pierian Press
All Rights Reserved

The Pierian Press
Box 1808
Ann Arbor, Michigan 48106

LIBRARY ORIENTATION SERIES
(Emphasizing Information Literacy and Bibliographic Instruction)

*   Pierian Press's ISBN identifier is 0-87650. This identifier should precede the number given for a book (e.g., 0-87650-327-X).

Table of Contents

Articles

Breakout Sessions

PREFACE

Instruction librarians are incredibly busy people. Not only do we teach multiple classes each week but we are also responsible for other areas of professional library work such as collection development, reference and committee assignments. To be sure, we'd like to engage in self improvement of our teaching skills; what professional wouldn't? But given our daily schedule, who has the time?! And why is it important anyway?

The 31st National LOEX Conference initiated a wake-up call for instruction librarians to make time for that self-assessment of our teaching, "....to take a step back for a moment and reflect on the very essentials of instruction: teaching and learning."[1] Teaching is not and should not become a static enterprise; rather we bring aspects of ourselves as individuals into the process. When we take the time to understand and reflect on how we teach, we can only foster more effective learning for our students. In this regard, the conference explored such topics as support for improved teaching, professional growth as teachers, collaborative learning, teaching to different learning styles, the passionate teacher and other thematic areas.

Our keynote speakers, Betsy Baker and Elizabeth Burge, set the tone for the conference, each reflecting in her own way on the art and practice of reflection. Betsy Baker, a library consultant and educator, who has been an academic librarian for over twenty years at the University of Illinois and Northwestern University, urged taking that seemingly non-existent time for reflection. With reflection we can begin to ask ourselves about the true meaning and purpose of our work. This, Baker states, "informs our answers to questions of what we need to do and how we should do it."[2] Liz Burge is a professor in the Faculty of Education at the University of New Brunswick, Fredericton, Canada where she works in adult and distance education research. Burge, a former librarian, used a metaphor to help "examine some assumptions about our own and our clients' learning" as well as assumptions having to do with instruction librarians professional worth and practice vis-à-vis our students.[3]

The selected papers which follow the keynote addresses in these proceedings showcase individual presenters' strategies, programs, and ways to incorporate self-improvement and assessment in teaching and through reflection. Discovering and then implementing ways to "nurture" our teaching selves will ultimately result in our students becoming effective learners and instruction librarians more fulfilled professionals. That....is a bottom line proposition.

Deb Biggs Thomas
LOEX Director

1. Reflective Teaching: A Bridge to Learning, LOEX 2003, Madison, WI. *Program*. 2003. Internet on-line. < http://loex2003.wisc.edu/program. > [13 September 2003].

2. Reflective Teaching: A Bridge to Learning, LOEX 2003, Madison, WI. *Program: Betsy Baker, Keynote Speaker*. 2003. Internet on-line. < http://loex2003.wisc.edu/program/Betsy_Baker.html >. [15 September 2003].

3. Reflective Teaching: A Bridge to Learning, LOEX 2003, Madison, WI. *Program: Elizabeth Burge, Keynote Speaker*. 2003. Internet on-line. < http://loex 2003.wisc.edu/program/Liz_Burge.html >. [16 September 2003].

THE MUSE IN THE MIRROR:
REFLECTION IN PROFESSIONAL PRACTICE

Betsy Baker

Good morning. I am very happy to be here with you today and am so honored to have been asked to be your keynote speaker for this wonderful conference. Being here with you at LOEX feels a lot like coming home. LOEX has such a special place in my heart; it was the very first professional conference that I attended after I became a librarian and began working in the Reference Department at the University of Illinois (UI). I have fond memories of traveling across the Illinois/Michigan countryside (or should I say interstate?) with a carload of other new reference librarians—Betsy Wilson, David King, Dana Smith, and Kathleen Kluegel, and our department head, Maureen Pastine—heading for Ypsilanti, Michigan. (We were in a University car and UI cars were at that time notorious for being held together with duck tape and paper clips. That we made it at all is a wonder. At one point, I was actually holding the rear view mirror in place so that Maureen could make a turn; I think someone else was in charge of the horn.) We are all to this day, very close friends.

I think the conference may have been somewhat responsible for the fact that we did become such good friends. We certainly bonded during the days we spent in Ypsilanti—staying in the dorm, eating in the cafeteria, hearing Evan Farber speak, and driving to Ann Arbor for the night life. I know that the same kind of bonding experiences have happened and continue to happen to so many others at LOEX. This is because LOEX is such a special community and creates such special conferences. Its mission has been unwavering over the years—promoting, fostering, and furthering instruction in libraries. When people come

together because of their belief in and the desire to be part of such a worthy mission, it is not surprising that synergetic and long-lasting relationships develop.

The Need for Reflection

The LOEX conference planners have, year after year, designed stimulating and imaginative conferences. I was very gratified to be asked to speak at this conference, not only because of the place LOEX holds for me, but also because the theme of this year's conference, "Reflective Teaching: A Bridge to Learning", really speaks to me and what I find most energizing about professional practice: the processes of reflection, problem solving, and inquiry in the field. The value of reflection in our profession and in our work, what reflection means, and what it can produce are vital topics. I really applaud Abbie Loomis and Carrie Kruse of the University of Wisconsin, Madison and the other planners for shaping this year's conference around such a meaningful theme. And, I can't imagine a more fitting place to address this topic than in a conference center that has as one of its rooms a "Hall of Ideas."

When I look back at my work over the years, what I have found most gratifying and engaging has been work in which I have felt the latitude and support to carve out new areas, initiate new projects, reflect on old projects, and revise things according to new information, new knowledge, and new needs. It is this emphasis on being a problem solver and a thoughtful member of the profession that has been most rewarding to me and that I most want to impart to students and to the people I work with, supervise, or mentor. In fact, it is interesting to me that when Abbie first contacted me about this conference, the topic of reflection was

---

Baker is a library consultant and educator formerly with Northwestern University.

already much in the fore of what I was doing. I was teaching a reference/instruction class at Dominican University for which the only text I required my students to purchase was "The Reflective Practitioner" by Donald Schon. My reason for choosing this text, rather than something that introduced the nuts and bolts of reference sources and services, is that I was attracted to its message about how one *approaches* a profession and *grows* in it and *what* this message would offer my students. Our discussions of reference took place in the context of what it means to practice what Schon calls "reflection in action," and by the end of the class, the students told me that they could see why I had focused the course around this theme. They could see that reference librarianship, and perhaps, by extension, any other professional field, requires a wide-open view that reinforces reflective thinking, theory building, and creative problem solving. We are not well served by approaches that emphasize fixed ends, tools and techniques. We need reflective approaches. We need big-picture thinking. We need to gain insight and perspective. Reflection gives us that. It helps us focus on questions of meaning and purpose. Being reflective about our work involves engaging in a dialogue between what we think, what we believe in, and what we do. It is through reflection that we can come to a clearer sense of the values that underpin our work and of who we are as professionals.

Donald Schon, is a professor at MIT who has written several books about reflection in professional practice and has done much to develop the concept of reflective practice as a way of being a professional. He proposes reflective practice as a way of understanding what he calls *knowing-in-action* (trusting what your experience tells you, but also realizing that you are bringing a certain frame of reference or perspective to what you are doing), *reflecting-in-action* (the on-going dialogue between reflection and practice in our lives triggered by what might be thought of as "snags" in the otherwise smooth fabric of our knowing-in-action), and *professional practice* (how we carry what we know and who we are into our interactions with our colleagues and clients). In this way, he says, reflective practice is a way of being professional that looks much more like artistry than science.

Schon's message is that there are real benefits to be derived from taking the time to sort through questions of meaning and purpose: "What am *I* doing?" "Why am *I* doing it?" "How am *I* doing?" "How is *my* work being received by others?" in *all* aspects and in an almost second nature kind of way in our daily activities. In my experiences as a teacher and as a department head, I felt that this is precisely where I needed and wanted to spend a lot of my time.

I found that I couldn't be a good department head, committee chair, teacher, or leader of any kind without being reflective. I needed to probe, question, and explore issues. I needed to provide a framework that defined the purpose of my own work and the work of those I was leading.

I have always been drawn to writers, speakers, thinkers, and colleagues who have helped me find ways to better talk about issues of mission and purpose. For me, one of these is Neil Postman. While he is a well-known social critic, noted for his commentary on the effects of technology on institutions and individuals in society, I was first drawn to his writings when I read an article in the *Atlantic Monthly* in which he talked about the importance of stories. Stories, he said, are necessary to our understanding of our mission and purpose. "A story," he said, "provides a structure for our perceptions; only through stories do facts assume any meaning whatsoever." This really spoke to me because I feel that this is what I have always tried to do. In my own work, I have been looking for stories, conceptual frameworks, models—something upon which to hang facts and information so that they make a cohesive whole.

Such stories can be of various scales. On one level, I have looked for stories to better enable me to communicate and teach. In library instruction, for instance, I have used the *database model* as a story to help students understand and retain the information they are receiving. In communications with faculty members and other librarians, I have used the *scholarly conversation model*, which is a story about what students are doing when they engage in research and writing projects (participating in the "great conversation"), to help me explain and define the purpose of library instruction. In a larger context, as the head of a reference department during the mid-1990s, an era when so much talk of "Rethinking Reference" was going around, I found I wanted to look for a story that really communicated the purposes and value of reference. I started working on this with two of my close colleagues in the reference department, Bill McHugh and Natalie Pelster. In our probing of the literature, we found some ideas that helped us to build a story of reference. We rooted it in a quote we found in a charming article from just before the turn of the last century, in 1897. Eleanor Woodruff, a reference librarian at the Pratt Institute, said that in short, the job of the reference librarian was to do anything and everything to "conduce" getting the right resources to the right users at the right moment. We found this to be a building block for our story.

It also became one of the cornerstones in the story of the learning library that I presented at the ACRL President's Program, "Imagining the Learning

Library," in 1997. This talk turned into the article in *Research Strategies* that is cited on the LOEX Conference Web site. For those of you who have read it, "conduce" is one of the four C's, along with "converge," "convey," and "community." The story of the learning library, with these four C's embedded in it, is one that I find to be especially compelling. It is an overarching story of what the library is all about and that can infuse everything that we do.

So, I have talked about three different scales of stories. The database model as a conceptual framework for instruction is a small scale story. The reference story is in the middle, so to speak. The learning library is a story for the big scheme of things. In the library literature, we sometimes find reflective thinkers who are laying out these grand stories that seek to give meaning and purpose to our entire enterprise. When I think of reflective librarians who have tried to frame "stories" of what the library is, two names jump immediately to mind. They are S. R. Ranganathan and Michael Gorman. Both of these men have done a tremendous service to the field by thinking, even "worrying", about the underlying values and purposes of our work. They have each put a lot of heart and soul into finding meaning to inform and fuel our work and thought. Ranganathan's five laws are really a story of the library. They came all at once, as a cohesive story in his mind. Michael Gorman says in his introduction to *Our Enduring Values,* "What I seek to do, and what, dear reader, I hope you will find in this book, is to illuminate and re-create the underpinnings of our profession to, at least, provide a framework for discussion and, at best, be a broad plan with which we may all proceed." The purpose of these reflective stories, whether large or small in scope, is to provide meaning and a framework, just as Neil Postman says they must. They tell us "what is important and what we can ignore."

A phrase that came to mind over and over again as I was putting this talk together was "really speaks to me". Initially, I thought I was using this too much and needed to change it. But then, I thought, why edit it out? Why not address it? The phrase keeps coming up because it points to something very important about stories. The important thing about a story is that you have to believe in it. It has to be true to you. *This* is what Neil Postman said in that initial article that so captivated me. "Stories have to be believed to work." If you cease to believe in your story, the bottom drops out.

This point was also made clear by Herb Kelleher, CEO of Southwest Airlines, when he spoke a few years ago at the Northwestern University Transportation Center's Patterson lecture series. My colleague, Natalie Pelster, attended the lecture, and came back with a quote that we put into our war chest of ideas. The idea was this—the story of who you are cannot be made up. It has to be true. Furthermore, it has to be true, and believed in by, the employees who represent the company and who have to sell that story to the customers. This concept of ideas "speaking to me" is essential. The ideas about "storying" rang true to me and became internalized and meaningful to the story I was writing or, perhaps more accurately, building about the purpose of the library.

For me it is interesting to think of reflection as the process of story-building. And I am definitely not alone in this. I recently read another book, *The Dream Society* in which author Rolf Jensen says that we are now moving from an information society to an imagination society. He says that the most important thing that leaders will do in the future is tell stories that give context, give a framework. He says that to a great extent the success of our enterprises will depend on the success of our stories. The story idea is so appealing to me that it is what I view the outcome of reflection to be. We reflect to understand, and the "story" is the expression of that understanding.

The Process of Reflection

We are at this conference to talk not only about the importance of reflection but also about how we can go about being reflective practitioners. When we look at people like Dr. Ranganathan, Michael Gorman, and Neil Postman, who are almost larger than life and the stories that they give us about the big picture, it can be hard to associate reflection with ourselves and what we do. Some of us may be thinking, "Reflecting on these large issues may be good, but "Me?" I have five classes to teach this week. How can I approach reflection with that on my plate?" Still, I have known many reflective librarians, some of whom do teach five classes a week. And reflection is something from which all professionals can benefit. Being a reflective practitioner doesn't mean that you are destined to lay out five laws or establish seven principles or articulate an overarching vision for the profession, but that you bring an inquiry into meaning and purpose into your daily work life. Reflective practice is an ongoing pursuit of questions and answers. Being a reflective practitioner means that you have found a way, or a medium for doing this.

Donald Schon says that finding a medium of reflection is very important. The medium can vary from person to person or from profession to profession. For some of us it might be journaling or writing. Many articles have been written about the benefits of professional journaling in helping to bring ideas to the surface. The key to professional journaling is to avoid being descriptive and factual in your writing. Don't just tell what you did that day; try, instead, to reflect on your day. Write about your reactions to the experiences you are having. Writing our thoughts often leads to being able to see things from a different angle or as Schon would say from a different frame of reference. It may even lead to a solution to a problem or help us be less anxious about a situation. Sometimes just writing about our thoughts and ideas can be very illuminating. One of my favorite quotes about this phenomenon comes from author Joan Didion, who in her essay "Why I Write" says "I write entirely to find out what I think." This sounds a lot like the title of this conference, "Reflective Teaching: A Bridge to Learning". For others, the medium of reflection might be talking to and collaborating with trusted colleagues, asking questions, reading books and articles, attending lectures, building up that "idea war chest." A colleague once told me that he goes to conferences looking for "an idea—not a solution to someone else's problem." He said that if he came home with one good idea, he felt that he had had an exceptionally successful conference. The medium of reflection for architects might be sketching. For therapists, it can be talking, listening, and drawing pictures. The important thing is to set some time for engaging in reflective thinking, however you decide to do it. How you organize your reflection time is up to you.

Whatever our medium, we can gain useful fodder for our reflections if we approach our projects and activities as we would approach a conversation. Schon calls this having a "conversation with a situation." And, with any conversation be it with a person or a situation, it is most productive if we are open to, what he terms, "back talk from the situation." We need to be open-minded and receptive to what we see and learn or what we are surprised or confused by from our questioning and conversing.

Maureen Clark, one of the many wonderful students in the reference class that I just finished teaching, reminded me that Carl Jung once said "Thank God, I'm Jung and not a Jungian." Like a good reflective teacher, Jung made many efforts in his writings to tell his students and followers to free themselves from any of his ideas or forms of practice that did not work for them. Jung's own sense of freedom to experiment and change directions when the "backtalk" was adverse, is what Jung is referring to when he professes his gratitude at not being Jungian.

Just finding the right questions involves thoughtful, complex framing processes. We can get some help in doing this, and in initiating conversations with situations, in the book *The Art of Focused*

Conversation from the Canadian Institute of Cultural Affairs. This book presents 100 different situations and how we can structure conversations with them, so to speak. For each situation, it presents a set of objective questions, reflective questions, interpretive questions, and decisional questions. This book provides a really good guide for organizing thinking around reflective questions. The editors, in their preface to the book, say that the idea for the book came out of all of the positive feedback that they had received about their use of focused conversations in their group facilitation courses. Some of the comments they received from the graduates of their courses were: "The conversation method is a tool that is constantly deepening the learning of my staff." "The sustained use of the focused conversation has changed the environment in our organization." "This is a method that enables us to deal with an issue before it turns into a major blow-up." John C. Maxwell, in a recently published book titled *Thinking for a Change: 11 Ways Highly Successful People Approach Life and Work*, further underscores the importance of questioning as a way to deepen one's understanding of a situation. He says that "the value you receive from reflecting will depend on the kinds of questions you ask yourself. The better the questions, the more gold you will mine from your thinking." He says that when he reflects, he thinks in terms of his values, relationships, and experiences. For example, in thinking about values, some questions he would ask himself would be: "What have I learned today that will help me grow? To whom did I add value today? How do I know I added value to that person? What did I do with someone else that made both of us better? Did I lead by example today?" Some of his questions about experiences are: "What did I encounter today to which I need to give more thinking time? What went wrong? Could I have changed it? What do I need to do differently next time? What went right? Did I create it? Is there a principle I can learn from the experience?" Questions about work relationships could be: "Have I spent enough time with my key players? What can I do to help them be more successful? In what areas can I mentor them?" I came upon a quote by Rainer Maria Rilke that, I believe, truly helps us embrace our questioning nature and also calms our fears about the unknown.

Be patient toward all that is unsolved in your heart and try to live the questions themselves like locked rooms and like books that are written in a very foreign tongue. Do not see the answers which cannot be given you because you would not be able to live them. And, the point is, to live everything. Live the questions now. Perhaps you will find them gradually, without noticing it, and live along

—BETSY BAKER—

some distant day into the answer.

On the bibliography I prepared for you, I have listed the URL for a folder I have at Mind University, a tool for organizing Internet resources to share with others. One of the links in my folder is to a site called "I Love Teaching," which is hosted at Ball State University. At this site, you will find ways of applying the various methods of reflection to teaching. I think it is a very helpful site with lots of ideas and hope you will get a chance to take a look at it. Reflection is a big topic in teaching right now, and there are many resources we can draw upon to help us build reflection into our work as instruction librarians. The Zeichner/Liston book is an especially good introduction to this topic.

Organizations and Reflection

We are all aware of how our organizations can either inhibit or encourage reflection in practice. We learn, by how we are treated and received in our organizations, about how we are expected to behave. A reflective organization or reflective leader isn't prescriptive and doesn't use dismissive language. It encourages questioning and listens to ideas. Michael Eisner, CEO of the Disney Company, says, "A company like ours must create an atmosphere in which people feel safe to fail. This means forming an organization where failure is not only tolerated, but fear of criticism for submitting a foolish idea is abolished. If not, people become too cautious. They hunker down...afraid to speak up, afraid to rock the boat, afraid of being ridiculed. Potentially brilliant ideas are never uttered...and therefore never heard."

This reminds me of something Peggy Van Pelt, creative resources director of Walt Disney Imagineering, said when she and I presented at the ACRL President's Program several ago at ALA. She said that ideas are fragile, delicate. When creativity is valued, ideas are handled with care. New ideas are viewed as seedlings. They don't get stomped on. Peggy even spoke of the shelf-life of an idea, saying how important it is to be patient and to respect ideas, knowing that even if they can't be used right now they may be very helpful in a month, a year, or even later.

While I don't want to come across as a Disney groupie—I have never even been to Disneyland or Disney World, although my two little boys are working to change that—many of their ideas and approaches address the value of reflection and the fostering of imagination. I was, in fact, first introduced to some of the kinds of ideas the Disney folk were discussing at an American Association of Higher Education conference, where members of the Imagineering Team were after-dinner speakers talking about the value of creativity and reflection for people directing the course of higher education. The thinking behind involving them in the ACRL program several years ago was that they had something to say to librarians as well. If you ever see them listed on a conference program, it's worth the time to hear them.

As much as we would like to think that this attitude toward fostering ideas and reflection is the norm, it is possible that your organization can thwart you, either overtly or subtly. The book, *The Nibble Theory*, talks about how we can get undermined little by little, in ways that don't seem dramatic at the time but that wear away our self-confidence and faith in ourselves as competent professionals. In time, in a nibbling environment, you may find you are not able to be who you want and deserve to be professionally. I put the word deserve in here very purposefully. By virtue of entering the profession, of being invested in your work and its outcomes, and participating, you have the right to bring your thinking, ingenuity, and imagination into your work environment and to have it met with respect and enthusiasm—not necessarily to be agreed with but to be appreciated for participating and contributing with the best you have to give.

If this is not the case, there are decisions that have to be made and realities that have to come into play. The idea of "think globally, act locally" comes to mind. The local might be you in the classroom with twenty students for fifty minutes, but in that setting you can do what you need to do. Maybe you cannot engage reflectively with the organization as a structure, but a relationship with a colleague can give you the support to nurture your ideas and creativity and to bring meaning to your work.

The truth is, most of us want to be reflective. We want to be contributing to the thinking that goes into the work that we are supposed to be doing. While some people may find comfort in being told what to do and how to do it, most of us find more support in an environment that validates and affirms who we are as professionals; we are people with judgement, experience, knowledge, ability, and beliefs. A really vivid example of this for me is the Rethinking Reference conferences in the early nineties. I attended the third go round of this (I can't speak about the first two) but by the third time, attendees were commenting that it was too prescriptive, that what they were hearing was "take notes on this new model and carry it back to your libraries." One person in particular said, "I came to be part of a conference titled "Rethinking Reference." This is more like "Reference Rethought." It's presented as done and we are just here to get our marching orders." Most of us want to be part of the blue print making not to just have the blue print handed to us. George Patton's often quoted comment: "Never tell people how to do things. Tell them what to do and they will surprise you with their ingenuity", comes to mind when I think about this.

Rewards of Reflective Practice

The rewards of being reflective are that your work becomes more interesting, exciting, alive, and full of ideas. You achieve better results for yourself, your users, and your organization. This is certainly what I have found for myself. Reflection enters the practice and, to use a word I used earlier in this presentation, *infuses* the work that we do. To illustrate this, I would like to share with you a short piece of one of my departmental annual reports:

As I sit down to write this year's departmental annual report and look over our goals from last year, the reports I have written over the past five years, and the activities and achievements that are in outline form before me, I find myself reflecting most deeply about the very nature of reference itself. Like every year, we have had a great deal of activity in instructional areas. We have also made great progress in bringing out more electronic resources for our users…Yet when I think about what it is that sets this year apart from other years; it is what might be thought of as traditional reference work, i.e. reference desk service and reference collection building. I can't help but think about the Harvard College conference that three of us from Reference participated in last spring. The title of the conference, "Finding Common Ground: Building the Library of the Future without Diminishing the Library of the Past," was meaningful to us because it suggested to us what we are always doing in Reference: bringing in new technologies, seeking new opportunities for outreach, and yet at the same time, maintaining a focus on the needs of our users and building a reference collection that answers those needs, regardless of format. As reference librarians we try to maintain intellectual control over the kaleidoscope of information sources available so that we can bring forward whatever source may be useful to a researcher when it is needed.

One of the benefits that working on the paper for the Harvard conference brought to me was a renewed interest in the fundamental questions of what reference service is and can be. The title of the conference, which juxtaposed the

ideas of the future and the past, and suggested that moving into the future might diminish the past, inspired us to look in the past for roots of reference service, to see just what reference service is meant to be, to see what it is that we have been doing that supports that mission, to see what we can do, and what technology can help us do, to advance rather than detract from that mission. One of the most succinct expressions of the reference mission that we found came from Eleanor Woodruff, reference librarian at the Pratt Institute Free Library, who, in 1897 wrote:

The aim of the reference department is, as you all know, to afford to readers the simplest, easiest, and quickest access to the resources of the library on any subject in which they may be interested or desire information. This may be accomplished by either introducing the inquirer directly to the books where his questions will be answered, or helping him to an understanding of the mysteries of the catalog, or explaining the use of indexes, bibliographies, and other library tools, or compiling lists for him , in short, by doing anything and everything which will *conduce* to getting him the right book at the right moment.

In the spirit of using this annual report as a means of sharing my thinking about reference, I want to focus this year on the "reference side" of reference services. What is happening at the Reference Desk? How are we developing the reference collection? How do our other services and activities support our overall reference goal of *conducing* getting the right resources to the right user at the right time?

The reflecting I had done with my department members informed our work and brought us together at a deeper level than just doing a variety of reference tasks. It also helped me to communicate with others in the organization just what we were doing and why it was important.

To me, the "learning library" is an important story and I continue to do a lot of reflecting about it. I think it really captures what libraries are all about—supporting learning. A big part of the learning library story has to do with the experiences we want users to have. This is why ACRL's program on the learning library brought in speakers from Disney and an architect as well as a librarian. The learning library is centered on "experience," and the design and offering of "experience" is what Disney and architects specialize in.

This focusing on experiences seems to be right in

line with what Joseph Pine and James Gilmore, co-founders of Strategic Horizons, are telling us to do in their book *Every Business a Stage: Why Customers Now Want Experiences*. "An experience," they tell us, "is not an amorphous construct; it is as real an offering as any service, good, or commodity. In today's service economy, many companies simply wrap experiences around their traditional offerings. To realize the full benefit of staging experiences, however, businesses must deliberately design engaging experiences." They acknowledge Walt Disney as the pioneer of the experience economy and say that Disney and the company he founded have creatively exploited the fact that experiences are what lie at the heart of their business.

Barry Braverman, Vice-President at Walt Disney Imagineering, talked about the same phenomenon that Pine and Gilmore are writing about. He said that at Disney, "as we look out across the competitive landscape we are more than a little concerned about the proliferation of themed entertainment offerings. Restaurants, once content to provide food and drink now feature artifacts and personalities from the movies, rock music, sports, and even high fashion. Night clubs employ elaborate theatrical devices to transport patrons to different eras and exotic locales. Even Las Vegas, once the exclusive Mecca of sin and sleaze, now markets itself as a family vacation destination complete with pirate ships, erupting volcanoes, and roller coasters. The trend has been called the theme parkization of everything."

While I don't think of the library as a theme park, I do think that considering the experiences users have in the library is vital to fulfilling the educational mission of the library. In libraries, we are much more likely to talk about services than about experiences, but the idea of the library offering engaging experiences has begun to arise almost in sync with the ideas of the experience economy. As an "experience-driven" vision of the library, the story of the "learning library" has profound implications for what we do in libraries. In reflecting on the learning library, we need to ask questions about what students and other users will experience when they stop at a service desk, attend an instructional workshop, and talk to a staff member. Among the things I want our users to experience and know are the following:

- You and your interest are important.
- You are not alone.
- You should have far-reaching expectations.
- There are ways out of apparent dead-ends.
- You can get assistance here.
- You can spend as much time as you want.
- Your time is important.

- This can be an enjoyable and invigorating experience.
- You can relax, browse, and sightsee here.
- The voices you want to listen to are included here.
- We do not censor or judge.
- All information is not digested.
- We are efficient, capable, caring, *and professional.*
- Resources are vast.
- There is an order to what you are being asked to do.

These messages can come through to people in many ways: through the physical environment, through their interactions with and impressions of the staff, through the resources offered and the way they are presented, and through our teaching and instructional programs.

As we reflect on what we are doing as library instructors, we look at what we are doing in individual library instruction sessions and information literacy courses, in our overall instruction programs, and in the library as a whole. I think that LOEX is a terrific venue for talking about and reflecting on the idea of the learning library because those of us involved in and valuing instruction have a lot to offer to an experiential view of the library that has learning at its base. I believe that LOEX can still fuel the same kind of synergistic and invigorating relationships that it did in my early career by bringing committed and reflective people together. During the course of my career, I have seen a continual momentum for instruction. As long as people bring energy and thought to the story of instruction, it will continue to grow.

I will close by saying that instruction librarians by virtue of their desire to teach and foster learning, bring a compassionate presence to the library. So I have a fifth "C" to add to my "C" words about the learning library, and that is "care". It is by being compassionate toward our users, really caring about them and their needs, that we bring the learning library to life and makes it a reality. I have one final quote for you, one that I feel truly sums up the importance of caring:

One looks back with appreciation to the brilliant teachers. but with gratitude to those who touched our human feelings. The curriculum is so much necessary raw material, but warmth is the vital element for the growing plant and for the soul of the child.

—Carl Jung

REFERENCES

Baker, Betsy. "Values for the Learning Library." *Research Strategies* 17, no. 2-3 (2000): 85-91.

Braverman, Berry. "Libraries and Theme Parks: Strange Bedfellows." *Research Strategies* 17, no. 2-3 (2000): 99-105.

Didion, Joan. "Why I Write." *The New York Times*, 5 December 1976, Section 7, 270.

Eisner, Michael. "Managing a Creative Organization: Never Being Afraid to Fail." *Vital Speeches* 62, no. 16 (1 June 1996): 502-505.

Gorman, Michael. *Our Enduring Values: Librarianship in the 21st Century.* Chicago: American Library Association, 2000.

Jamison, Kaleel. *The Nibble Theory and the Kernel of Power.* New York: Paulist Press, 1984.

Jensen, Rolf. *The Dream Society.* New York: McGraw Hill, 1999.

Maxwell, John C. *Thinking for a Change: 11 Ways Highly Successful People Approach Life and Work.* New York: Warner Books, 2003.

Pine, Joseph and James Gilmore. *Every Business a Stage: Why Customers Now Want Experiences.* Boston: Harvard Business School Press, 1999.

Postman, Neil. "Learning by Story." *Atlantic* 264, no. 6 (December 1989): 119 - 124.

Ranganathan, S. R. *The Five Laws of Library Science.* Bombay, New York: Asia Pub. House, 1963.

Ranganathan, S. R. *Reference Service.* London: Asia Pub. House, 1961.

Schön, Donald A. *The Reflective Practitioner: How Professionals Think in Action.* New York: Basic Books, 1983.

Stanfield, Brian R. *The Art of Focused Conversation: 100 Ways to Access Group Wisdom in the Workplace.* Toronto: New Society Publishers, 2000.

Van Pelt, Peggy. "Putting Talent to Work in the Creation of the Learning Library." *Research Strategies* 17, no. 2-3 (2000): 93-98.

Woodruff, Eleanor. "Reference Work." *Library Journal* 22 (1897): 65-67

Zeichner, Kenneth M. and Daniel P. Liston. *Reflective Teaching: An Introduction.* Mahwah, NJ: L. Erlbaum Associates, 1996.

Visit *MindUniversity.com* (bbaker login) and open the *LOEX* folder for links to some useful Internet sites. http://www.minduniversity.com

BRIDGING ACTION AND REFLECTION: STRATEGIES AND QUESTIONS FOR TEACHING LIBRARIANS

Elizabeth J. Burge, Ed.D

Introduction

Do you have any wicked professional problems? Peter Rowe (1987, 41) defined them as having four features: they resist clear definition, any proposed solution only creates more questions, different descriptions of the problem will generate as many different answers, and alternative solutions can be equally plausible.

We expect that expert professionals know a lot about 'wicked' problems. I have learned to approach some of my own 'wicked' problems by stepping aside from the heat of the moment and engaging in critically reflective thinking. It's not an easy task, especially for a time and workload challenged intuitive thinker. Heather Menzies, a nationally respected and astute analyst of the effects of technological change on humans and their life contexts, shows her concern for how we perceive time now: "Not just the fast forwarding of time through the speed-of-light pace made possible by online communication...But, equally important, the erosion of shared time and a pace of living attuned to our embodied existence –plus the deconditioning or desensitizing that this entails." (2001, 2) After ten years as a full-time academic, I agree with Heather's assessment of professors under pressure: "They're overextended. They can't even slow down enough to be in touch with themselves, and get their bearings on what's important to them...." (2001,1) Alan Lightman, the U.S. physicist, essayist, novelist (who eschews email use, by the way), is not

---

Burge, a former librarian, is now Professor, Adult Education, Faculty of Education at the University of New Brunswick, Atlantic Canada.

immune either to time-shortages: "All around me, everywhere I go, I feel a sense of urgency, a vague fear of not keeping up with the world, a vague fear of not being plugged in." (2002,R1)

Sound familiar to you too? If so, let's use this conference time together to step away from immediate pressures and habitual trains of thought and try to "get (our) bearings on what's important...."

This paper has three parts: some challenges facing university libraries; thinking about reflection itself; and various strategies and questions to sustain you on your own critically reflective journey.

Some challenges facing university libraries

My first career, librarianship, influences my current interest in what libraries are doing. That career helped me develop a profound respect for freedom of information and for easy and sustained access to reputable information. It helped me learn how adults learned without professional educators or in spite of what some educators did to them. It raised unsettling questions about where librarians are seen by others to bridge into and across the landscapes of formal higher education. It pointed to the need to establish built environments that promote learning. In Finland and mid-Sweden, for example, I've used public libraries where the ambience alone drew me to return, *viz*, the new Viiki library and the elegantly restored Rickardinkatu library in Helsinki, and the Sambiblioteket in Härnösand.

As a colleague of an Ontario librarian not scared of thinking outside the box—Judith Snow (University of Toronto Education Commons (U of T)), I've heard stories both poisonous and poignant of how librarians perceived themselves to be marginalized in educational settings; to be, by default, built out of course designs and curriculum models (Burge, Snow, and Howard 1989). Later, in a 2000 paper Judy and I discussed the factors inherent in current flexible learning contexts that impinge upon library services, especially regarding the huge challenge of disintermediation, i.e. the lack of stable bridges across divided educational territories (Burge and Snow 2000).

Post-2000, at the "Libraries Without Walls" (LWW4) 2001 conference in Greece, organized by Professor Peter Brophy, Director of the Center for Research in Library and Information Management (CERLIM), <www.cerlim.ac.uk> (Brophy, Fisher and Clarke 2002), I explained how some universities are promoting their learner advisory and library services as integral aspects of their distance and flexible learning activity (Burge 2002). The Open University is the world leader here <www. open. ac.uk> but there are other single and dual mode universities beyond the United States with decades of distinguished educational experience and the conviction that fast and flexible library services are essential.(See, for example <www. athabascau.c;www.lib.unb.ca;www. deakin.ac.au/ library/>.

Accompanying all these activities are my own observations and experience as a professor in adult and distance education and as an academic library user. Three things emerge from my reflections: some confusion and angst, librarians who instruct, and librarians who seem to disappear from my sight. Feelings of confusion and angst may arise very quickly as I try to navigate my way around all the new databases and understand all the new terminology that some librarians speak these days. Joanne Smyth, one of the innovative librarians here at University of New Brunswick, feels some pity for innocent users: "we invent new jargon, and more than one term to describe what are really simple phenomena, and expect our users to keep up. It's impossible!" Joanne did confide that, while working online now as a learner doing her second Master's degree (her first is in Education) from a prominent U.S. university, she is experiencing the administrative snafues and labyrinths that must be negotiated before her significant learning can begin. She also has to learn "the code" (all the acronyms and special university terms) before she can navigate more effectively on screen.

Librarians who instruct seem to deliver their information and its impressive acronymic scaffolding while their audience listens politely, before asking questions based on their own information needs and phrased in their everyday terminology. Hear Joanne Smyth again—with feeling: "People don't come here

[the library] to learn the library; they come to learn [their discipline]". Some students are free of current information literacy skills with its attendant jargon and they feel apprehensive; others see the open Internet as their instant salvation.

Librarians who disappear return to a place that has lost some ambient attraction. To even reach it physically often involves parking problems or icy pavements. Once inside, I typically engage with friendly circulation staff but notice too the 'hum' from younger students using the library for gossiping, group assignments and peer tutoring. The reference librarian on duty sits behind a big counter/desk and seems always to be intently reading a screen. The library keyboards and 'mice' are never as clean as I would wish. Given my time and energy pressures, not to mention my preferred ambience for thinking, I go to the 'library-as-place' only when I have to; otherwise I stay office-bound, using the 'library-as-e-service' and e-mailing as needed our helpful specialist librarian, Lesley Balcom.

Others' experience and opinions indicate additional overt and covert challenges for academic scholarship. You may know about the Academic Integrity surveys being done in Canada and the United States, managed by Dr. Don McCabe at Rutgers University <http://teachx.rutgers.edu/integrity/facult y.html#>. My university is now processing its own results and they promise to command attention, if not some shock, about how cheating is construed and applied. But that's another tale; and I'm sure you know at least 75% of it!

Several issues regarding library 'presence' are worth noting here. The top issues facing academic libraries—see for example, *College and Research Libraries News*, 63, no. 10 (2002)—contain few surprises: technical and personnel issues link to the thorny ones around human and material deficits such as lack of information literacy skills, reduced higher education funding, too few librarians available for hiring, and lack of awareness and appreciation of what libraries and librarians can do. A very recent Canadian article (Crawley 2003) reported a recent United States study by the Pew Internet and American Life Project showing that "nearly three quarters of U.S. college students use the Internet more than the library". The article also reported (p. 28) a 12% drop in the average number of reference queries between 1998-2001 in the libraries associated with the Canadian Association of Research Libraries. Thousands of Canadian university professors now have read this line: "...technologically savvy students may think older librarians have nothing to teach them about electronic resources." (p. 28). The *Chronicle of Higher Education* (CHE) continues to report various budget cuts to libraries, stories of how "[s]tudents and faculty members turn first to online library materials..." (CHE, 18 Oct 2002, A37), or questions such as "[d]o libraries really need books?" (CHE, 12 July 2002, A31). If I scan the indexes of many international books about open, flexible and distance learning, looking for any mentions of librarianship, it's a very rare day when a chapter appears, but a typical day when I lobby for librarianship to be included. My point here is not so much the content of such writing or my ongoing lobbying, but more the long-term, covert impact on readers. Are some of the reports and surveys quietly but surely worsening the disintermediation of librarians, marginalizing them into nice-to-have teachers of information literacy skills—if there is enough time in the curriculum?

We have to be confronting some wicked problems here. I don't see them going away with activities equivalent only to digging the same holes deeper or fine-tuning the *status quo*. But I do see an opportunity for stepping back, thinking reflectively, and getting some new compass bearings. How many different definitions of which problems might we develop? If several plausible solutions are proposed, which consequent problems might present themselves, especially around the complexities associated with introducing change in organizations?

It was quite reassuring to recently find more evidence of librarians promoting the concept of partnership (Frank and Howell 2003) and arguing for more assertive behavior by librarians—to be named "information consultants"—who would move out of their libraries and generally display the characteristics of proactive and communicative consultants. Yes, indeed; Judy Snow and I argued for that in 2000, and Judy comments now on her recent experience:

> Since our 2000 article, I/we have been trying hard to stress the need for change in the role of librarians—discussing the need for the partnership function and true involvement in curriculum design and delivery. I can't say that this is happening everywhere, but there have been some definite initiatives on each of the three campuses of U of T. Librarians are partnering with faculty and becoming an actual part of the course offerings—rather than just a one-time visitor. I think that this is easier to do on a smaller campus and within a faculty. The real challenge at U of T is making this happen within the vast realm of the Faculty of Arts and Science....There has been some success with 'information specialists' getting out of their libraries and

into faculty meetings, etc. but this is still a challenge. There has been quite an active project in the science library here—with varying results. Some faculties are thrilled and welcome the info professionals—some have asked people not to return. So there needs to be work on all sides, it seems. Success in the humanities and social sciences has been more limited. There needs to be much more work done in this area. (Of course, I am commenting here on the U of T situation—other places might have had more success). (Personal communication, 29 April 2003).

Therefore, several questions haunt me. How will these consultants gain adequate education training and actual practice in the facilitation of adult learning, and do so without being perceived as a threat to the teaching faculty members? How might the librarians be helped to explore different models of teaching (Pratt and Associates 1998) and experiment more with overtly learner-centered ones? (Barr and Tagg 1995; Land and Hannafin 2000) And what are the real chances of librarian-as-learning-consultant being based with their clients so that they avoid the 'out of sight, out of mind' problem?

Plausible answers will create more plausible questions, so it's probably time to step back and sideways to move towards reflection itself.

Thinking about reflection

The concept of reflection for enhancing professional practice has gained considerable attention in the United Kingdom, Canada, United States, Australia, and other countries over the past two decades, with, of course, due recognition of John Dewey's foundational work (1933). These authors are engaging and practical: Colin Beard and John Wilson 2002; Gillie Bolton 2001; David Boud and Nod Miller 1996; Evelyn Boyd and Ann Fales 1983; Stephen Brookfield 2000,1998,1995; Natalie Ferry and Jovita Ross-Gordon 1998; Jack Mezirow 2000; John Mason 2002; Nod Miller 2000; Parker Palmer 1998; Russell Rogers 2001; Jovita Ross-Gordon 2002; and Donald Schön 1995, 1987, 1983.

On our side of the Atlantic Ocean, the concept of the "reflective practitioner" really gained salience after Donald Schön's first book in 1983. He argued for moving away from seeing professional knowledge as "technical rationality" i.e., "instrumental problem solving made rigorous by the application of scientific theory and technique" (Schön 1983, 21) and moving toward "an epistemology of practice implicit in the artistic, intuitive processes which some practitioners do bring to situations of uncertainty, instability, uniqueness, and value conflict." (48) He also argued that reflection-on-action was as important as knowing-in-action, but it often needed a trigger--some discontinuity or surprise (even a bit of wickedness)--in order for such questioning and analysis to begin (1995). He used a metaphor to distinguish two areas of professional practice: "In the swampy lowlands, problems are messy and confusing and incapable of technical solution. ...[they are] the problems of greatest human concern." Opposing the swamp is "the high, hard ground...[where] manageable problems lend themselves to solution through the use of research-based theory and technique". Schön valued reflective analyses of the "indeterminate zones [that are our everyday] practice [and which are full of] uncertainty, complexity, uniqueness, conflict." (1995,3) Practitioners who choose to struggle in the swampy lowlands use "experience, trial and error, intuition, or muddling through" in order to respond to various situations (as distinct from waiting for theoretical or action-based guidance from others). I do like this swamp concept: it resonates with my landscapes of practice (Burge, Laroque, and Boak 2000) and those of valued colleagues (e.g., Cavanaugh, Ellerman, Oddson, and Young 2001; Cowan 1998; and Campbell-Gibson 2000).

While Stephen Brookfield acknowledges that we all engage in 'reflection' during our practice, for example, thinking about whether to make surface-level changes in technique or contextual features, he quickly separates this kind of thinking from critical reflection:

> "...reflection becomes critical when it has two distinctive purposes. The first is to understand how considerations of power undergird, frame, and distort educational processes and interactions. The second is to question assumptions and practices that seem to make our teaching lives easier but actually work against our best interests." (1995,8)

Hmmm...that's not easy work at all...and there have to be significant costs, so why go critical? Brookfield has six reasons (1995, 22-26) and I particularly like these two: avoidance of self-laceration, and emotional grounding. We benefit when we confront the contextual factors and habits of mind that, unless we reflect carefully enough, push us into impossible goals or impose inappropriate stress.
As others do, Brookfield sees the costs:

> A critically reflective stance towards our practice is healthily ironic, a necessary hedge against an overconfident belief that we have captured the one universal truth about good practice. [It]...makes us mistrustful of grand theories ...We realize the contextuality of all practice and the limitations of universal templates...One consequence of this realization is that we learn humility regarding the possibility of our ever "getting it right," of ever attaining a peerless state of perfect grace as practitioners .... (2000, 46-47)

UK colleagues have produced thoughtful and sometimes witty reflections on reflection for professional practice (e.g., Atkinson and Claxton 2000; Bolton 2001; Hillier 2002; Mason 2002; Miller 2000; and Moon 1999). John Mason rather dryly points out that reflection is the "vogue term for intentionally learning from experience, but it is more talked about than carried out effectively." (29) He promotes "noticing": methodological (not mechanical) noticing "...[is] a collection of practices both for living in, and hence learning from, experience, and for informing future practice." (29) For you and I to notice any opportunity to act appropriately "[needs] three things: being present and sensitive in the moment, having a reason to act, and have a different act come to mind." (1) Yvonne Hillier explains various types of reflection, as well as the need to unearth informal theory or common sense in order to render such knowledge explicit before it can be examined with a critical mind set. (12) She knows that reflective thinking denies quick conclusions: "Reflective practice means that you can never be sure that ideas have been fully explored and developed. It is relentless in its quest for making explicit the tacit thoughts and feelings about your practice." (2002, xi) Gillie Bolton knows that reflective practice is not for the faint-hearted, since we need to embrace "uncertainty as to what we are doing and where we are going; confidence to search for something when we have no idea of what it is; [and] the letting go of the security blanket of needing answers." (2001, 15) To further challenge our equilibrium, she suggests that we assess our own relationship to various current models of teaching, including the "chalk and talk" model (should that now be the 'mouse and mouth' model?), the "*fofo*" model (f***off and find out), the "hey presto" model (attract the consumer with innovation), and the "looking-glass" model with its "three foundations...[of] certain uncertainty...serious playfulness...[and] unquestioning questioning." (24-35)

It's time now to draw back from these writers and experience critical reflection for ourselves. In a nutshell, what's it like 'on the ground'?

—ELIZABETH J. BURGE, ED.D—

Characteristics of critical reflection

I can only speak personally here, and give you my list-in-progress.

Critical reflection is:
- A process more than an outcome
- Located in diffuse and chaotic contexts
- Gaining mental and temporal 'space'
- Feeling ready to engage in critical inquiry
- Recognizing and using a trigger event
- Recalling details from "swamp" experiences
- Finding new 'glasses' for seeing new things
- Giving voice
- Seeing new relationships
- Maintaining self-esteem
- Feeling OK when the answers don't come
- Letting go of assumptions without feeling guilty
- Tipping over the 'rocks' of tradition or habit
- Seeing actions, feelings, and thoughts as interrelated
- Using uncertainties and discombobulations
- Looking in the familiar for what may be missing
- Problematizing actions—asking 'why' before 'how
- Confronting illusions
- Searching for paradox
- Redefining wicked problems and rehearsing solutions
- Peeking into dark corners
- Deciding on potential changes in practice (action research)
- Feeling exhilaration when an insight is gained
- Being energized

Now it's time to apply all the ideas above: to 'walk this talk' and develop some specific questions to help you reflect about your work and concerns. Feel free to walk right past any sections below that do not attract you, but don't throw them out altogether: you may want to slide past them later to see what sticks. For now I give the equivalent of a cognitive vaccination, but how much better would be a stress-reduced reflective 'cure' at a spa!

Questions/Strategies to Promote Critically Reflective Thinking

Section A: Generic Strategies and Questions
- Look for hegemonies—those assumptions about 'normal' practice that appear to act in the clients' best interests or that adhere to fine traditions or unquestioned common sense; for example, that it is the best idea to gather all the paper, the librarians, and their expertise into a building called a library and then wait for the 'patrons' to come. Or, that good teaching should mean keeping all students happy all the time. Or, that students should be able to leisurely enjoy the atmosphere of a scholarly edifice and experience serendipity as they stroll between the shelves.
- Seek out antinomies—those situations holding conflicting and apparently irresolvable forces or dynamics. For example, regarding online interaction: 'one person's freedom to message is another's information overload'; or regarding online teaching: "The desire to reflect on a student's communication before responding is always in conflict with the urge to respond quickly so that the student knows they have been 'heard'. (Kirkup 2003,7) Ask not what I should do to the antinomy, but what the antinomy might do to me.
- Develop similes, metaphors, images or analogies that challenge familiar mindsets or enable the unpacking of traditional labels or practices. Asking "Is my teaching at all comparable to jazz improvisation?" or "How might a teaching librarian be like a cat?" enables us to unpack multiple sub-concepts in 'jazz' and 'catness' and use them as possible 'bridges' into new ways of seeing our daily behaviors. A key Canadian colleague, Margaret Haughey explains that "for me insights often come through images embedded in stories"... and she uses another teacher's metaphors of paddling (in part looking forward) and rowing (looking backward) to gain new insights:

"The paddler seems to focus on the currents around the canoe, whereas the rower focuses on the rowing. I saw how we could be so caught up in our own work that other ways of seeing are lost to us. Like the rower, we focus on the rowing more often than the goal." (Haughey 2001,5)

- Invent axioms and maxims that provoke by reversing the familiar; e.g., reverse Kurt Lewin's famous axiom "There is nothing so practical as a good theory." (Hunt 1987, 30) Or enjoy wry humor from witty minds, e.g., "If you can't solve a problem, at least give it an abstract title." (Hunt 1987, 13)
- Assess the impact of "ideological homogeneity" or "groupthink" (Brookfield 1998, 138) on collegial discussions. Which canons of librarianship are most often used to defend current practice? How are they helping us to flourish? How often do I feel safe in raising unpopular questions in staff meetings? How easily can I keep my subversive ideas to myself? And should I?
- What I feel depends on how I react to change and to everyday events. And how I react depends on my values, my past history of behaviors and rewards, and my current expectations. How useful now are those histories and expectations for planning services to new generations of students?
- Look for thinking confusions; for example, that teacher talking means student learning, or that movement of data means movement of minds.
- Seek out a mentor or a trusted teaching colleague in another discipline who, without getting involved in the gory details of my practice, can help me reflect and examine various perspectives on teaching. (Pratt and Associates 1998)
- Look for ethical dilemmas and figure out which kind of reasoning I most often use: is it ends-based, rules-based, or care-based? (Kidder 1995)

Section B: Focusing on Educational Matters:
- When I was an undergraduate student, how did I generally prefer to learn? Generally, how did my teachers prefer to teach? Are my answers relevant now?
- My model of instruction can best be described as...
....
- Its origins lie in ....
....
....
- Which words and acronyms tend to sprinkle my speech most often? What might the answers tell me?
- How often have I had to go to highly competent professionals, on their territory, and confess my ignorance or lack of skill?

- Recall a recent particularly good teaching moment: what bursts into the foreground? What makes that particular factor/element so prominent?
- In my current professional life, the two things that give me the most pleasure are ....and.......................…... ....because.. ....
- The two things about my work that give me uneasy feelings are ....and.. ....because.............................. ....…..
- When I encounter my own uncertainty or confusion in a work effort, how do I usually manage myself?
- When I am giving a mini-lecture or a demonstration, what things do I most often notice in the context?
- What might happen if next time I'm listening to a colleague or client and want to respond with "Yes, but...", I said instead "Yes, and furthermore..."? (Mason 2002, 79)
- When I was last confirmed as a competent professional, what actually happened? How was 'competence' defined, and who defined it?
- Which constants in my professional life sustain, and restrain, my thinking?
- "We think and write about what we perceive to be practical. And what we see as practical depends on our fundamental beliefs about education." (Wellington and Austin 1996, 307) Hmmm: which three teaching principles do I value most?
- Is there a word or phrase in my practice that I would dearly like to debate, amend, or jettison? If 'yes', which one, and why?
- Where are the energy leaks in my daily practice? And the energy intakes?
- If I gained a three-month study leave to enhance my professional significance, I would..… ....

Section C: Focusing on Learning and Learners:
- From my own experience, what seem to be the academic drivers of our younger learners? How far do any of these motivators apply to older learners? What implications do the answers have for what I want to do?
- How do I feel about the newest generation of undergraduate students? Well, to be perfectly honest, in three adjectives:

—ELIZABETH J. BURGE, ED.D—

....and....................and
....
- These feelings mean that I am most likely to
....
....
- If I were to walk around the campus looking for student 'learning energies', i.e., the small group interactions, peer tutoring, friendly advice, and collegial comfort for the cognitively afflicted, where might I most often see them? Wherever I find those energies, what does each location say about preferred learning contexts?
- Should I first try to get inside a learner's head to better understand how she/he has constructed knowledge, or should I focus on giving my expert constructions and waiting for questions? What do I tend to do?
- Recently, I was quite surprised when a young undergraduate student..............................
....
....
- Now where did that surprise come from?..
....
- What kinds of relational or identity connotations lurk behind these terms: "professional practice," "instruction," "lesson," "pedagogy," "patron," "learner support," and "lecture"?
- Recently I did something in a session with learners that made me cringe somewhat. It happened because ....
- I'll try to prevent the occurrence again by...
  But something might stop me:...
- If e-technologies make plagiarism for essays and cheating in exams easier, and if so many learners are time-stressed, how do those factors influence my place in the educational landscape?

Section D: Focusing on Colleagues:
- Thinking about two of my best colleagues: which teaching tasks do they carry out very well? How far do their 'excellencies' differ from mine? What might account for that difference?
- How do my colleagues interpret emerging signals about large-scale societal, institutional and client demographic changes? Which assumptions, needs, and habits appear to drive my colleagues' thinking? And with whom

don't I agree?
- How far do my leaders encourage critical questioning of the status quo, or even any outrageous lateral thinking? What's driving them to do so?
- What does the collection of papers at this LOEX 2003 conference, or at ACRL 2003, indicate about our professional preoccupations? Do any other topics lurk silently beneath our radar screens, needing attention?

Section E: Focusing on Other People's Literature:
- How far is/could be the design of my instruction deliberately related to issues and practices around adult learning, adult development, experiential learning, and facilitation literature?
- Recalling Tenner's revenge effects of technology applications (1997): How often do I experience any educational effects of recomplication (e.g., the phone messaging labyrinths we get trapped inside), recongestion (e.g., techno-litter in small office spaces) or regeneration (e.g., the rising expenses and use of plain paper)? Are any students involved in pilot testing our web site designs?
- If I was asked about how my instructional activity related to constructivist learning or to various models of adult cognitive development, what might come to mind?
- Avoid seduction-by-technology, or, as Joanne Smyth says, "being distracted by the format." Interrogate changing technological contexts using McLuhan and McLuhan's, four *Laws of Media*. The "it" refers to any selected change.

  What does it enhance or intensify?
  What does it render obsolete or displace?
  What does it retrieve that was previously [made obsolete]?
  What does it produce or become when [pushed] to an extreme?"
  (McLuhan and McLuhan 1988, 7)

- Rogers's work (1995) on the attributes for sustaining the adoption of any innovation looks interesting when I think of changes. Any innovation must prove Relative Advantage over existing methods, be Compatible with the everyday needs, functions and goals of its potential users, have low Complexity (as in, for example, producing minimum "revenge" effects, be Trial-able, i.e., developed and tested with the intended users (as distinct from being imposed as is), and be Observable in the users' contexts, i.e., be highly visible in places where the intended users most easily congregate. So, in a context of serious challenges to conventional librarianship, planning for such attributes means cheerful and courageous critical reflection. How sturdy are my contextual supports for doing such thinking?

Section F: Other institutional matters

- Why is my work tethered to the library building? How did that edifice-centric policy originate? How far does the rationale still apply?
- What kinds of factors and dynamics are hindering my 'getting through' to faculty members? Don't they understand my language and the intrinsic 'good' of a library?
- Do the professors talk much about their teaching and its challenges? If I cannot easily answer, what does that indicate to me?
- Deep down, how comfortable do I really feel about talking with faculty members about their course designs and learners' assignments?
- How often do I talk with colleagues in the university's teaching and learning center? Or go to their conferences; for example, conferences of POD (Professional and Organizational Development Network in Higher Education) <www. podnetwork .org>, SEDA (Staff and Educational Development Association) <www. seda.ac.uk> or STLHE (Society for Teaching and Learning in Higher Education) <www.tss.uoguelph.ca/STLHE/information .html>
- What might happen if my computer and I worked where my clients work on campus?
- What are our gate statistics telling us? If users are not visiting us in person as much we had hoped, whose problem is that?
- What would have to happen to better enable me to regard faculty members as educational partners?
- How far does my work context support reflective study circles held in work time?
- In the old days, librarians persuaded people that they and their collections were an intrinsic good waiting to be maximized. Nowadays, librarians think about disintermediation and help people learn information literacy skills. What lies ahead?

The end

Enough questions. Let us find some time, a metaphorical compass and canoe, and paddle closer to existing features in the landscape, not to mention the obstacles to our better travel. We surely can design better bridges between action and reflection, and between librarianship and the wider higher educational enterprise.

REFERENCES

Atkinson, Terry, and Guy Claxton, eds. *The Intuitive Practitioner: On The Value of Not Always Knowing What One Is Doing.* Buckingham, UK: Open University Press, 2000.

Barr, Robert B., and John Tagg. "From Teaching to Learning: A New Paradigm for Undergraduate Education." *Change* 27 (1995): 12-25.

Beard, Colin, and John P. Wilson. *The Power of Experiential Learning: A Handbook for Trainers and Educators.* London: Kogan Page, 2002.

Bolton, Gilly. *Reflective Practice: Writing and Professional Development.* London: Paul Chapman Publishing, 2001.

Boud, David, and Nod Miller, eds. *Working with Experience: Animating Learning.* London: Routledge, 1996.

Boyd, Evelyn, and Ann Fales. "Reflective Learning: Key to Learning from Experience." *Journal of Humanistic Psychology* 23 (1983): 99-117.

Brookfield, Stephen D. "The Concept of Critically Reflective Practice." In *Handbook of Adult and Continuing Education,* ed. Arthur W. Wilson and Elizabeth Hayes, 33-49. San Francisco, CA: Jossey-Bass, 2000.

Brookfield, Stephen D. "Against Naïve Romanticism: From Celebration to the Critical Analysis of Experience." *Studies in Continuing Education* 20 (1998): 127-142.

Brookfield, Stephen. D. *Becoming a Critically Reflective Teacher.* San Francisco, CA: Jossey-Bass, 1995.

—ELIZABETH J. BURGE, ED.D—

Brophy, Peter, Shelagh Fisher, and Zoë Clarke, eds. *Libraries Without Walls 4: The Delivery of Library Services to Distant Users.* London: Facet Publishing, 2002.

Burge, Elizabeth. J. "Behind-the-Screen Thinking: Key Factors for Librarianship in Distance Education." In *Libraries Without Walls 4: the Delivery of Library Services to Distant Users,* ed. Peter Brophy, Shelagh Fisher, and Zoe Clarke, 7-15. London: Facet Publishing, 2002.

Burge, Elizabeth J., Daniel Laroque, and Cathy Boak. "Baring Professional Souls: Reflections on Web Life." *Journal of Distance Education* 15 (2002): 81-98.

Burge, Elizabeth J. and Judith Snow. "Candles, Corks and Contracts: Essential Relationships Between Learners and Librarians." *The New Review of Libraries and Lifelong Learning* 1(2000): 19-34.

Burge, Elizabeth J., Judith Snow, and Joan Howard. "Distance Education: Concept and Practice." *Canadian Library Journal* 46 (1989): 329-335.

Campbell-Gibson, Chére C. "The Ultimate Disorienting Dilemma: the Online Learning Community." In *Changing University Teaching: Reflections on Creating Educational Technologies,* ed. Terry Evans and Daryl Nation, 133-146. London: Kogan Page, 2000.

Cavanaugh, Catherine, Evelyn Ellerman, Lori Oddson, and Arlene Young. "Lessons from Our Cyberclassroom." In *Using Learning Technologies: International Perspectives on Practice,* ed. Elizabeth J. Burge and M. Haughey, 61-71. London: Routledge Falmer, 2001.

Cowan, John. *On Becoming an Innovative University Teacher: Reflection in Action.* Milton Keynes, UK: Society for Research into Higher Education/Open University Press, 1998.

Crawley, Devin. "Libraries Need to Reach Tech-Savvy Students, Say U.S. Studies." *University Affairs* (April, 2003): 28.

Dewey, John. *How We Think: A Restatement of the Relation of Reflective Thinking to the Educative Process.* Lexington, MA: Heath, 1933.

Ferry, Natalie, and Jovita Ross-Gordon. "An Inquiry into Schön's Epistemology of Practice: Exploring Links Between Experience and Reflection." *Adult Education Quarterly* 48 (1998): 98-112.

Frank, Donald G., and Howell, Elizabeth. "New Relationships in Academe: Opportunities for Vitality and Relevance." *College & Research Libraries News* 64 (2003): 24-27.

Haughey, Margaret. "Using Learning Technologies: An Introduction." In *Using learning technologies: International perspectives on practice,* ed. Elizabeth J. Burge and Margaret Haughey, 3-12. London: RoutledgeFalmer, 2001.

Hillier, Yvonne. *Reflective Teaching in Further and Adult Education.* London: Continuum, 2002.

Hunt, David. E. *Beginning with Ourselves: In Practice, Theory and Human Affairs.* Cambridge, MA: Brookline Books/OISE Press, 1987.

Kidder, Rushworth M. *How Good People Make Tough Choices: Resolving the Dilemmas of Ethical Living.* New York: Fireside, 1995.

Kirkup, Gill. "Cyborg teaching." Unpublished paper. 2003.

Land, Susan M., and Michael Hannafin. "Student-Centered Learning Environments." In *Theoretical Foundations of Learning Environments,* ed. David H. Jonassen, and Susan M. Land, 1-23. Mahwah, NJ: Erlbaum, 2000.

Lightman, Alan. "Prisoners of the Wired World." *Globe & Mail,* March 10, 2002, Section R, 1, 9. Mason, John. *Researching Your Own Practice: the Discipline of Noticing.* London: RoutledgeFalmer, 2002.

McLuhan, Marshall and Eric McLuhan. *Laws of the Media: The New Science.* Toronto: University of Toronto Press, 1988.

Menzies, Heather. "The Over-Extended Academic in the Global Corporate Economy." *CAUT Bulletin,* January, 2001. www.caut.ca/english/bulletin/2001_jan/comment.asp

Mezirow, Jack. *Learning as Transformation: Critical Perspectives on a Theory in Progress.* San Francisco, CA: Jossey-Bass, 2001.

Miller, Nod. "Learning from Experience in Adult Education." In *Handbook of Adult and Continuing*

Education, ed. Arthur W. Wilson and Elizabeth Hayes, 71-86. San Francisco, CA: Jossey-Bass, 2000.

Moon, Jennifer. *Reflection in Learning & Professional Development: Theory and Practice.* London: Kogan Page, 1999.

Palmer, Parker. J. *The Courage to Teach: Exploring the Inner Landscape of a Teacher's Life.* San Francisco, CA: Jossey-Bass, 1998.

Pratt, Daniel D., and Associates. *Five Perspectives on Teaching in Adult and Higher Education.* Malabar, FL: Krieger, 1998.

Rogers, Everett M. *Diffusion of Innovations.* (4th ed.). New York: Free Press, 1995.

Rogers, Russell R. "Reflection in Higher Education." *Innovative Higher Education* 26 (2001): 37-57.

Ross-Gordon, Jovita M., ed. "Contemporary Viewpoints on Teaching Adults Effectively." *New Directions for Adult and Continuing Education, #93.* San Francisco, CA: Jossey-Bass, 2002.

Rowe, Peter G. *Design Thinking.* Cambridge, MA: The MIT Press, 1987. Reprint 1991.

Schön, Donald A. "Knowing in Action: The New Scholarship Requires a New Epistemology." *Change* 27 (1995): 26-34.

Schön, Donald A. *Educating the Reflective Practitioner: Toward a New Design for Teaching and Learning in the Professions.* San Francisco, CA: Jossey-Bass, 1987.

Schön, Donald A. *The Reflective Practitioner: How Professionals Think in Action.* New York: Basic Books, 1983.

Tenner, Edward. *Why Things Bite Back: Technology and the Revenge of Unintended Consequences.* New York: Vintage Books, 1997.

Wellington, Bud, and Austin, Patricia. "Orientations to Reflective Practice." *Educational Research* 38 (1996): 307-316.

—ELIZABETH J. BURGE, ED.D—

BREAKOUT
SESSIONS

THE DIGITAL DIFFERENCE: WHAT OPPORTUNITIES FOR INNOVATION, STUDENT INTERACTION AND REFLECTION DOES A WEB-BASED COURSE OFFER?

Jeanette McVeigh

Creating instructional sessions for in-class learning is challenging enough. Creating instruction through the medium of the World Wide Web demands more. At the University of the Sciences in Philadelphia the information science faculty was presented with the opportunity to create a for-credit course using a virtual learning environment or courseware. The course was designed with the cooperation of the occupational therapy department and intended as a capstone experience for graduating students who were participating in their final field experience. Since the field experience could be anywhere in the United States, the course, except, perhaps, the first and last class sessions, had to be online.

The members of the information science department have always taught class sessions in the courses of other departments and teach two in-person courses "Introduction to Online Sources" and "Introduction to Web Page Design" already in the curriculum. With a curriculum focused on the sciences, particularly the health sciences, the information science department chose the clinical journal article as the lynch-pin upon which many of the class sessions would hang.

McVeigh is the Coordinator of Outreach Services and Electronic Resources at the University of the Sciences in Philadelphia, Philadelphia, PA.

The article and its publication, the journal or magazine, offered a natural starting place for students to develop skills in analyzing the article for format, language, structure and their relationship to the intended audience. From article analysis, students continuously built knowledge and skills by searching their chosen topics in health databases, learning the need for their practice to be evidence-based, developing strategies for locating articles as a non-affiliated health professional using Loansome Doc and the services of their professional association, and finally navigating the murky waters of health Web sites. Piggy backed on the search for professional sources was a rare opportunity for a student in a professional program to examine typical sources of information used by the general public and to understand what guidelines are necessary to sort sources that are appropriate and correct from those that are questionable.

Creating a completely new course for online delivery offered opportunities for innovation at many levels. The course was a cooperative venture between the occupational therapy and information science departments with input from the humanities in focusing the initial sessions on the article and audience. Working with and through the courseware gave the instructors new ways to look at their instruction. The technology, WebStudy for the first semester and Blackboard for succeeding semesters, was the instructor's voice as well as her classroom. Exploiting the features the courseware offered, the connectivity and interconnectedness, along with the support for a variety of file types, created a dynamism much needed by the computer screen. Short modules took the place of in class experiences and lectures. Assignments were rethought to be shorter and more connected with the modules and succeeding weeks' experiences. Methods of engaging the students, including anonymous surveys and discussion board postings were incorporated.

Another innovative opportunity afforded by the online course is the asynchronous nature of the delivery. Students in a fairly rigid professional curriculum appreciate the opportunity to learn at a time of their choosing. Many work and participate in mandatory pre-professional experiences in addition to intense laboratory and lecture classes lasting hours. The online class offers them the independence of managing their time more efficiently.

How does a "live" class session go online? The first class of "Information Strategies for Health Care Professionals" evolved from a class on the scientific journal taught to third year chemistry students. In this class, the students, having gone to a Web site that discusses the importance of the journal article to science, were given an article from a chemistry journal. Together with the instructor, the students took yellow and pink high lighters and marked the parts of the article—Introduction, Methods, Results and Discussion, (IMRaD)—in pink and discussed the function of each part. They then nominated other parts that supply additional critical information, such as the abstract and references and discussed why they were important. These were marked in yellow.

As the opening to the new online course, this session was changed in two ways. First, it was broadened to not only emphasize the scholarly publication, in this case the clinical rather than scientific journal article, but also to include comparisons with the popular press. Many professionals must not only be able to communicate with peers but they must also be able to understand and be understood by their patients or clients. To do this they need an exhaustive base of medical, scientific, and clinical information. They must also know the limitations of their patient's knowledge and the sources of their patient's information or misinformation. For good or ill, students in the sciences are exposed to the scientific literature sometimes as early as their first year. From that point on, the popular press is prohibited as a source of information. In this course, they are given the permission to examine the popular

article in the same way they do the clinical, for format, structure, language and appropriateness to audience.

A limitation of working online is what the students can do from their end. It is easy for the students to highlight sections of an article in class. This is far more difficult to do online. To compensate for this loss, the session online exploited the Web's ability to connect to other files and other locations. A reading created in FrontPage™ explained the parts of the article and allowed for examples by creating links within the reading to scanned pdf files of different articles' IMRaD sections. Other parts of note, such as the abstract, statement of peer review, authors, and references, were also discussed with examples. Since this was a course that students in any of our health programs could take, the examples were drawn from a variety of disciplines, including occupational therapy, physical therapy, and pharmacy. This served an additional purpose of exposing the students to the language of other professions and also reinforced the durability of the IMRaD structure across many fields of inquiry.

Once the reading was conceived and constructed, the student's part seemed too passive. To address this shortcoming, questions throughout the reading asked for specific information about the examples but also asked students to connect to their prior experience, for example, by discussing an instance in their past course work or clinical experience, when they used an abstract, either from a database or a journal article, to reject an article. Another question asked if someone not well-acquainted with statistics could skip the Results section and overlook the figures and tables. It was explained that "yes" or "no" were not acceptable answers.

Not present in the live class and introduced here were examples from the popular press, from an opening quote from *Good Morning America* to a pdf of a first page from an article in a popular magazine. Students were asked to compare this first page with a first page of a clinical article on the same subject. They were further asked to reflect upon what appeal this article would have for their patients.

Although not an intended purpose, this first session has also served as a "shakedown" of the technology. While the students do have a "live" class this first week, the intent of this class is to introduce the instructors and the students to each other and to understand the basics of Blackboard, the courseware. It takes place in a computer lab on campus. Their assignment for this week is the reading and questions posted on Blackboard and it offers an opportunity for

—JEANETTE MCVEIGH—

the students to report what works and what doesn't. Since it uses a variety of file types, HTML and ftp, including a zipped file, it is a good estimator of how well things will go in future sessions. Can they get into Blackboard? Can they open the files? Do things time out?

In a second change from the "live" class, the one session was expanded to two. In the second session, additional attention was given to the publication itself, its sponsoring association, if from a professional association, its article acceptance policy, and its typical types of articles (review, research, professional practice, news). This session linked directly to examples of a complete review article and an article that applied clinical theory to practice. As an assignment, students began work on their final project by selecting particular articles that they identified as one aimed at a peer in their profession, one aimed at a health professional in another field and one that was aimed at the patient. Their final project is a 10 minute presentation on a disease or treatment aimed at their professional peers and the creation of a brochure for a patient on the same topic.

Reflection on content has altered the course each of the three semesters it has been offered. The first opportunity for reflection and change came with the realization the intended audience, occupational therapy graduating students, did not make up the majority of the enrollment. The instructors were convinced of the broadness of the appeal of the class when far more pharmacy students enrolled than any other. This necessitated additions and changes to several of the class session. In this last semester, comments from the students have led us to incorporate a brief review of basic statistical topics, such as P values and confidence intervals. Based upon students' responses on their assignments, this session that began as a one session "live" class will be expanded into a third session as more emphasis is placed on the publication and the students' choice of articles. In the assignment for the second online session, the students filled in a form for each of the three types of articles (peer, other health professional and patient) identifying specific information. This form has been reconstructed several times but still seems to confuse the students. The additional class will incorporate a discussion using the Discussion Board and will ask the students to cite the articles and discuss what elements of format, structure, and language led them to make their choices. It will also allow other students to comment on the appropriateness of the choices

Discussion boards are frequently cited as a way of opening the students to more reflective thinking. Discussions can be used to share real-life experiences direct from fieldwork. They work best when they have value, such as class participation, grades, and guidelines with rubrics, such as two postings per student and grade A for original thought with explanation or references to course readings, etc. Still, for courses that are elective and outside the student's major, the student may, and some will, make the decision not to participate. The hope is that making the discussion their major assignment and grade for the week will encourage students to actively participate. However, at a post course interview with students, several indicated that they viewed the mandatory discussion board postings as just one more thing to do. The intention of focusing reflection or providing inter-action, seemed forced to them.

During these early stages in creating and maintaining an online course, reflection, by both the students and the instructors, is on the technology as well as the content. Students comment that what constitutes an individual class online session is more involved and takes more time than what they would expect from a usual "live" class. This is, in part, due to the complex nature of connections and files and the various levels of familiarity and comfort with the technology that a class of students brings to the endeavor. Perhaps too, there is an expectation that everything on the Web is fast and easy and happens quickly.

It is important to understand why students are taking your course. Is it required? How many credits does it have? "Information Strategies for Health Care Professionals" is an elective course with three credits. As previously stated, it is also offered outside the restriction of the class schedule. At a predominantly professional school, with a heavy emphasis on the sciences, students view non-program courses as a way to boost their GPA and expect the courses to be easier than the science courses in their curriculum. The instructors always hoped that the students would do the course work to the best of their ability, but with other "must pass" courses in their professional program competing for the students' time, the student engagement was not always there. Both instructors and students had some adjusting to do. Although there were frequent opportunities to redo assignments, they were not always taken and grades suffered.

In the ideal world, the online class sessions would be engaged in over the period of a week, a module or assignment at a time. In the real world, students, particularly undergraduates, access the course information about three hours—and frequently less—before the deadline. Problems with connecting to the courseware, opening files and understanding assignments abound. The instructors found that a willingness to renegotiate due dates is necessary. It is sometimes impossible to detect on whose part (the course's or the student's) the technology failed, so it is wise to be flexible. Promptness in assigning a new deadline is of the essence, because it is so easy for a student to fall behind and drift out of contact as other assignments come due. The dialog of response to questions, misinterpretations, and reflections works online as it does in real time. The key is timeliness. The response must be in time to reinforce the importance of a concept or an assignment before it is lost in the next week's work.

There is much discussion about the assessment of online courses. From the student side, our university uses a standard twenty-one questions evaluation form for evaluating the teaching of every instructor for every course. When the instructors reviewed the questions, only six questions were deemed appropriate for the online course. Questions about the instructor's voice and command of the English language, in addition to use of classroom media, were clearly irrelevant. In addition, for "Information Strategies for Health Professionals" there is no "live" equivalent, no control group to which achievement can be compared. As new versions of Blackboard become available and the instructors exploit more of the features and other software, such as Camtasia, the class itself is constantly changing.

Finally, if you savor the give and take of the classroom, you will miss that in an online class. However, the technology does offer compensations. It encourages the instructor to be innovative and more involve in the delivery of the content as well as the content itself. Typical of a relatively new technology, it reveals limitations fairly quickly and allows for revision, almost on the fly, with no more waiting until next class. It also focuses attention on the individual student, since the online experience at this juncture, can be so individually different. It makes the instructor the facilitator, helping the student negotiate, react to and interact with the content. It encourages the student to be independent learners by giving them autonomy over when they learn. The learning can take place at 11 at night or 2 in the morning. It requires good listening and much reflection. Students have requested, and the instructors are considering, uploading and making visible all instructional material for the entire semester all at once. Our students have commented that the ability to work on assignments ahead of time, to avoid "overload" during test weeks and times when major projects are due, would be appreciated. We respect our students' concerns about their time and will make much, if not all, of the course available all at once this fall. If this is effective or foolhardy, we will learn—and change.

—JEANETTE McVEIGH —

Library Instruction for All: Exploring Ways to Accommodate All Learning Styles in and Out of the Classroom

Vivienne Piroli

Knowing about information literacy and knowing how to incorporate the ACRL standards and performance indicators into instruction sessions is not always sufficient to guarantee student learning success. It is the quest for understanding that should motivate us as teachers, as standards and principles will remain the same no matter what changes occur to an information source or the media through which it is delivered. Being motivated by this quest is tempered by the responsibility we bear to find and create paths of understanding through which students can successfully achieve lifelong learning. Learning is a complex process, but it is important to emphasize that achieving student-learning outcomes is not the only measure of teaching success. Teaching processes play a large role in ensuring student success also. Teachers need to receive training on the tools that help develop intrinsic learning and get adequate support for trying new pedagogical approaches

The bibliographic instruction group at the Simmons College libraries is made up of instruction and reference librarians. Designed as a support to all librarians involved in instruction, its purpose is to act as a resources exchange and a think tank. Group meetings allowed us time to discuss the problems inherent in trying to teach library skills and concepts to all levels of undergraduate students, graduate students,

non-traditional students, and to students in off-campus programs. The problems were all the more challenging given the fact that there is no curriculum based library instruction program at Simmons. With the exception of the first year students, all other students are taught through one-shot sessions. Clearly a new model of teaching and a fresh approach was required.

Suggesting instruction opportunities was simple enough; ensuring that they were workable, required closer examination. ACRL provides *Guidelines for Instruction for Academic Libraries* in which they list Identification of Modes of Instruction—"Instruction takes place in many ways using a variety of teaching methods. These may include, but are not limited to: advising individuals at reference desks, in-depth research consultations and appointments, individualized instruction, electronic or print instruction aids, group instruction in traditional or electronic classrooms, Web tutorials and Web-based instruction, asynchronous modes of instruction (e-mail, bulletin boards), synchronous modes of instruction (chat software, video conferencing), course management software, and hybrid or distributed learning or distance learning, employing combinations of the previous methods."[1] The bibliographic instruction group began to explore learning styles as a teaching option. The librarians were receptive to the idea of meeting students' needs based not on whether they were an undergraduate or a non-traditional student, Generation X or Y, but rather on the basis of

Piroli is Reference/Instruction Librarian at Simmons College, Boston, MA.

how they learned best. The "librarians' challenge is to match instructional styles to their student populations because students not intrinsically motivated learn better when taught in accordance with their learning style preferences."[2]

David Kolb is one of the main exponents of learning styles and explained a theory of experiential learning in his 1984 book, *Experiential Learning*. In this book he outlines and explains the four principle stages of his theory: Concrete Experience (CE); Reflective Observation (RO); Abstract Conceptualization (AC); and Active Experimentation (AE). Each of these stages is cyclical in nature, with experiential learning occurring as a result of the student's participation in the learning event. Kolb defines learning as, "the process whereby knowledge is created through the transformation of experience."[3]

Kolb developed a learning style inventory aimed at placing people on a continuum between concrete experience and abstract conceptualization and again between active experimentation and reflective observation.[4] He had identified that perception and processing are two key elements of learning with concrete experience and abstract conceptualization being two opposite types of perception and active experimentation and reflective observation, two opposite types of processing.[5] Learners tend to have a preference for one type of perception and again for one type of processing. It is these preferences and strengths that determine the way in which individuals learn. Kolb was able to identify four distinct styles based on varying combinations of the experiential learning cycle. He named them diverger, assimilator, converger, and accommodator.

Divergers are learners who favor a concrete experience and reflective observation. They like to answer the question "why" and typically prefer to reason situations with specific factual types of information. In the classroom divergers like the lecture format that presents pros and cons concerning the subject matter. They enjoy the opportunity to have hands-on time with a project or material to adequately explore it. They like to have guides and concise summaries of the material being taught. They also like to find patterns and are skilled at organizing information into a cohesive format.

Assimilators learn through reflective observation and abstract conceptualization. They want to answer the question, "what is there to know?" They prefer to have information delivered to them in a very organized and systematic way and rely on the instructor to give them correct and authoritative material. They tend to believe that every problem has a definitive answer. They like a lecture format in class and like when answer keys accompany lessons.

Convergers learn best through active experimentation and abstract conceptualization. The question this learning style seeks to answer is, "how?" They enjoying analyzing information and are generally quick to arrive at decisions based on the analysis they have done. They try to understand the information so that they can apply it and maximize its usefulness. In the classroom convergers do best when the environment is interactive. They like to be able to make connections with ideas and concepts and see them applied in a practical way. This group responds well to electronic resources and Web-based tutorials. They like to work their way through problems and set exercises.

Accomodators learn through concrete experience and active experimentation. The question this style of learner asks is, "what would happen if I did this?" This group is good at understanding complex relationships between things. Their learning experience has to be meaningful and they draw on the experience of others as well as their own when learning new material. They generally take an intuitive rather than analytical approach to problem solving. They are action oriented and like to put theory into practice. In the classroom they require feedback to keep them focused on the problem they are working with.

While Kolb identified four distinct learning styles, his theory didn't imply that every person fell neatly into one of the categories. As instructors we knew we would have to make it our goal not only to provide instruction for all the styles but also to gently push students into learning in ways that might not be their dominant style. Sonia Bodi writes, such an approach, "will help students to learn in their own styles and to develop abilities in all four quadrants of the circle, thus increasing their effectiveness as learners."[6] Ultimately we wanted to use the Kolb approach for all our instruction interactions but due to time and staffing constraints we had to prioritize where our efforts would go first. Unanimously we opted to try it out in our classroom settings. We believed the classroom offered us a better chance to experiment, reflect, and assess our experiences. We choose an instruction series that allowed us access to the same group of students twice in the one academic year. These were the students in the first year Multidisciplinary Core Course (MCC).

MCC is a first-year program where the content

of the course surrounds multidisciplinary topics designed to encourage students to explore and learn about multiculturalism while also learning about research and writing processes. To facilitate and support the goals of the course library jeopardy (based on the popular television game show) was introduced. These goals included getting first year students into the library early in the fall semester, giving them a friendly introduction to the librarians and the libraries' services and service points, showing them the library's collections and catalog and having them check out books. Library jeopardy therefore had to be much more than just a quiz game. It involved a self-guided tour of the library using explanatory posters. The instruction team prioritized the areas, collections, and services that students needed to know about and developed a series of thirteen posters to illustrate each of them. The content focused on things such as how to print, finding periodicals in the stacks, to what students needed to check out a book. The questions for the library jeopardy game were based on the content of the posters. One of the posters based on the library catalog had index cards attached to it. Each card contained an MCC related topic. During the tour students took one of these cards, searched the catalog for a book on the topic, went to the stacks to retrieve it, and finally to the circulation desk to check it out.

The second semester workshops were held in computer classrooms. After the fun and novelty of library jeopardy, expectations for an engaging workshop session were high. Librarians planned them with a high active learning quotient. Snavely in *Designs for Active Learning* notes, "This active engagement helps students integrate new material with what they already know. It helps them form new ideas in their own words and it helps students with a variety of learning styles understand the material in ways they would not if it was delivered in a lecture format. In short it increases student's learning."[7] The workshops needed to be able to guide students through the research process.

Librarians and students worked as a group to brainstorm ideas, create a keyword grid, and identify sources to search. Librarians developed a Web-based course guide, which acted as the backbone of the class with all of the activities being anchored to it. Students learned how to brainstorm a topic an exercise, that produced keywords used for creating concepts maps and later keyword grids. The keyword grid provides a useful segue into teaching the concepts inherent in Boolean operators. We turned this into an activity. Librarians held up signs with words such as "jeans" and "glasses" as well as "jeans" or "glasses." Students were asked to be records in a database and had to stand if they matched the particular Boolean query. This way they had a visual and experiential understanding of the concepts. They were also able to see how the operators controlled the search elements in the keyword grid. During the hands on search period librarians and faculty roved around the classroom answering questions, making suggestions, and reiterating some of the earlier content. Students were given research logs to track their own progress through the workshop. Given that much of the curriculum and pedagogy was based on our understanding of Kolb's experiential learning, we can see how the MCC library jeopardy and workshops embodied an active effort to incorporate activities to appeal to the four main types of learning styles and their combinations.

The self-guided tour of the library and the game of library jeopardy appealed in particular to those who were Divergers. The posters guiding the tour could be approached in any order and the information on them was discrete. During library jeopardy the entire section was able to collaborate on the answer to each question. While the answers to the questions in library jeopardy were designed to avoid ambiguity, the fact that there were a variety of questions within each category meant this group had a chance to look at topics from a variety of angles. The brainstorming and keyword grid activity fulfilled the Divergers needs for such stimulation. It satisfied their need for bringing people and ideas together with the goal of solving a problem.

Assimilators belong to the group that likes to learn through observation and by thinking about the problem. In library jeopardy the success of a section depended on teamwork just as much as it relied on the intelligence or domination of any one learning style. Even if Assimilators were not active participants in library jeopardy or the classroom activities they benefitted from the experience of the self-guided tour, checking out a book, and brainstorming in class as all of these activities helped to create their theoretical framework for understanding the services and resources of the library. The Web-based course guide gave them a chance to revisit the content of the workshops after they were over. In their own time they could assimilate the information and if they needed further help they could e-mail or call a librarian. The experience was an initial introduction to the library and one, which they could build on, in their future use of its resources.

The active learning approach was suitable for Convergers. As their preference is for thinking and doing, the tour of the library combined with the information on the posters allowed them to get a picture of the layout of the library and how the services and resources intersected with the physical space. Their desire to see information used in a practical way was well served by the exercise where they took the index card, looked up the topic printed on the card, found a book, retrieved it from the stacks, and checked it out. The activities in the workshop made the links between the process and the practice from the brainstorming and keyword grids to then having an opportunity to apply these skills and concepts in real database searches.

Accomodators preferred approach is one based on trial and error methods and less likely to occur as a result of reasoned thinking. Active experimentation helps this group to learn optimally. For them the self-guided tour, library jeopardy and the research workshops provided the active learning experience. The catalog search and finding a book in the stacks gave them ample opportunity to try to achieve the objective using a variety of methods. The brainstorming and keyword grids in the workshops provided them with a lot of freedom in choosing strategies to apply in their database searching. This experience gave the Accomodators challenge and action, both of which they respond to favorably.

The overall response to the MCC program has been a positive one. Faculty are pleased to see their students engaged in the learning and research process. While the emphasis in designing the curriculum was to incorporate elements to appeal to all of Kolb's learning styles we have not assessed the impact the experience has had on individual styles. To assess the learning that has taken place for each learning style would require us to administer pre and post tests. This is something that time does not currently permit. Additionally its value is questionable, as it is not as important to know how each student experienced library jeopardy or the workshops as it is to know what they took away from both. The area for assessment is in the curriculum development. This internal type of assessment ensures that we continue to offer learning opportunities to MCC students with all learning styles.

In 2002 the Simmons College Libraries received an internal grant to start live digital reference. The software provided librarians and users with the ability to chat, co-browse, and share applications via computer. It was the live aspect of digital reference that heightened interest in its potential as a teaching tool. Typical transactions involved students clicking on the call button from the libraries' Web page or from their course pages in WebCT.

Analyzing the service in terms of its learning potential indicated that it offered a variety of ways for the librarian to teach the user about the library and its resources. While accessing digital reference required the user to have a significant comfort level with computers and technology. The types of questions asked indicated that computer literacy or fluency did not equate with information literacy. Many users required the librarian to do much of the work towards answering their question while others wanted to avail themselves of the co-browsing features in the software and get the information they required in a collaborative partnership with the librarian.

Within digital reference, users representing all of Kolb's learning styles have an opportunity to learn in a way that suits them best while remaining exposed to other approaches. Convergers who prefer to deal with things rather than people may have derived delight at not having to deal with the librarian face to face. When they asked a question they received not only the text response from the librarian through the chat feature, but they also got to see the concepts being explained through a practical demonstration. The interactive nature of the co-browsing also allowed them the opportunity to try out their own searches and test their ability to follow the librarian's example in a guided environment where feedback was available.

Accomodators benefitted from the concrete aspects of being able to see and do their own searching. As a group they like to be able to determine the relevance of the material they find. The approach of the librarian was to let the user choose the entries they wanted to see through co-browsing. As a service, digital reference can provide an immediate response to a remote user. Accomodators appreciate this type of availability as they try to solve problems. They too like the Converger benefit from the availability of the librarian to offer comments and guide them through the search until their question is answered.

Divergers preferring to think about their information needs first, were given an opportunity to discuss the nature of their request through the chat function and see a search done by the librarian before they tried one themselves. The chat piece was particularly important to this group as they could brainstorm their topic and refine the nature of their information request before actually doing any searching. While not a face to face interaction, it did give this group a live connection to a human being. As

—VIVIENNE PIROLI—

they like to deal with people, the live digital reference interaction was preferable to e-mail reference.

Assimilators like the lecture format and concrete documents. Providing some of our print guides in digital form gave this group some specific bodies of knowledge that they could refer to later. The transaction for this leaning style may have been too rushed for them to fully absorb the process and content at the time, but having the transcript e-mailed to them gave them an account of everything that took place. This they could review and implement in their own time and at their own pace. The search process done by the librarian did not require them to be actively involved. It was an opportunity to observe the research process and absorb the strategies used to find information, which they could later emulate.

Just as the learning styles were considered when developing digital reference policies and procedures, so too were they considered when we took a fresh look at our reference interview techniques. Many librarians argue for the separation of reference and instruction, but with the previously mentioned absence of a formal instruction program in the Simmons College curriculum, we had to find ways to extend instruction at every point of contact. Using a problem solving approach to each transaction often occurred at the reference desk so it was a matter of raising awareness among reference desk staff on how our behavior and actions could affect student learning.

Many reference transactions take place in more than one segment with students asking an initial question and coming back with follow-up queries. This behavior is typical of Convergers who like to think about the problem they are dealing with before acting on it. Reference staff now understood this behavior as a learning style rather than seeing it as a student who was unable to formulate her research question. Working with this type of learner at their workstation was very beneficial as they could listen to the suggestions of the librarian and then try their own searches and refer back to the librarian for additional guidance as needed.

Accomodators we noticed were the students that spent a long time at the workstation or roaming in the stacks. Usually the furrows in their brows drew kindly reference staff to ask them if they needed help. As they are active experimenters, it is not unusual that they were reluctant to ask questions as they expect they will figure things out on their own. Again, when working with them, librarians generally let them take over the keyboard even at the reference desk.

Working with students to help them brainstorm their topic was a useful approach for Divergers. It is not unusual for a student to come to the desk asking for information on a broad topic such as pollution, or access to healthcare, for which they have no focus, research question, or hypothesis. The activity of teasing a focus out of the topic through open-ended questioning works for Divergers. They can see their subject matter in different lights. Talking to them about possible information sources sets up a framework from which they can begin to search for information on their topic. Offering a handout on criteria for assessing information lets them control the examination for credibility and reliability in the sources they use.

Assimilators are another group that make good use of the handouts and research guides offered by the libraries. Librarians made special attempts to turn computer monitors towards the student when showing library resources or executing a search. This allowed them to see the process before they replicated it.

To ensure library staff approached the reference interview and transaction in a consistent way, we built the model into our new staff training and staff refresher sessions. In this environment we could effectively show how student behaviors were not indicative of intelligence levels and abilities but rather of the way in which students learn. Staff then had a rationale for proceeding with this teaching approach while doing reference.

Learning is continuous for both the students we teach and for us as we explore ways to make our teaching relevant, meaningful, and seamlessly present in our reference and instruction services. We must acknowledge as Chickering and Gamson have that, "Learning is not a spectator sport. Students do not learn much just by sitting in class listening to teachers, memorizing prepackaged assignments, and spitting out answers. They must talk about what they are learning, write about it, relate it to past experiences, apply it to their daily lives. They must make what they learn part of themselves."[8] This statement mirrors the principles of information literacy acquisition, which is our prime focus as instruction librarians. Given that the learning styles of most librarians are those of Assimilator and Converger it is important that librarians are open to the various ways people learn and extend their teaching repertoires to meet the challenge.[9]

Knowledge and understanding of learning style theories can help the library profession to present students and users of libraries with the means to achieve information literacy. It is important that librarians continue to refine the way they teach and remain active in their approaches to teaching and learning. Reflecting on past experiences and willingly experimenting with new and proven methodologies can help to keep an instruction librarian energized and enthused by their profession.

NOTES

1. Policy Committee of ACRL's Instruction Section, "Guidelines for Instruction Programs in Academic Libraries," *College & Research Libraries News* 63, no. 10 (2002): 733.

2. Kate Manuel, "Teaching Information Literacy to Generation Y." *Journal of Academic Librarianship* 36, no. ½ (2002): 196.

3. David A. Kolb, *Experiential Learning* (Englewood Cliffs, NJ: Prentice Hall, 1984): 26.

4. David A. Kolb, *The Learning Style Inventory: Technical Manual* (Boston: McBer, 1976).

5. Sonia Bodi, "Teaching Effectiveness and Bibliographic Instruction: The Relevance of Learning Styles." *College & Research Libraries* 51 (March 1990): 116.

6. Bodi, 117.

7. Loanne Snavely, "Active Learning in the Library Instruction Classroom," in *Designs for Active Learning: A Sourcebook of Classroom Strategies for Information Education,* ed. by Gail Gradowski, Loanne Snavely, Paula Dempsey (Chicago: Association of College and Research Libraries, 1998): vii.

8. A.W. Chickering and Z.F.Gamson, "Seven Principles for Good Practice in Undergraduate Education," *AAHE Bulletin* 39 (1987): 7.

9. J.M. Choi, "Learning Styles of Academic Librarians," *College & Research Libraries* 50 (November 1989): 691.

—VIVIENNE PIROLI—

PATTERNS OF SELF-ASSESSMENT
FOR TEACHING AND LEARNING

Janice Krueger

A frequent temptation for those in professional roles as teachers and librarians is the development of direct instructional approaches aimed at introducing large amounts of information and implementing a host of activities theoretically connected to all the topics covered in the allotted time. Librarians particularly, succumb to this temptation when given only one class period per semester to familiarize students with the gamut of library resources. All too often the enduring concept, goal, or principle is lost, allowing whatever seems to work for the moment to become fossilized for fear of change or lack of time and personnel to do so. Time for reflection and evaluation of the process in light of the results is not set aside due to the varied demands of busy schedules.

Professional educators have wrestled with this same issue on an even larger scale when developing standards, establishing curriculum, and selecting classroom materials. Throughout the last six decades curriculum developers and educational reformers have proposed strategies and formulated questions to direct teachers' focus on maintaining enduring concepts and relevant practices. Particular curriculum theories and practices formulate mechanisms with inherent reflection and assessment tools to foster and understand patterns of learning. Librarians can benefit from these

strategies as they engage in planning and designing the one time opportunity during a semester, partnering with faculty for a semester course, or implementing a separate information literacy course.

Summarizing and bridging the ideas begun in the late forties and recently practiced by educators is a question posed in the mid-sixties by John Holt, a leader in educational reform, "Where are we trying to get, and is this thing we are doing helping us to get there?" (Holt 1964, 134). Posing this question before, during, and after designing any course of study or instruction session can prompt teachers and librarians to focus on the essential concepts and employ the principles embodied in the backward design approach. This method, put forth by Wiggins and McTighe, forces educators to uncover the essential, enduring concepts of a lesson or course and to determine the acceptable evidence or proof of understanding of these concepts. Therefore, one starts thinking like an assessor instead of an activity planner (Wiggins and McTighe 1998, 86; Black 2001). The authors attribute this approach to Tyler, who formulated his ideas on curriculum while teaching at the University of Chicago (Wiggins and McTighe 1998; Marsh and Willis 2003). One can note the similarities between both methods by studying the following criteria of each.

Krueger is the Electronic Resources and Serials Librarian at the University of the Pacific, Stockton, CA.

Tyler (Marsh and Willis 2003, 71)	Wiggins and McTighe 1998, 9
--What educational purpose should the school seek to attain?	--Identify desired results.
--How can learning experiences be selected that are likely to be useful in attaining these objectives?	
--How can learning experiences be organized for effective instruction?	--Determine acceptable evidence.
--How can the effectiveness of learning experiences be evaluated?	--Plan learning experiences and instruction.

The key similarity between the two is the clear identification of the purpose, outcomes, and results of the educational experience from the beginning of the planning stage. Once identified, the next task is to determine what constitutes proof that learning has taken place. Then, and only then, are the learning experiences and activities planned, reading materials selected, and appropriate resources gathered.

Wiggins and McTighe have extended and modernized Tyler's rationale of looking at the ends and means together into a Backward Design model applicable to many different disciplines and uses. Wilcox and Wojnar (2000) employed the direction of Backward Design in the development of their online teacher preparation course. Moore and Hinchman (2003) recommend the process in developing meaningful units of instruction to handle the current emphasis for standards based outcomes. Given the strict standards developed in most states, Backward Design can build on them and facilitate the remaining aspects of curriculum planning.

One value of the Backward Design model is that it provides a structure for positively satisfying the demands of the current standards based movement for educators. Since the objectives are already embedded within the standards, teachers can then extract the enduring concepts, figure out the most effective assessments, plan the necessary learning experiences and activities, and select the necessary materials and resources. Another value is that, even though it provides a well-defined and structured approach, it is open-ended and applicable to a variety of situations. The planners, teacher, librarian, or administrators, make the initial determinations on the essential content. The first stage, Identifying Desired Results, allows the designers to determine worthwhile knowledge, overarching concepts, formulate essential questions, and determine applicable knowledge and skills. The second stage, Determine Acceptable Evidence, provides the opportunity to decide what assessment pieces will provide acceptable proof and evidence of learning. Depending on the situation and discipline or topic, this could be anything from quizzes, papers, labs, portfolios, etc. that give the learner the opportunity to demonstrate what they have learned through the required reading, experiences and activities. The third, final stage is reserved for the actual planning of the resource material, experiences, and activities that will facilitate the desired outcomes. Wiggins and McTighe also recommend six facets of understanding, explanation, interpretation, application, perspective, empathy, and self-knowledge, for incorporation into the planning process and design of learning experiences and activities. A reminder for key practices and the overall process is summarized in their design tool using the acronym WHERE explained below (Wiggins and McTighe 1998, 190).

W How will you help students know *where* they are headed and *why*?

H How will you *hook* students through engaging and thought provoking experiences?

E What learning experiences will *engage* students in exploring the big ideas and essential questions?

R How will you cause students to *reflect* and *rethink* to dig deeper into the core ideas? How will you guide students in *revising* and *refining* their work?

E How will students *exhibit* their understanding through final performances and products? How will you guide *self-evaluation*?

The formulation of this design tool into the acronym WHERE replicates in a more defined, pointed, and detailed way the heart of the question asked by Holt over thirty years ago. Deriving the essentials and heart of the topic at hand is an important accomplishment for educators and librarians, especially during this time of high stakes testing, reduced budgets, and "any information anywhere" mentality. Also built into the planning is an opportunity to set aside time for reflection and self-assessment for both the student and teacher.

Implications for Librarians

The three stages of the Backward Design model of planning can be incorporated into the type of instructional situations librarians are called upon for guidance, participation, and implementation. They provide a framework to focus on the desired objectives and outcomes of an information literacy course required by some institutions to meet competency requirements. The stages can also work well in a more integrated approach in which librarians work closely with faculty to weave research and information literacy skills into the content of a semester long course. Finally, using these three stages for a one time instruction session can prevent information overload, guiding the librarian to focus on the essential points. In these situations, the amount and types of assessments are limited and may require partnering with faculty to review course products in general.

Furthermore, three of the six facets of understanding are core to the nature and type of "subject matter" dealt with by librarians. The rubrics established for the facets of explanation, application, and self-knowledge are applicable to a progression and demonstration of comprehension of library and research skills required by the dynamic nature of resources, particularly electronic materials. Self-knowledge even becomes important for librarians as they try to cope with new products, new ways of integrating resources, and new ways of structuring information and retrieval. They have to be in tune with what they do and do not know, how to apply old methods of retrieval with new ways of building information, and how to revitalize instructional strategies and techniques to match differences in prior knowledge of younger students and faculty.

An added benefit is the spiral curriculum approach that results from implementing this model (Wiggins and McTighe 1998). There is a continual interplay and building on what already exists in a student's prior knowledge so the student moves into a new level of understanding. An integration with what is already known as essential offers a foundation for deeper levels of understanding as students progress along a continuum.

Discussion of Course Example

Attendees of this session participated in a discussion of the Backward Design model in relation to a University of the Pacific freshman seminar course as it was taught when I was working with the faculty to develop the library segment of the course approximately two years ago. The course as a whole and the annotated bibliography assignment were redefined according to the Backward Design model and are described here.

The Freshman Course (according to Backward Design)

Desired Results
    Awareness of Social Issues
    Realization of possible solutions to improve quality of life
Acceptable Evidence
    Small research assignments on an introduced topic
    Debates on social topic
    Participation in small group discussions
    Annotated bibliography
    Incremental pieces of larger paper
    Culminating group policy paper
Learning Experiences
    Rotating leadership of group discussions
    General sessions with invited speaker
    In class debates
    Larger debate competition with entire freshman class
    Library assignments

The Annotated Bibliography (according to Backward Design)

Desired Results
    Identify keywords for topic
    Locate a variety of scholarly resources
    Evaluate the credibility and usefulness of the resources
    Format citations correctly
    Write descriptive, critical and evaluative annotations

Acceptable Evidence

Annotated bibliography

Additional library assignment

Learning Experiences

Group work

Library research

Meeting with professor/supplemental instructor

Participants were asked to either create an accompanying library assignment for the bibliography activity or a separate library activity for the course according to Backward Design principles using the WHERE design tool, keeping in mind that faculty requested all 700 plus freshman be given an instruction session during the first three weeks of the semester. The group chose to work together instead of breaking up into smaller groups in the interest of time, but also asked for clarification regarding topics, requirements for the annotated bibliography, and group work. Their essential findings were as follows:

- Smaller assignments focusing on specific databases, or resources, were needed.
- The timing of instruction should have been closer to when students need the library resources.
- Parameters for topic selection would guide students towards positive results.

After noting overall faculty dissatisfaction with the library portion of the course, I had an opportunity to propose a new implementation for library research skills through a university grant. Since the course traditionally employs the use of supplemental instructors (SI)—older students, to act as teaching assistants—I requested some instruction sessions with them along with the chance to have them test a new online tutorial for integration with the course. The basic purpose was to give the SIs enough background to act as peer mentors and participate in small instruction sessions as the need for a particular resource was encountered. I did receive the grant to work with the SIs, but, since there were a number of new aspects to implement in the seminar course, I actually had only one instruction session with them. The course, however, took a definite turn for a more integrated model when the professors took responsibility for providing research instruction according to smaller lessons and assignments designed by the librarian working with the faculty on the

planning committee. I strongly feel that this was an outcome of my proposal and attempt at using a peer-mentoring model designed around shorter visits to individual class sections by the SIs and librarians.

Future Possibilities

The reflective and self-evaluation aspects of this model coincide with key points of the Action Research approach to curriculum implementation. While Backward Design aids in curriculum design and planning, Action Research can be the mechanism for full implementation. Although originally conceived as a method to involve teachers in tackling larger social and political issues in education, such as race, gender, equity, and social justice in formal classroom situations, it can engage educators in personal and professional reflection resulting in dynamic, rather than static, educational programs (Marsh and Willis 2003). It has actually assisted teachers in solving their own problems, growing in their own self-awareness of personal learning patterns, learning about discrepancies in their own beliefs and their actual practices, and understanding their students' thought processes (Zeichner and Gore 1995). Action Research particularly calls for elements of discussion, reflection, rethinking, and evaluation of teaching practices and learning experiences for improvement (Marsh and Willis 2003). The cyclical nature of Action Research supports and reinforces the spiral curriculum of Backward Design. Both allow educators and administrators to move the curriculum and students along a continuum of higher order thinking and give students the opportunity to grow in self-awareness of their own learning patterns, becoming self-directed life long learners.

WORKS CITED

Black, Susan. Stretching Students' Minds. *American School Board Journal,* 188 (June 2001): 31-33.

Holt, John. *How Children Fail*. New York: Pitman Publishing, 1964.

Marsh, Colin J., and George Willis. *Curriculum: Alternative Approaches, Ongoing Issues*. 3rd ed. Upper Saddle River, NJ: Merrill/Prentice Hall, 2003.

Moore, David W., and Kathleen A. Hinchman. *Starting Out: A Guide to Teaching Adolescents who*

—JANICE KRUEGER—

Struggle with Reading. New York: Allyn and Bacon, 2003.

Wiggins, Grant, and Jay McTighe. *Understanding by Design*. Alexandria, VA: Association for Supervision and Curriculum Development, 1998.

Wilcox, Bonita L., and Linda C. Wojnar. "Best Practice Goes Online." *Reading Online* 4 (August 2000): 1-19. Internet on-line. Available from <http://www.readingonline.org/articles/art_index.asp?HR EF=/articles/wilcox/index.html>. [26 April 2003].

Zeichner, Kenneth, M., and Jennifer M. Gore. "Using Action Research as a Vehicle for Student Teacher Reflection: A Social Reconstructionist Approach." In *Educational Action Research:Becoming Practically Critical,* edited by Susan E. Noffke and Robert B. Stevenson, 13-30. New York: Teachers College Press, 1995.

TEACHING AS AN ACT OF COURAGE: TAKING OUR TEACHING TO THE NEXT LEVEL

BethAnn Zambella and Susan Barnes Whyte

Introduction

Susan and I know how scarce time for reflection is, so we wanted to spend the next hour giving you a lecture about "the 7 habits of highly-reflective people".... Not. But we do feel your pain. At Wellesley College, I'm what's known as a "working manager." That means I'm supposed to spend 50 percent of my time administering my group and 50 percent of my time doing the actual work of my group. It breaks down to more like 75/75. Time for what I would call ordinary thinking, let alone 'reflection,' gets knocked off the bottom of my to-do list every day. What we want to do today is to give you some tools to work with, so you can jump-start your reflection (isn't that an oxymoron?!) and maybe your whole group's reflection, in the limited time you may be able to carve out for it. In the March 2003 issue of *American Libraries*, Walt Crawford wrote a column about the "Century's Most Vital Technological Device." Did anyone read that? Can anyone guess what he chose? It was the "off" button.

Susan and I spent time together last year at the Frye Institute in Atlanta. We had some impassioned conversations about Parker Palmer (instead of about leadership in higher education, which was the theme of the Institute), and that's how the idea for this workshop began. Since we decided on this topic, I've been seeing

---

Zambella is Research and Instruction Group Manager at Wellesley College, Wellesley, MA and *Barnes Whyte* is Library Director at Linfield College, McMinnville, OR.

signs of it everywhere. On the flight here, the airline magazine had an article about a journalist who was accustomed to interviewing CEOs and other bigwigs. He talked about one interview that just wasn't going well. The CEO was giving one-word answers, no matter what the interviewer asked. Finally, he took a good look around the CEO's office and saw that he was interested in cars. He said, "Well, I see you're interested in cars..." and thought that would break the ice. The CEO said, "Yup." Finally, in desperation, the interviewer said, "Well, I'm restoring a '67 Thunderbird myself, and my wife thinks I'm nuts." That's what opened up the conversation. The interviewer had to reveal something of himself. Parker Palmer says teaching is all about knowing yourself and revealing some of that to your students. I'll let Susan tell you more about how Parker Palmer's message resonates with the theme of reflective teaching.

Here's how this workshop is going to work. First, Susan will talk briefly about Parker Palmer's first chapter in his book *The Courage to Teach*. Then we'll do three different participatory exercises: a metaphor exercise to pop our brains open a bit, a reflection on best and worst teaching moments, and an exploration of the concept of organizational blasphemies.

Parker Palmer's Acts of Courage

Welcome to this workshop which is focusing on teaching as an act of courage. All of us are probably nervous when we teach. Why? Teaching is a courageous act for many people because, in the end, despite your best PowerPoint or web page design, you still need to connect with the people in the class, to make those students care about the material. We work in a culture, higher education, which values expertise and does not allow for possible failure in teaching. One way we all cope with possible failure in the classroom, when we might appear to be stupid or even wrong in front of students, is to fill up our classes with content, in order to demonstrate to ourselves and to our students what we *do* know. This filling-up of class time and space does not necessarily open up the space for our students to learn, as Parker Palmer says (Livsey and Palmer 1999, 9). The filling-up of a library instruction section with the details of the perfect search or with all the many delightful ways people can search in any given database can often bore students, because there is little chance for them to connect with the content, much less to connect with us.

Good teaching—where the students and the teacher leave the classroom thinking that the experience worked—does not come from filling the space up. Good teaching comes from connecting with the students. In order to connect with students, you must have a strong sense of who you are, identity and integrity as Parker Palmer says in the first chapter of *The Courage to Teach* (Palmer 1998). Neither can you succeed as a teacher by trying to teach like someone else whose approach to teaching you admire. Each teacher needs to figure out through trial and error those classroom techniques that work. And, because some techniques don't work, failure plays an important role in this developmental process. Being a good teacher means thinking about what works for you. What techniques fit with your identity? What methods suit your integrity? Which ones challenge and favorably expand your presence as a teacher? If you're uncomfortable with a certain approach in the classroom, students will know it, immediately.

As Palmer says: "The connections made by good teachers are held not in their methods but in their hearts—meaning heart in its ancient sense, as the place where intellect and emotion and spirit and will converge in the human self" (Palmer 1998, 11). Reflective teaching isn't just about affect, it's about bringing a sense of who you are to the classroom, to the students, because people connect with people and then connect with the knowledge. It is an act of courage to go before people every day, each semester. It's a risk that we all take. Sometimes it works, sometimes it doesn't. The challenge in teaching is to balance your expectations and theirs and to understand that the best is rarely achieved, but that often we can reach students if we let them reach us.

In order to fully explore who you are as a teacher, it's useful to talk about teaching with your colleagues in the library and in various departments across the campus. Yet this conversation is difficult to start, much less sustain in a meaningful fashion. Academic culture distrusts conversations about personal experience, as Parker points out in his lead chapter (Palmer 1998). Often we're taught to view knowledge objectively and at a distance from who we are. Yet I imagine that all of us remember our favorite teachers as those who were vividly human, who lived their knowledge. I remember my piano teacher in college for whom music was the essence of being, my high school field hockey coach who taught me the importance of focus and why that was important in the moment, and my French literature teacher who kept asking me to think deeper and harder, to go below the surface of the words on the page, as he did in each class. One way to start reflective conversations about teaching is with the non-threatening but powerful tool of metaphor.

Metaphor Exercise

At this point, we asked everyone to take part in an exercise using metaphor. We led off with some examples of our own: For example, Barbara J. Phillips, a professor at the University of Saskatchewan, says "For me, teaching is like stuffing a back-pack." Author and teacher Melannie Svoboda has titled her book, *Teaching is like—peeling back eggshells*. BethAnn posited that teaching is like "playing a game of 'energy ping-pong,' because you throw your energy out into the classroom and hope that someone will return the volley." For Susan, teaching is like "playing improvisational jazz: the theme may remain constant, but the variations are many and sometimes unexpected."

At their tables, individuals wrote down their own ending to the sentence "Teaching is like…" and then talked about what their metaphors meant to them with others at their table. Some themes that resonated around the room included the idea that teaching is like a performance. Teaching was described as "dancing with someone you don't know, performing in a play, performance art, a cabaret act, an audition, cantoring at a church service," and "dancing in your living room with the neighbors watching through the window."

Another theme focused on uncovering mysteries: for those participants, teaching is like "inviting students to share in a wonderful secret, hunting for treasure, and helping solve a mystery." For many, the metaphors revolved around journeys and navigation:

—BETHANN ZAMBELLA AND SUSAN BARNES WHYTE—

"traveling to a familiar destination on a new freeway, being the tour guide at a large and fast-growing nature preserve, trying to navigate the parking lot at Disney World, canoeing down a stream where you don't always know what's around the next bend, paddling white water on a good day." Further themes includes playing games, gardening, interior design, images of water, light, chaos, cooking and chemistry. One participant connected with the reflective theme of the workshop by saying, "Teaching is like becoming reacquainted with a part of yourself you've lost track of."

Best and Worst Moments

Parker Palmer asks us to think about which aspects of our identity and integrity feel most supported by and engaged with the teaching that we do (Livsey and Palmer 1999, 17). And, conversely, to think about what aspects of our identity and integrity feel most threatened by our work. Truly reflective teaching takes place in those moments of thought, fleeting or intentionally-prolonged, when we ask ourselves what happens in the classroom, why it happens, what we want to change. Reflective teaching requires a certain amount of risk, because change is an intrinsic piece of the thinking-through, figuring-out, asking-why and trying-out process that teaching and learning are all about.

As John Dewey said, reflective teachers ask themselves why they are doing what they do, as they approach their teaching with a "wholeheartedness." In other words, "teachers who are wholehearted regularly examine their own assumptions and beliefs and the results of their actions and approach all situations with the attitude that they can learn something new" (Zeichner and Liston 1996, 10). Aha! Reflective teaching can mean trying something new, expanding our repertoire of approaches or methods. Doing the same old 45-minute lecture in that 50-minute instruction session not only bores the students, it bores us the teachers. Doing something new requires that we take risks and refuse to label the things that don't work as failures.

Best and Worst Exercise

We asked participants to think about their best and worst teaching moments on a "spectrum" represented by a long piece of paper on the wall, from best, to pretty good, to bad, to worst. Participants wrote down their moments, then a few shared their moments with the rest of the group.

Some worst moments included a student flossing continually, teaching to an assignment that the students had already turned in that very day, or working with students to brainstorm topics with concepts maps. During the map exercise, the faculty member crossed out one of the group's maps, saying that they were all wrong.

Bad moments ranged from mistyping a URL and having a porn site appear on screen in front of the class, to having 30-minutes' notice to teach a class that the librarian had never taught before and having the faculty member not even come to the class. Another bad moment happened when a participant misspelled words on the board and didn't notice it for 15 minutes; meanwhile, students were taking bets on when she would finally notice. And, one of the funniest, a participant had loudly asked a student to stop perching on the top of a chair; he was on a stool.

Pretty good moments happened when students stayed after class to discuss other applications of what they learned or when the technology failed and students had to listen and participate. One wonderful story emerged from a librarian attached to an oxygen tank. During one class, she had walked away from her cart and the oxygen got disconnected. The class, filled with nursing students, spent the class time researching the librarian's medical condition.

Best moments were fewer, but one librarian mentioned "The Grandmaster Flash Moment" and the "Lens Bias Moment." I would love to hear about more about what these mean. Another talked about teaching a class to choose a database by letting the class discover it for themselves. A few mentioned applause from the students.

Going into this workshop, we did not really know what to expect from this exercise. We guessed that perhaps everyone would focus on the worst rather than the best, because it's easier to remember what went wrong than what worked. And we did have more examples of the worst rather than of the best. What *did* work though was the sharing of stories. The spirit of this group at LOEX was superb. Everyone was eager to think and speak and listen. And some participants enjoyed the best/worst exercise the most. One liked hearing others' stories of bad things happening in the classroom. One felt that the experience was cathartic. One librarian new to teaching appreciated this approach because it made her feel "okay about not being perfect." Several folks shared examples of "worst" moments, that, through flexible, creative and humorous thinking on their parts, actually became "best" moments, thus emphasizing the thin line that divides our perceived successes from our perceived failures. During our debriefing, we emphasized Palmer's belief, and ours, that you can't be a good teacher without experiencing some moments of failure.

Organizational Blasphemies

Organizational blasphemies are "a phrase or slogan so alien to what the group represents, that the members will squirm in their seats when they hear it" (McNulty 1983). Organizational blasphemies question assumptions about organizational and cultural values. Parker Palmer says, "in a culture of technique, we often confuse authority with power, but the two are not the same. Power works from the outside in, but authority works from the inside out." (Palmer 1998, 32) Academic culture, especially administrative culture, is great at using external power to set limits, describe known limits, and point to history. How many of you have ever made a suggestion at a meeting and heard, "We tried that—it didn't work"? Sometimes we need to turn the culture on its head to do some true reflection. There are a few folks who do it for me in the library literature—Walt Crawford, Will Manley (on a good day), Cheryl LaGuardia, Herb White. They are irreverent in a way that rigid thinkers feel borders on the blasphemous.

What are some organization blasphemies we might come up with? For a group like this, I like to start with the statement, "There *are* dumb questions." What makes you uncomfortable about that? What hits home?

After exploring some of the "dumb questions" that do get asked ("Do these stairs go up?" "Do you have any history books?" "Is your online catalog available online?"), we talked about ways that such a discussion could lead to improvements. For example, if your dumb question is "Do you have a restroom?" you might decide to improve the signage at your library. Likewise, if pen requests lead your hit list, you could get a vending machine that sells pens. If the plethora of repetitive questions drives you wacky, you might decide to develop an FAQ on your web page. Being irreverent can have an up-side, and, not only that, it builds authority, the real from-the-inside-out kind.

The full exercise on organizational blasphemies is supposed to be done in about 3 ½ hours (McNulty 1983). In the interests of giving you only a small taste of it, and of relieving gray-matter compression and threat, I thought that we would try a looser but related form of brainstorming, called "No Rules." Let's see

what we can do with it.

"No Rules" Exercise

We asked participants to brainstorm about what could happen at their libraries if there were no rules, no buts, no policies, no shortages, no fear and no baggage. Each table wrote their ideas on flip charts. What follows is just a sampling from those charts.

If there were no rules, we could
—truly challenge the status quo
—admit that teaching is messy and noisy
—hold more than one session
—stop trying to be "experts"
—make instruction a priority
—listen to each other
—get rid of the nay-sayers
—have sexy, trendy libraries
—become more student-centered
—create "discovery zones"
—team-teach every class

If there were no fear, we could
—be encouraged to make mistakes
—acknowledge that some people are inherently better teachers than others
—earn more respect as professionals and be given more autonomy
—count on faculty support

Conclusions

Our experience with this workshop proved that these three exercises are easy ways to get people to talk about their teaching. The metaphor exercise broke the ground, because it was somewhat abstract, yet personal all at the same time. The best/worst teaching moments required more self-revelation, but the metaphor exercise had already created an easy climate within the group of 50 people. And then the blasphemies exercise provided a window to thinking outside of the veritable box. This workshop revealed our human moments and was fun. In the best Parker Palmer tradition, we shared bits of who we are with each other and, in the process, learned a bit more about who we are as teachers.

—Bethann Zambella and Susan Barnes Whyte—

If there were no space or time constraints, we could carry this conversation on and on. As it is, we hope that the attendees at LOEX and readers of these proceedings will continue to think about these issues, will try some of the exercises on their own and with others, and will keep reflecting on their own practices with courage and wholeheartedness.

REFERENCES

Crawford, Walt. The Crawford Files: The Century's Most Vital Technological Device. *American Libraries*, 34 (March 2003): 84.

Livsey, Rachel C. and Parker Palmer. *The Courage to Teach: A Guide for Reflection and Renewal*. San Francisco: Jossey-Bass, 1999.

McNulty, Tony. "Organizational Blasphemies: Clarifying Values." In *The 1983 Annual for Facilitators, Trainers, and Consultants*, eds. L.D. Goodstein and J.W. Pfeiffer, 77-79. San Diego, CA: Pfeiffer & Company, 1983.

Palmer, Parker J. *The Courage to Teach: Exploring the Inner Landscape of a Teacher's Life*. San Francisco: Jossey-Bass, 1998.

Zeichner, Kenneth M. and Daniel P. Liston. *Reflective Teaching: An Introduction*. Mahwah, NJ: Lawrence Erlbaum, 1996.

THE LIBRARY-RESEARCH PAPER: A HISTORY, A CONTEXT, AND A SPECULATION

Donna J. Gunter

As a library instruction coordinator, "disconnect" is the word I would use to express the anguish I have long heard from library instructors over teaching library research methods to basic English composition classes. The received wisdom of library instructors, of course, is to encourage a library instruction session in the context of an actual library research assignment. However, library instructors often feel frustration over requests for a "basic introduction to the library." Surely more than one library instructor has fought the temptation to respond, "Giving a basic library introduction is like introducing American literature in 45 minutes." Equally frustrating is the writing faculty's pronouncement that "students can write on anything they choose" in a tone of voice that reveals the writing instructors' own dismay with the library research assignment. The instruction session turns into a generic library orientation in spite of all the best efforts to make it meaningful for the student. Soon, the library instructor burns out and turns to other professional opportunities.

This conflict is especially exasperating because English Composition classes are often the foundation and core of a library's information literacy program; after all, eighty percent of basic writing programs require a basic library-researched paper.[1] The purpose of this session is to make some sense of this "disconnect" through a discussion of the history and conceptualization of the research paper assignment. The session concludes with a speculation on the research paper assignment and library instruction.

Gunter is the Library Instruction Coordinator at the University of North Carolina, Charlotte, NC.

History of the Library-Research Paper: It's Place in the History of Education

To place the research paper assignment in its proper context, we must go back, prior to the twentieth century when education was rooted in the stability of religion and primarily for the upper classes. Those who were educated entered law, the ministry, or medicine through the study of a unified curriculum; students did not choose elective courses.[2] Additionally, few research libraries, and language skills, rooted in classical rhetoric, were tested orally. There was no such thing as a literacy crisis.[3]

At the beginning of the twentieth century, the influence of religion declined as the influence of science soared. With the excitement of science came the professions, and education segmented into departments; students could choose elective courses and the curriculum was no longer unified. Research libraries also appeared. As colleges admitted students from the middle classes, a literacy crisis ensued.[4]

To address the literacy crisis that happened with the admission of the middle classes to college, Harvard University created the first freshman writing course, called English A. Seated in the English Department, English A became the only required course by 1900. English A existed to serve other academic departments, which were preparing students for the professions.[5]

The History of the Library Research Paper: The Role of the Teaching of Literature

Complications for the teaching of the library-research paper arose because the teaching of writing and the teaching of literature were both seated in the English department. Professional departments offered a "discipline," and English departments needed a "discipline" to match other departments in stature, so they would not be viewed as a mere "service" departments. Literature was the "discipline" offered by English departments. Taught in the "New Critical" approach, which was based on scientific methodology, the teaching of literature offered a "credence" in a world of scientifically-based professions. The teaching of writing, however, instead of being a "discipline" worthy of scholarly study and analysis, was a skill that was taught in service of students preparing for the professions. Whereas the study of literature evolved through various approaches and methods, the teaching of writing stagnated in method because it was seen as secondary and service-oriented. [6]

The Library-Research Paper: From Objective Models to Subjective Models

Around the middle of the twentieth century the library research paper began its development, along with the teaching of writing in general, from a methodology that was not theorized or analyzed, to methods that are discussed in scholarly literature. Those methods are a movement from the more objective models of the first part of the century to the more subjective models of the latter part of the century.[7] Finally, composition studies became a discipline, and currently 66 doctoral degrees (38 states) in Rhetoric and Composition are offered in the United States.[8]

The Library-Research Paper: Objective Models

Objective models of teaching writing, and specifically the library-research paper, focus on writing as an end product. As the oldest models of teaching writing, they are still practiced in today's classroom, though no longer exclusively and without criticism. The term *current-traditional* method, coined in 1959, had been in practice since the early part of century. The current-traditional method, emulating scientific methodology, assumes the stability and objectivity of truth; language is assumed to convey the truth, and does not mediate it in symbol or metaphor. Since ideas are not created, but discovered, the current-traditional model focuses on the arrangement of ideas, not on the creation of ideas.[9]

A library-research paper written in the current-traditional method frequently features the thesis/defense style of organization. Since the current-traditional method assumes the transparency of the truth, the writer poses as an expert in order to set up a problem and solve it. All texts, including those used for sources, are read uniformly, and texts consulted for research are usually privileged ones found in the library. Language is distant, formal, and academic, negating the use of the first-person personal pronoun. A sense of specific audience and reader are not apparent. Correct grammar, punctuation, and citations are more important in the current-traditional method than in the methods developed toward the latter part of the century.[10]

The teacher of the library research paper, using the current-traditional paper, focuses on the end product of the paper and not on the process of creating the paper. The student must choose a topic, often from a list. Topic selection does not often emerge from a process of uncovering a deep, immediate interest or need. Another typical method is that the student is assigned a topic, with the notion that the purpose of the course is that the student learn how to organize an idea and not create one. A thesis is formulated near the beginning of the writing period, and the student is expected not to modify it. The teacher may spend a significant amount of time teaching the student how to outline, with the expectation that writing the paper will simply involve filling in the blanks of the outline. Another conventional focus of instruction is on creating note cards and proper paraphrasing techniques, and on using library resources, with little emphasis on evaluating and engaging with outside sources. The research paper is often taught as an assignment that is isolated from other writing assignments.[11]

Library research in a paper written in the current-traditional method uses academic resources, relying on texts that are privileged and found in a library. Library instruction guides the student to find information, and not toward finding and evaluating "voices." The library instructor is assumed to train students in a skill that is adjunct to the research process, and not an organic part of it.[12]

The Library-Research Paper: Subjective Methods

By the 1950s, the current-traditional method began to see competition, as composition emerged as a discipline. As a discipline, it emerged in response to a lot of frustration over the traditional term-paper assignment and with the perception that cut-and-paste methodology was too common. It became obvious that novice writers cannot be experts.[13]

Out of the emergence of composition as a discipline came more subjective models of writing. Writing specialists developed methods based on the instability of the truth, which do not try to emulate scientific methodology. Language is seen as the mediator of truth, not as a mere carrier of the truth.

—DONNA J. GUNTER—

Since language is not considered a transparent carrier of the truth, ideas are created, and texts are not uniformly read; instead they are the subject of engagement and creativity.[14]

The features of a paper written from a more subjective model may include experimentation, speculation, open-endedness, and even collaboration. Since subjective models are not based on the stability of the truth, the writer does not pose as an expert; instead, she may act as a "seeker." The paper may show evidence of awareness of the audience and reader, in which the first person pronoun "I" may be used. Outside resources may or may not be library based.[15]

One who teaches a library-researched paper using a more subjective model may lead students through a long inventive process in order to unearth personal and practical interests. Those activities might include brainstorming and free writing. The focus/thesis of the paper would possibly modify throughout many weeks of research, taking place throughout the writing process; in fact, research would help modify the focus. Research is generative and recursive. Students learn to "engage" with texts as "voices," not as mere facts, through a process of multiple drafts and peer editing.[16]

The research in a paper written in a subjective model would be guided by curiosity and inquisitiveness and not hurriedly picked from a list of potential topics. In fact, the student may not write a single, isolated research paper, but may write many connected projects, with some of them involving research. Research is not "assigned" in rote segments, such as three peer-reviewed articles and two books, all from the library, but emerges from the paper as needed. The definition of research could be expanded beyond library resources; a "source" could be the narrative of a nursing home resident. Library instruction is seen as an organic part of the research process because the research process is seen as an organic part of the writing process.[18]

Examples of a library research paper in a more subjective model include the I-Search paper, started by Ken MacRorie; this is a narrative paper that does not focus on the results of the research but on the research process itself.[19] Another type of narrative paper that presents not only the results of the research but the research process is an ethnography which would be the study of a culture, with the assumption that the writer brings personal experiences to the research.[20] A third example would be the multi-genre paper, which consists of many genres and sub-genres, each being an isolated unit of writing, yet connected by a theme.[21]

The Library Research Paper: The "Disconnect" Revisited

Certainly, the models described in this session are at the far ends of the spectrum. A current-traditional, objective paper could have some subjective characteristics; for example, a teacher could assign a topic, require a thesis and defense model and yet allow a fluid amount of research to come from the library or outside the library. A subjective paper could have some current-traditional characteristics; for instance, a teacher could lead students through a sophisticated inventive process and still require a paper that is written in a strict thesis and defense style with discrete research requirements.

Most library-research paper assignments probably fall somewhere in the middle of the spectrum. My personal observation is that English department faculty members assign papers using a mixture of models. One teacher assigns the same research topic to every student every semester. The library instructor's role is assumed to show students the "skills" of using databases. Another teacher spends many weeks, unearthing interests of students, determined that students' topics must come from them and not from an arbitrary list of topics. In this model, the library instructor invites students to become acquainted with "perspectives" housed in the library stacks and through the databases.

At the beginning of this session, I mentioned the "disconnect" I hear from library instructors when working with English writing classes. I think many library instructors secretly feel guilty that they cannot "fix" what they perceive to be a "generic" paper assignment. Perhaps this disconnect comes from being involved with different models of writing that assume different views of the place of research within the writing process. Still, some teachers may be using a model in which they remain unhappy with the writing and research results. Other teachers may be largely trained in the reading of literature and may not have a conceptual basis for teaching the library-research paper—a possibility that is dying out. The onus of the library instructor is to identify not only the assignment being addressed, but to analyze the assignment for that writing instructors' view of research. We, as library instructors, may not always be happy with the writing instructors' choices, but we can be happy that we have done our best to conceptualize our own views of the research process and to integrate our instruction with their teaching models.

NOTES

1. P. Zemliansky, "Genuine Training in Academic Discourse or an Artificial Construct?" Reconsidering the Past, Present, and Future of the College Research Paper" (Ph.D. diss., Florida State University, 2002),

2. Zemliansky, 6.

3. K. Spear, "Controversy and Consensus in Freshman Writing: An Overview of the Field," *The Review of Higher Education* 20 (1997): 320. MUSE. Internet on-line. Available from <http://muse.jhu.edu/journals/review_of_higher_education/v020/20.3spear.html>.

4. Spear, "Controversy and Consensus in Freshman Writing: An Overview of the Field."

5. Spear, "Controversy and Consensus in Freshman Writing: An Overview of the Field."

6. James Berlin, *Rhetoric and Reality: Writing Instruction American Colleges, 1900-1985* (Carbondale: Southern Illinois University Press, 1987), 26-27.

7. Berlin, 6-7.

8. University of Nevada at Reno Graduate Programs. "Doctoral Programs in Rhetoric and Composition." Internet on-line <http://www.unr.edu/artsci/engl/program/graduate/wrc/links/links-programs.htm>. [30 May 2003].

9. Zemliansky, 82-90.

10. Zemliansky, 82-90.

11. Zemliansky, 82-90.

12. Zemliansky, 82-90.

13. Zemliansky, 62-63.

14. Zemliansky, 92-93.

15. Zemliansky, 106-108.

16. Zemliansky, 91-117.

17. Zemliansky, 91-117.

18. Zemliansky, 91-117.

19. Zemliansky. 164-168.

20. Zemliansky., 181-190.

21. Zemliansky, 195-202.

—DONNA J. GUNTER—

STONE SOUP: A RECIPE FOR COLLABORATION AND SUPPORT

Jim Kinnie, Mary C. MacDonald, and Amanda Izenstark

Introduction

Welcome to *Stone Soup: A Recipe for Collaboration and Support*. There are only three of us here today—you know what they say about too many cooks—but our recipe affects several more librarians at the University of Rhode Island (URI). In that sense, the more "cooks" there are, the better.

When we saw the LOEX conference theme, we realized that several of us, as new instructors in the library, were beneficiaries of just such reflective teaching at URI. Amanda and I are here to share our experience with the program of collaboration and support for instruction that had grown out of URI's Information Literacy program which Mary oversees. Overall, it's a recipe that has helped us all become better teachers and build a strong instructional team within the library by bringing everyone to the table to share their secret ingredients to really spice up our instruction.

Our instruction retreat and other support mechanisms reminded me of the old tale, *Stone Soup*. It's the story of three soldiers who were walking through an unknown country returning from the wars. They hadn't eaten for several days so they were happy to come upon a village where they might be able to get something to eat. But the villagers saw them coming and since they were afraid of strangers and knew the soldiers would want food (they barely had enough for

themselves), the villagers decided to hide their food. They put it in lofts, down wells, in covered bins and in cellars.

The soldiers arrived and went from house to house asking for food but the villagers gave many excuses why they didn't have any. The soldiers went off to talk among themselves and came back to announce that they would make stone soup for everyone. The villagers sounded interested and they brought out a large pot, filled it with water and started a fire under it. The soldiers asked the people to gather some round smooth stones which they threw into the pot.

When the water got hot the soldiers stirred and tasted the soup and one of them said, "What this soup needs is some salt and pepper." A couple of children ran off and brought back some salt and pepper. The soldiers tasted again and said, "This soup would be really good with some onions." A woman in the crowd said, "I think I have a few," and ran off to her cellar to fetch some onions for the soup. The soldiers stirred and tasted and said, "Some carrots would be really good in here," and a man in the crowd brought some carrots back. And so it went with potatoes and cabbage and other vegetables.

The villagers were really impressed. The soldiers were making a rich man's soup from stones, just like magic. After a while even the villagers were saying, "Some of my cider and bread would really go well with this soup."

That night they all had a big feast with the soup made from stones. All the villagers thanked the soldiers. They knew they would never go hungry again now that they knew how to make soup from stones.[1]

Kinnie is Reference Librarian; *MacDonald* is Information Literacy Librarian and *Izenstark* is Reference Librarian at the University of Rhode Island, Kingston, RI.

As instructors in the URI library we are here to share our recipe for our own stone soup. It is made up of our ingredients, but substitutions are allowed and even encouraged; you can stew over it or chill out with a gazpacho or even turn it into a casserole. It allows for local taste and can be doubled or halved. In other words, it is not carved in stone.

Stone Soup Ingredients

LIB 120, Introduction to Information Literacy, is a 3-credit course that was taught for the first time in fall of 1999. It was part of the URI Plan for Information Literacy that was eventually approved in 2000.[2] The Plan is much larger than the one credit course, but the course has had the most impact on the curriculum, and on us! There was a need on campus for a course such as ours. It was requested by deans and faculty and so more sections were added over the next several years.

There was fairly quick growth. We went from one section in fall 1999 to six sections in fall 2002 adding one on WebCT during the summers. LIB 120 became an option in the University College General Education in fall 2000, guaranteeing full enrollment each semester.

Uh-oh! This meant a rapid learning curve for the Information Literacy Librarian...and for all the instructors!

Now we can generally expect 4-6 sections a semester. Faculty librarians teach the course. In fact, librarians at URI all do lots of teaching, but formal credit courses require stamina, and continual resources of energy and ideas to keep the dynamics going, so teaching LIB 120 is on a voluntary basis.

At first, we weren't familiar with traditional support resources for teaching faculty. We envisioned ourselves bringing our strengths and weaknesses to a place where we could share, prepare and learn. We recognized the informal and formal methods that we had for coaching each other through the process of becoming a teacher and we identified among ourselves some grassroots co-mentoring or peer mentoring techniques.

Who teaches? Since teaching is not mandatory, only the willing were "recruited." We began with two, then three original instructors. Then we added a select group: GSLIS "RefStuds", students trained in reference and experienced in teaching freshmen level library instruction; assistant professors, some who were the original course developers and some who came on board in 2000; an assistant professor who has

been steeped in information literacy since her appointment and who coordinates the program; an associate professor who works primarily with adult learners in a continuing education college. The make-up of the LIB120 teaching faculty now consists of part- time, full-time, temporary lecturers, assistant professors on the journey to tenure, and associate professors who can lend support and experience.

There was lots of enthusiasm, lots of resources, but little experience teaching a 3-credit course year round. Our support system was very organic at first, mainly in the form of hallway conversations and e-mail messages. We met in the "meeting before the meeting" and at the "meeting after the meeting." We were able to add instructors, whether tenure line or temporary, but new instructors were overwhelmed with advice and suggestions, and oriented in a very unorganized manner.

We began sharing existing exercises and assignments with new instructors by assembling and distributing common assignment binders for everyone to use, mutilate, spindle, change and annotate. As more sections and more instructors became involved however, the details of teaching became an everyday event, and university requirements became a monster to tame—a necessary chore that none of us was used to.

We planned a day off-site to gather together and begin to coordinate our efforts, bringing everything to the table and to create and fortify a community of learners and teachers. We had a few initial ingredients that we brought to our gathering. Getting together as a group was a great idea; there was lots of sugar, no phones, a few jokes, Play-Doh and other party favors, and some real work.

Each of us, whether new instructors or experienced instructors, shared our experiences and we learned from one another. Some of us had previous careers that can flavor this recipe. By the time of our first retreat we had all the makings of Stone Soup!

Here are the ingredients for the recipe—adjust yours to taste: 4-6 librarians, 1-day retreat, 40 lbs assignment binders, various syllabi, practices and experiences, 40 laptops, 4-6 sections LIB 120.

Directions

Pour librarians into retreat. The retreat was a great opportunity for instructors to bring their experiences and backgrounds to the table in an informal setting from which to learn. There was plenty of homemade food to fuel our endeavors and Play-

—JIM KINNIE, MARY C. MACDONALD, AND AMANDA IZENSTARK—

Doh to keep our minds active. We had a chance to chat off the record, share good gossip and create a real camaraderie among instructors. After all the formal library meetings and procedures, this was different, very informal. But it was also a dose of reality. It was a time to hash out the course and discuss classroom management and teaching in general.

Add assignment binders. The binders contain copies of assignments and in-class worksheets, created by each instructor, that were used and were using in their classes. The materials were often multiple copies of the same assignment that each had adapted to suit a particular need. Some even included hand-written notes on the copies: "This was great!" "This was too tedious!"

Add new worksheets and exercises. The retreat gives each instructor an opportunity to share new worksheets and exercises of their own. Some are just revisions or updates of earlier assignments, while others are entirely new, created to emphasize a particular lesson.

Add generic syllabus. The public services department asked for a generic syllabus which includes the basics of the required components of the course and a suggested set up for the university requirements. This was a great help to new instructors as it gave an underlying structure for their classes and gave a clear sense of the components they needed to include. Each instructor tweaks the syllabus to highlight the elements that each considers priorities. For example, one might give homework a much heavier weight than exams, to encourage students to do the exercises and to revise them.

Add best practices. We each learned classroom techniques from other instructors at the retreat and adapt them. Since we try to emphasize active learning and student engagement in the classroom, we share and contribute to successful exercises. For example, in an information organization lesson students are asked to classify, with subdivisions, various collections by category, alphabet, time, location etc. Instructors all contributed their collections of toys, postcards, political buttons, personal care products, building blocks and beads.

Add classroom management issues. Along with serious discussion of managing our classrooms, Mary brings her party favors to the retreat to help us teach and in some cases, help us cope: A Whatchamacallit – what students call you when you're teaching them; A compass – to steer the class in the right direction; Fireballs – to engage and "fire up" your students; Glow-Sticks – the pointer that will keep their attention;

Bubbles – to capture their thoughts; Life Savers – For those who may drift in late; Pencils – For those who forget to bring one; Fuzzy Pipe Cleaners – For those of us who procrastinate instead of grading; Pay Day – The feeling you get when they all earn As in May; Happy Harmonica – For us to play on the way to the Registrar's Office with our grades.

Add technical support. Collaboration on technical support is essential in keeping classes on schedule. Instructors bring their own background and experience to the team and even new instructors can add their support to the others. Jim had a career in television and audio-visual services so he makes sure all the others are proficient in using instructional media; Amanda has computer experience so everyone turns to her to troubleshoot their hardware and software problems.

Add other impact on teaching. The academic calendar is discussed during the retreat to make sure everyone knows which Mondays are really Wednesdays, when religious observances occur, and when to meet important university deadlines. We also share strategies in dealing with student athletes who miss class for events as well as what to do when students skip class because of bad weather, and good beach weather.

Allow to sit 5-6 hours. Of course we break for lunch.

Add additional ingredients. To keep us in the loop and introduce new ideas for our planning and teaching, we try to get together for half-day refresher retreats. We meet with Writing Across the Curriculum Faculty from the writing center to improve our understanding of the purpose of certain kinds of writing assignments. Instructors are encouraged to attend the IDP, or Instructional Development Program, series of workshops in August. All of the informal hallway conversations and e-mail correspondence still are very important. We are all available to proctor exams or substitute for each other's classes.

Combine retreat mixture with LIB 120 sections, adding laptops as needed. We bring the ideas we have discussed in the retreats back to the classroom. Since our 40 wireless laptops require some time setting up (removing the laptops from the cupboard, plugging and unplugging the power cables), instructors have another opportunity to help each other and to talk about how each other's class is going.

Simmer 14 weeks. Student reaction, in general, has been very positive. Some examples of student testimonials: "I think LIB 120 should be mandatory—it helped me with all of my other classes and will definitely always come in handy." "Regardless of the stress that I have felt in taking this course, I know that this one class will benefit my whole life." "Doing research papers is not the hassle it was before, and I feel well-versed in the library system. I enjoyed the class so much that I think I'm going to go into information sciences and skills myself."

Leftovers from this recipe are easily applied to our other instruction in subject-specific and freshman library classes. Collaboration has improved all of our instruction. It has enabled us to improve our plan for information literacy and it has strengthened our community of instructors. It has made us better teachers even when we feel fried, cooked or even burnt out.

ENDNOTES

1. Marcia Brown, *Stone Soup: An Old Tale* (New York: Charles Scribner's Sons, 1947).

2. Joanna Burkhardt, Mary MacDonald, Andrée Rathemacher, J. Laurence Kelland and Michael Vocino. *Plan for Information Literacy at the University of Rhode Island. University of Rhode Island,* University Libraries, Library Strategic Planning Task Force for Teaching and Research, 2000. Published as ERIC Document ED455849. Citation and abstract appear in *Resources in Education* 37, no. 1 (January 2002).

Further Reading on Collaboration, Co-Mentoring, and Support From and For Teaching Librarians

Bergeron, Pam, and Mike McHargue. "Recent Advances in Retreats: Adapting the Great Teachers Seminar Model to Serve an Entire College." *New Directions for Community Colleges* 120 (Winter 2002): 75-83.

Jipson, Janice and Nicholas Paley. "Because No One Gets There Alone: Collaboration as Co-Mentoring." *Theory into Practice* 39, no. 1 (Winter 2000): 36-42.

Litten, Anna. "We're All in This Together: Planning and Leading a Retreat for Teaching Librarians." In *Information Literacy Programs: Successes and Challenges*, ed. Patricia Durisin, 57-69. Binghamton, NY: Haworth Press, 2002.

Frank, Polly, and Lee-Allison Levene. "Everyone in the Pool: Staying Afloat with a Good BI Team." *The Upside of Downsizing: Using Library Instruction to Cope*, ed. Cheryl Laguardia, Stella Bentley, and Janet Martorana, 107-125. New York: Neal Schuman, 1995.

Mullen, Carol A. "Constructing Co-Mentoring Partnerships: Walkways We Must Travel." *Theory Into Practice* 39, no. 1 (Winter 2000): 4-11.

Palmer, Parker. "Learning in Community: The Conversation of Colleagues." In *The Courage to Teach*. San Francisco: Jossey-Bass, 1998.

Rymer, Jone. "Only Connect: Transforming Ourselves and Our Discipline Through Co-Mentoring." *Journal of Business Communication* 39 (July 2002): 342-363.

—JIM KINNIE, MARY C. MACDONALD, AND AMANDA IZENSTARK—

Toss the Bag of Tricks: Fostering Motivation in Library Instruction

Michelle Twait

Introduction

Motivation is an elusive concept. It cannot be touched or measured. In educational psychology terms, it is a hypothetical construct. It is a concept that has been invented to provide causal explanations for behavior. In essence, to be motivated is "to be moved to do something"[1] or "to direct energy in pursuit of a goal."[2] This paper hopes to provide a theoretical background, while offering practical suggestions for classroom practice.

Identifying Motivation

While motivation may be difficult to quantify, behaviors can be observed and inferences can be made. Readers may recall students encountered at the reference desk or in the classroom that were clearly motivated. What behaviors signaled motivation? What did these students do (or, perhaps, *not* do) that made them seem motivated? In some cases, it may have been evidence of persistence—a refusal to give up despite obstacles encountered. In other cases, it may have been the enthusiasm or energy displayed. Often, motivated students can be identified by the time and effort they are willing to expend. All of these behaviors can indicate the presence of motivation.

Twait is the Reference Coordinator and Instructor at Gustavus Adolphus College in St. Peter, MN.

So What?

Why should instruction librarians care about motivation? First, and not surprisingly, there are many students who are not inherently interested in research or fascinated by libraries. Reaching those students and providing successful instruction will, therefore, depend upon the inclusion of elements designed to foster motivation.

Secondly, certain types of motivation have been shown to improve students' academic performance. Intrinsic motivation refers to performing a task because one enjoys it or finds it inherently interesting. In classrooms where intrinsic motivation is enhanced, students tend to achieve more academically, be more curious, more creative, and seek out challenges.[3]

Extrinsic motivation refers to performing a task because it will lead to some other outcome. A student exhibiting autonomous extrinsic motivation will perform a task in order to achieve some other outcome, but the student also sees value or "buys into" the instruction. Fostering a more autonomous extrinsic motivation in students has been shown to increase their academic achievement, willingness to persevere, and levels of engagement.[4]

By catalyzing these two types of motivation, librarians can encourage future interest in library research. Students that have had motivating learning experiences are more likely to become lifelong learners.[5]

Learning Theories and Motivation

Behaviorism, social constructivism, and cognitivism are three learning theories that offer different, yet related, perspectives on motivation. Each can inform our understanding of this elusive concept.

According to behaviorism, learning is "the development of associations between stimuli and responses."[6] Desired behaviors are rewarded and undesired behaviors are punished. Behaviorism presumes that learners are passive creatures and motivation to learn is linked to rewards. The issue of rewards has been hotly debated. Some scholars have argued that this use of rewards is problematic and may diminish students' intrinsic motivation.[7] Others feel that the influence on motivation is determined by the type of reward and how the reward is administered.[8]

In social constructivism, learners take a much more active role. Students, while interacting with others, construct their own understanding of the material. Cooperative learning strategies are an example of applied social constructivism. Problem-based learning and discovery learning are two other examples. These strategies emphasize the process of learning, rather than solutions or answers. One social constructivist has coined the phrase "continuing impulse to learn" to describe the motivational affects of these strategies.[9] Research has shown that both cooperative learning[10] and optimally challenging problems[11] foster motivation.

Cognitivism is another learner-centered theory. According to this theory, learning is facilitated as connections are made between prior knowledge and new information. Instruction may include strategies to help make the learning more meaningful for students or it may involve teaching metacognitive skills (e.g. problem-solving techniques). Motivation can be fostered through personally meaningful instruction and by developing students' metacognitive abilities.

Ryan and Deci's Self-Determination Theory (SDT),[12] derived from cognitivism, can be useful in understanding the nuances of intrinsic and extrinsic motivation. This theory is split into two subtheories, Cognitive Evaluation Theory (CET) and Organismic Integration Theory (OIT). The first subtheory, CET, examines the factors that foster or diminish intrinsic motivation. Rewards, threats, deadlines, and competition have been found to diminish intrinsic motivation.[13] The factors that foster motivation (both intrinsic and autonomous extrinsic) will be discussed in the next section. The second subtheory, OIT, considers the varying degrees of autonomous extrinsic motivation. The authors place extrinsic motivation on a continuum, pointing out that the various degrees depend upon the level of "buy in" or the degree to which the task is integrated with one's values or needs.[14]

Characteristics of Motivating Instruction

Using these theories and several research articles, I adapted and expanded the four characteristics of motivating instruction identified by Paris and Turner.[15]

Challenge. Students may be challenged in various ways. As mentioned earlier, problem-based learning can create moderate challenges for students. Ideally, challenging problems should be those that "students can complete but only with some effort, so as to engender feelings of competence and pride."[16] Challenge may also refer to "challenging [students'] beliefs, actions, and imagination."[17] For example, one might ask students to create a search strategy and then predict what might happen if that search was executed. Stimulating students' curiosity is another way to challenge learners. For example, an instructor might ask students unexpected questions about the familiar (e.g. "Do you know what the yellow pages have in common with the library's catalog?").

Choice. Choice involves students' freedom to choose their own learning goals, select a course of action, determine the amount of effort to expend, and so on. It is a fundamental aspect of motivation for a number of reasons. First, through the very act of selection, students assume some responsibility for their choice and will be more accountable for their actions. This can enhance students' willingness to persevere. Second, by choosing, students indicate that they have an interest in that topic or path. Since interest is related to intrinsic motivation, the element of choice can help foster motivation. In addition, studies have shown a strong interest-achievement correlation in male students.[18] For example, if a female student takes a class she is not interested in, this will not affect her achievement in the course. However, a male student's disinterest can affect his achievement. As mentioned earlier, many students do not have an inherent interest in research. Offering an element of choice is one way to foster autonomous extrinsic motivation and possibly even intrinsic motivation. Applying this element to practice can be as simple as allowing some time at the end of a session for students to work on their own.

—MICHELLE TWAIT—

Control. Although closely related to choice, control represents an expansion of choice. Studies on motivation and control have found that "students who are overly controlled not only lose initiative but also learn less well."[19] Control takes choice a step further and turns it into self-regulated and autonomous learning. Students direct their own learning and the instructor becomes less of a "sage on the stage" and more of a "guide on the side."[20] Two variables influence the element of control: prior knowledge and individual ability. Students with a high level of prior knowledge and/or high ability should be allowed greater control over their own learning.[21] In contrast, it is perfectly acceptable to exercise a little more instructor control in, for example, a library session for first year students.

Connections. Although cognitivism's emphasis on connections has already been discussed, connections play a significant role in motivation. It is important to relate library instruction to students' needs and goals. Also, whenever possible, librarians should try to make instruction personally meaningful to students. For example, an instructor might demonstrate a database search by using examples related to course content or students' lives. An instructor might also ask students "So what?" or "Who cares?" and ask learners to explain why the concept is important. In addition to connections between the students and the material, it is also helpful to have students connect with one another. Increased motivation is one of the many benefits of cooperative learning.[22]

Competence. Stipek writes, "Students enter each new classroom with a set of achievement-related beliefs, including expectations for success, perceptions of academic competence and self-efficacy, perceptions of control over achievement outcomes, and perceptions of the cause of those outcomes."[23] This quote nicely sums up the variables influencing students' feelings of competence. Self-efficacy can be defined as belief in one's abilities. Students may enter a library session believing they are very capable researchers or may feel as though they are doomed to fail in any research pursuit. Perceived locus of causality refers to whether one attributes success or failure to internal or external causes. In other words, does a student blame a failed search on lack of effort (internal) or the database (external)? Motivation is fostered when students have a strong sense of self-efficacy and an internal perceived locus of causality.

Conclusion

By incorporating elements that foster motivation into information literacy instruction, librarians can help improve student achievement and build the foundation for lifelong learning. This information can also clarify the role of the instructor in student motivation. As Nuhfer wrote, "We cannot motivate other people, but we can create environments in which people can motivate themselves."[24]

NOTES

1. Richard M. Ryan and Edward L. Deci, "Intrinsic and Extrinsic Motivations: Classic Definitions and New Directions." *Contemporary Educational Psychology* 25 (January 2000): 54.

2. Raymond J. Wlodkowski, "Motivation and Diversity: A Framework for Teaching," in *Motivation From Within: Approaches for Encouraging Faculty and Students to Excel: New Directions for Teaching and Learning,* ed. Michael Theall (San Francisco: Jossey-Bass, 1999), 7.

3. Deborah J. Stipek, "Motivation and Instruction," in *Handbook of Educational Psychology*, eds. David C. Berliner and Robert C. Calfee (New York: Macmillan Reference USA, 1996), 96.

4. Ryan and Deci, 63.

5. Raymond J. Wlodkowski, *Enhancing Adult Motivation to Learn: A Comprehensive Guide for Teaching All Adults*. (San Francisco: Jossey-Bass, 1998), 5.

6. Marilla D. Svinicki, "New Directions in Learning and Motivation," in *Teaching and Learning On the Edge of the Millennium: Building On What We Have Learned: New Directions for Teaching and Learning*, ed. Marilla Svinicki (San Francisco: Jossey-Bass, 1999), 5.

7. See: Edward L. Deci, "Effects of externally mediated rewards on intrinsic motivation." *Journal of Personality and Social Psychology* 18 (1971): 105-115. See also: Edward L. Deci, *Intrinsic Motivation*. (New York: Plenum, 1975).

8. Judy Cameron and W. David Pierce, *Rewards and Intrinsic Motivation: Resolving the Controversy.* (Westport, CT: Bergin & Garvey, 2002).

9. Penny Oldfather and Jane West, *Learning Through Children's Eyes: Social Constructivism and the Desire to Learn.* (Washington, DC: American Psychological Association, 1999).

10. Theodore Panitz, "The Motivational Benefits of Cooperative Learning," in *Motivation From Within: Approaches for Encouraging Faculty and Students to Excel: New Directions for Teaching and Learning*, ed. Michael Theall (San Francisco: Jossey-Bass, 1999), 59-67.

11. Oldfather and West, 17.

12. Ryan and Deci, 55.

13. Ryan and Deci, 59.

14. Ryan and Deci, 62.

15. Scott G. Paris and Julianne C. Turner, "Situated Motivation," *in Student Motivation, Cognition, and Learning: Essays in Honor of Wilbert J. McKeachie*, eds. Paul R. Pintrich, Donald R. Brown, & Claire E. Weinstein (Hillsdale, NJ: Lawrence Erlbaum, 1994), 221-227.

16. Stipek, 89.

17. Ruth Kanfer and Barbara McCombs, "Motivation: Applying Current Theory to Critical Issues in Training," in *Training and Retraining: A Handbook for Business, Industry, Government, and the Military*, eds. Sigmund Tobias and J.D. Fletcher (New York: Macmillan Reference USA, 2000), 100.

18. Kanfer and McCombs, 93-94.

19. Ryan and Deci, 59.

20. Alison King, "From Sage on the Stage to Guide on the Side." *College Teaching* 41, no. 1 (1993): 30-35.

21. Mable B. Kinzie, "Requirements and Benefits of Effective Interactive Instruction." *Educational Technology Research and Development* 38, no. 1 (1990): 11.

22. See: Panitz. See also: David Johnson, Roger Johnson, and Karl Smith, *Active Learning: Cooperation in the College Classroom.* (Edina, MN: Interaction Book Company, 1998)

23. Stipek, 95.

24. Edward B. Nuhfer, "Motivation in Interdisciplinary Programs," in *Motivation from Within: Approaches for Encouraging Faculty and Students to Excel*, vol. 78 of *New Directions for Teaching and Learning*, ed. Michael Theall (San Francisco: Jossey-Bass, 1999), 80.

REFERENCES

Cameron, Judy and W. D. Pierce. *Rewards and Intrinsic Motivation: Resolving the Controversy.* Westport, CT: Bergin & Garvey, 2002.

Deci, Edward L. "Effects of Externally Mediated Rewards on Intrinsic Motivation." *Journal of Personality and Social Psychology* 18 (1971): 105-115.

Deci, Edward L. *Intrinsic Motivation.* New York: Plenum, 1975.

Johnson, David, R. Johnson, and K. Smith. *Active Learning : Cooperation in the College Classroom.* Edina, MN: Interaction Book Co., 1998.

Kanfer, Ruth and B. McCombs. "Motivation: Applying Current Theory to Critical Issues in Training." In *Training and Retraining: A Handbook for Business, Industry, Government, and the Military*, edited by Sigmund Tobias and J. D. Fletcher, 85-108. New York: Macmillan Reference USA, 2000.

King, Alison. "From Sage on the Stage to Guide on the Side." *College Teaching* 41, no. 1 (1993): 30-35.

Kinzie, Mable B. "Requirements and Benefits of Effective Interactive Instruction." *Educational Technology Research and Development* 38, no. 1 (1990): 5-21.

Nuhfer, Edward B. "Motivation in Interdisciplinary Programs." In *Motivation from Within: Approaches for Encouraging Faculty and Students to Excel.* Vol. 78 of *New Directions for Teaching and Learning*, edited by Michael Theall, 79-86. San Francisco:

—MICHELLE TWAIT—

Jossey-Bass, 1999.

Oldfather, Penny and Jane West. *Learning Through Children's Eyes: Social Constructivism and the Desire to Learn*. Washington DC: American Psychological Association, 1999.

Panitz, Theodore. "The Motivational Benefits of Cooperative Learning." In *Motivation from Within: Approaches for Encouraging Faculty and Students to Excel*. Vol. 78 of *New Directions for Teaching and Learning*, edited by Michael Theall, 59-67. San Francisco: Jossey-Bass, 1999.

Paris, Scott G. and Julianne C. Turner. "Situated Motivation." In *Student Motivation, Cognition, and Learning: Essays in Honor of Wilbert J. McKeachie*, edited by Paul R. Pintrich, Donald R. Brown, and Claire E. Weinstein, 221-227. Hillsdale, NJ: Lawrence Erlbaum, 1994.

Ryan, Richard M. & Edward L. Deci. "Intrinsic and Extrinsic Motivators: Classic Definitions and New Directions." *Contemporary Educational Psychology* 25 (2000): 54-67.

Stipek, Deborah J. "Motivation and Instruction." In *Handbook of Educational Psychology*, edited by David Berliner and Robert Calfee, 85-113. New York: Macmillan Reference USA, 1996.

Svinicki, M. D. "New Directions in Learning and Motivation." In *Teaching and Learning On the Edge of the Millennium: Building On What We Have Learned*. Vol 80 of *New Directions for Teaching and Learning*, edited by Marilla D. Svinicki, 5-27. San Francisco: Jossey-Bass, 1999.

Wlodkowski, Raymond J. *Enhancing Adult Motivation to Learn: A Comprehensive Guide for Teaching all Adults*. San Francisco: Jossey-Bass, 1998.

Wlodkowski, Raymond J. "Motivation and Diversity: A Framework for Teaching." In *Motivation from Within: Approaches for Encouraging Faculty and Students to Excel*. Vol. 78 of *New Directions for Teaching and Learning*, edited by Michael Theall, 7-16. San Francisco: Jossey-Bass, 1999.

WORKSHOP ON EDUCATING REFLECTIVE USER INSTRUCTION LIBRARIANS

Jana Varlejs and Eileen Stec

According to the librarians who attended this LOEX conference workshop, very few had taken a formal course in library user instruction while studying for a library or information science master's degree. This is not surprising, as there are not many courses on this topic offered in the 49 ALA accredited programs in the United States. In the spring of 2003, a quick review of the library schools' Web sites uncovered not quite two dozen courses that are devoted to user instruction. This seems to be quite an advance over the number reported by a 1991-1992 study conducted by members of the ACRL Bibliographic Instruction Section. According to documents saved by Esther Grassian, who served on the Section's Education for BI Committee from 1992-1993, ten courses were identified at that time (personal communication, 23 April 2003). The idea then had been to develop a model course, with the objective of encouraging an increase in the number of courses available. In 2003, there is greater demand for more user instruction in all kinds of library settings, but there is not yet a commensurate number of courses preparing LIS graduates to deliver this service. Further, there has not been much discussion of what such courses should be like. The LOEX 2003 theme suggested exploration of one aspect of course design, that is, the extent to which a course fosters education of reflective teachers.

Varlejs is Associate Professor, School of Communication, Information and Library Studies and *Stec* is Instruction and Outreach Librarian at Rutgers—The State University of New Jersey, New Brunswick, NJ.

Workshop Proposal

Using several syllabi, participants will identify aspects of courses currently taught in library schools that foster development of reflective teachers. They will propose criteria for course design that can also be applied to in-service and continuing education.

Objectives

How does one learn to be a user instruction librarian? For most, the answer probably is on-the-job or continuing education. Recently, however, an increasing number of library schools have courses on user instruction. Are these courses designed to produce "reflective" teachers? The objectives will be to identify aspects of courses that appear to foster reflective teaching, and to develop criteria for course design.

Design

As facilitator, I will obtain the cooperation of several library school faculty who teach user instruction. With their permission, I will use their syllabi to create two "courses" as case studies. The sources will remain confidential. Workshop participants will be introduced to the case studies, and asked to categorize the course contents, assignments, etc., on a continuum of low to high probability of producing reflective teachers. Participants will be in small groups for this exercise, and told to report back to the whole group in 20 minutes. After a debriefing, participants will reassemble into small groups to develop criteria for course design (15 minutes). For the remainder of the hour, the criteria will be prioritized by the entire group.

Results

Participants will have clarified their definition of "reflective" teaching and identified factors likely to foster the development of reflective teachers. They will have produced a rough list of criteria that can be used as a base for course design by library school faculty who are teaching user instruction, and also adapted for staff development and continuing education.

As it turned out, the LIS educators who were willing to let their courses be used in the workshop wanted to be identified and credited. Their courses differed from each other more than expected. Given these factors, it seemed best to give up the idea of creating two fictional case studies, and instead to use four representative course syllabi, albeit edited and condensed. The four that were used were Diane Nahl's from the University of Hawaii, Emily Okada's from Indiana University, Irene Percelli's from Pratt, and Jana Varlejs' from Rutgers. Each workshop participant received two syllabi to read, as time was limited. The group as a whole, however, had four examples to explore for factors fostering the development of reflective teachers.

Since the purpose of the workshop was to have attendees try to identify aspects of course design that would result in students eventually becoming reflective teachers, they were first asked to write down their own definition of reflective teaching. They were then asked to note for each case, items in the course content and in the assignments that they felt fostered students' reflection on themselves as teachers. This exercise was followed by small group discussion and then a report to the group as a whole in order to identify commonalities.

Given Betsy Baker's key note address earlier in the day, a number of workshop participants found it fairly easy to articulate what characterized reflective teaching for them. An example of a response to this opening question was:

• ... constantly learning from successes and failures, from students; changing, adapting what is taught and how you teach; and consideration of **why** you teach.

Those elements of course content that were seen as fostering students' reflection on themselves as teachers were:
- Learning styles
- Learning theories
- Teaching styles
- Self and peer evaluation methods
- How to observe
- Outcomes evaluation

Elements in assignments that were singled out as helping students to develop reflective habits were:
- Journaling
- Video taping presentations
- Exercises in diagnosing learner needs
- Apprenticing to instruction librarians
- Practicing instruction
- Taking learning style, personality teaching style inventories
- Writing debriefing essays

At the conclusion of the workshop, participants were asked to write on 3" x 5" cards their responses to two questions. On the lined side of the card, they were to state what they planned to do with what they learned from the session. On the blank side of the card they were to say what they wished would have been done differently. Some interesting "will do" comments were the following:
- Structure an anticipatory reflective activity for teachers
- Build peer observation into informal staff evaluation
- Create some kind of journaling or summarizing for our teaching staff
- Add more reflective exercises to a class that I teach
- Provide a more proactive mentoring program for new librarians
- Talk about self-assessment during library instruction meetings

It is clear from these comments that what LIS educators model in their courses on user instruction can have some application in practice—a gratifying outcome.

On the blank sides of the cards, where participants told us what they wished we had done, or not done, or done differently, the common thread was that one hour was too short to explore adequately the complexities of educating reflective user instruction librarians. Furthermore, there was a desire for advice on how to take some of the ideas in the LIS course syllabi and adapt them for staff development. For example:

- I wanted more on working with current staff, who already teach, and are not very reflective, open, and flexible to user needs
- How to translate the exercise of creating a reflective teaching library school class into how to create a reflective teaching library staff
- Specific ideas/strategies to introduce reflective teaching to colleagues

In addition, there were some comments about the structure of the workshop. One complaint was that instructions about how to proceed were not entirely clear, and another criticism was that it was difficult to distinguish between content and assignment elements when examining a course for reflective teaching stimulators.

As reflective presenters of this workshop, what do we conclude from our own observations and from the comments of the participants? First, a single hybrid syllabus would have been more effective in eliciting the criteria that we were after and would have saved time. Second, a concluding discussion about how to take ideas from LIS courses and adapt them for staff development would have given participants something concrete to take home to try out with their colleagues. It is impossible, of course, to know what —if anything—those in attendance at this workshop will actually do with whatever impressions they took away with them. The presenters, on the other hand, feel that they now have a mandate to pursue the question of how to translate some of the reflection-fostering aspects of LIS courses into practice in user instruction and information literacy programs in libraries.

The most challenging comment we received on our 3" by 5" cards was this:

- I am intrigued by this connection: how do reflective teachers help students become reflective learners....

The assumption is, after all, that librarians who are in the habit of examining their own motives, performance, and results will be more likely to succeed in teaching their students (or patrons, or clients) to be competent information resource users. Much of that competence is directly related to the critical self-questioning that is demanded by the process that begins with the defining of the information need and proceeds through the several stages of resource exploration, evaluation, and selection, ending with analysis based on the weighing of evidence and arguments not necessarily congruent with one's beliefs. It is difficult to imagine how a librarian who has not engaged personally in this kind of struggle can encourage a learner to go down that stony path. The habit of reflection can be an antidote to the cynicism and burnout that can afflict instruction librarians, insofar as it keeps the focus on the "why" and on the "how" the user is helped. The librarian's habit of questioning, one hopes, can lead the learner to ask questions as well and thus to become a more reflective thinker.

FURTHER READING

Loomis, Abigail, and Deborah Fink. "Meta-Learning: A Transformational Process for Learning and Teaching." In *New Ways of "Learning the Library" —and Beyond,* eds. Linda Shirato, Elizabeth R. Bucciarelli, and Heidi Mercado, 19-25. Ann Arbor: Pierian Press, 1996.

Meulemans, Yvonne, and Jennifer Brown. "Educating Instruction Librarians: A Model for Library and Information Science Education." *Research Strategies* 18 (Winter 2001): 253-264.

Schon, Donald A. *Educating the Reflective Practitioner: Toward a New Design for Teaching and Learning in the Professions.* San Francisco: Jossey-Bass, 1987.

CROSSING THE BRIDGE WHEN YOU GET TO IT: HOW TO USE PUBLIC SPEAKING SKILLS TO IMPROVISE AND IMPROVE YOUR TEACHING

Sarah Statz

One cow said to the other: "So, what do you think of this mad cow disease?"
And the second cow replied, "What do I care? I'm a helicopter."

Opening a presentation with a joke is always a risky maneuver. Opening a presentation by making one of the participants tell the joke can be riskier still, but taking risks to interact with your students, and responding immediately to those interactions, is what "crossing the bridge when you get to it" teaching is all about. Getting the time to reflect on your teaching skills after or outside of your classes may not be an option, but observing and reflecting upon your students' behavior and feedback during class is. Increasing immediacy by enacting planned responses in your classes, asking questions to encourage spontaneous examples, and studying education and communication theory are just three (of many) ways to use traditional public speaking skills to motivate your classes and have more fun teaching.

Before the terms feedback and immediacy can be defined, it is imperative to understand one of the most basic—and groundbreaking—models of communication. In 1949, two telecommunications engineers named Claude Shannon and Warren Weaver published their theory (for our purposes, the following is a simplified version) that messages flow from a sender to a receiver (Shannon and Weaver 1949, 7). Since 1949, a number of variables have been added to that model; one of those variables is known as "noise," and can be any factor that

interferes with the receivers hearing all of the message (e.g., if it's your students' last breakout session of the day and they're hungry). Another concept that was added to Shannon and Weaver's linear model was that of feedback. Feedback has been defined in literally hundreds of different ways, but can be understood as referring to "those messages sent from listeners and received by speakers which enable speakers to gauge their effect on their receivers." (DeVito 1976, 219). Adding feedback to the model of communication means that while your students are watching and listening to you, you can also be observing and listening to them and their reactions. Feedback can also be more broadly defined in terms of verbal and nonverbal participation from your listeners. Asking a class participant a question such as "Are you enjoying being in Madison?" and receiving the answer "Yes, thank you." illustrates the principle that "feedback," in the form of student and teacher interaction, can be requested and encouraged by the teacher in a number of different ways.

Responding appropriately to and encouraging feedback from your students can be one of the easiest ways to achieve immediacy in your classroom. Immediacy, a concept that was first introduced by Albert Mehrabian, has been described as the "degree of perceived physical or psychological closeness between people" (Richmond and others 1991, 205). Why should we strive to achieve immediacy in our classes? We should because there is some evidence that teacher immediacy (verbal and nonverbal) is positively associated with student motivation to study (Christophel

Statz is a Librarian at the Madison Public Library, Madison WI.

1990, 323-340).

We now know that feedback allows the sender of a message to respond immediately to a student's reaction to that message, and that the use of immediacy behaviors in the classroom can help motivate our students to learn what we have to teach. The stage is thus set to consider three ways to interact with our classes, and to allow enough flexibility in our course structures to achieve active student learning. I refer to these three methods as my speaking tricks of the trade: easing into interaction by eliciting a planned response from your students, opening it up in the classroom by asking questions and allowing the answers to dictate the course of the instruction, and making any number of other discussion methods your own by reading communication and education theory research.

Most instruction librarians learn on the job, and have never had the luxury of being taught how to teach. This lack of theoretical training can lead to a situation in which teaching librarians might prefer to write and read from a script rather than teaching extemporaneously. If this is the case, one way to ease into the practice of asking for feedback is to plan some sort of action or response from your students, as well as a way to enact it. To begin this presentation, I wanted to tell my favorite joke, but I also wanted to find a way to immediately engage my audience members by making one of them tell it. I accomplished this by writing the joke on a note card and giving it to one of the session participants, and when I asked the person with the blue note card to read the joke, she was kind enough to do so. This plan had the double benefit of adding a bit of interest to the introduction ("How will she get an audience member to tell HER favorite joke?") as well as immediately making the point that in this session, the students were not intended to be merely passive receivers of information.

The glory of planning an interaction in this manner is that, while you have encouraged your students to take an active role in the class, you have also provided for yourself the safety net of knowing what they're going to say. I have used this technique many times in the past, both as a way to introduce the subject, but also as a way to break up what might otherwise become boring lectures. For the purpose of this workshop I used jokes; in previous classes I have distributed quotations on slips of paper and asked students to stand and read them at various times during the class, just to change the momentum of the class enough to regain their attention even

momentarily. The flip side of this method is that it requires a good deal of preparation time. You must plan the response and how to achieve it--for example, handing out note cards with the jokes, neatly typed in a large typeface, on the back, before the class began. Having a back-up plan (as well as a back-up plan for the back-up plan) is essential. In the case of this workshop, I distributed not one, but three differently colored note cards with different jokes to three different participants. Had the first participant been unable or unwilling to read their card, I was ready to ask the second or third participant to read theirs. Having the ability to "read" your students and their verbal and nonverbal behavior before and during your class is also necessary to use this technique successfully. As I stood at the door of the workshop room, distributing my session handouts (three of which had my joke note cards paper-clipped onto them), I had to carefully observe my attending colleagues, and make an educated guess as to who might not be adverse to being asked to stand and read a joke to a roomful of people. To accomplish this, I used indicators like who was making eye contact with me; who smiled and responded verbally to my "thanks for coming," and other signs that I believed showed a willingness to participate. The more students and classes a teacher observes, the more obvious these indicators become.

Planning for a known response, or stacking the deck, can be a very effective way to invite student participation. However, the time will come in any class when you will want to open the session to questions, the formulating and answering of which can actually form the basis for your entire class. The efficacy of this particular method was showcased during the session by asking the participants this question: "Why might it be hard to ask questions of your students during your classes?" A number of answers were offered, among them the fears that asking questions would make it harder for a teacher to control the direction of the lecture, that no students would answer the questions and this would be embarrassing for the teacher, and that a failure to answer questions immediately, or to dictate the content of the session, would constitute a failure on the part of the teacher to impart the proscribed knowledge. These are all valid fears. In response I could only ask, is showing students the possibility of failure the worst thing that can happen? How many times can undergraduate students sit down at the catalog, or at any database, and type in the perfect search phrase on the first try? For that matter, how often do librarians chance upon the perfect search on their first try?

—SARAH STATZ—

I challenged the group to give up the notion that showing students the perfect search example is the best way to teach them how to use the library. Instead, I asked, why not show them that constant failure, really, eventually leads to more comprehensive research? What better way to help them internalize the fact that if they fail, they must try, try again, than to show them in your class that you're not afraid to answer their questions on the spot, and formulate your search strategy as you go along? This is what asking questions allows a teacher to do. And I don't mean asking questions like, "What's another word for 'cars' that we could type into this database?" I mean asking questions like, "You've got a term paper on the latest development of hybrid engines for cars due in a week. Where would you start looking for information?" Being willing to let students' questions form the outline of a class doesn't mean a teacher can't prepare; in fact, preparing for students' questions can often take longer than sitting down, finding that perfect example, and writing down a "script."

Once again it is imperative to read students' verbal and nonverbal communication cues to interact with them. Calling on the student who is avoiding making eye contact with anyone is probably not the best way to earn the trust of the class; however, calling on the student who is nodding along, or leaning forward in their chair (and providing them with plenty of enthusiastic reinforcement for responding to questions) will engage them and display to other students that participating doesn't have to be painful. It's also a good idea to use open-ended questions whenever possible, and not to have any one specific answer in mind. When I ask where a student will first turn when researching a paper, I try not to expect any certain answer, although I may suspect that they will answer, "the Internet," "the library," "books," or any number of other answers that I've most likely heard from other students, in other classes. The pure logistics of learning how to ask questions and wait for their answers can also be important to consider. Researchers have found, for example, that pausing for one second after asking questions resulted in student replies of about eight words, while pausing for three full seconds resulted in replies that averaged twenty-seven words (Rowe 1974, 90). Knowing this has enabled me to try and use pauses after questioning more effectively so I can get more comprehensive answers. Addressing the problem of non-responsive students can also be accomplished through research; for example, Wilbert

McKeachie suggests having students write down, and then read, their answers to the class (McKeachie 1994, 43). This is a technique I myself would never have thought of before reading the book; but that didn't stop me from putting pieces of paper on all of the tables before the breakout session, just in case the attendees would have been more comfortable writing down their answers to my query regarding the fears inherent in asking questions.

As always, reading about and trying out new techniques of encouraging class participation will only help you, as a teacher, if you are prepared to try out a variety of methods and adopt those that are well suited to your personality and style. If you aren't comfortable calling on students who have not volunteered, don't force yourself to do so! Just because you've seen someone else successfully have students read quotations from note cards, don't do it if you would feel uncomfortable doing so. Instead, devote some time to learning about and reflecting upon questioning methods before your classes; start reading books like McKeachie's *Teaching Tips*. Don't forget to read up on the theory regarding nonverbal communication cues; becoming proficient in "reading people" is not intuitive (if it were, books like *Reading People* by Jo-Ellan Dimitrius and Mark Mazzarella, would not be *New York Times* bestsellers). A serendipitous browse in any academic library's psychology section will help you find textbooks like *Nonverbal Behavior in Interpersonal Relations*, in which can be found any manner of helpful tips like "the teacher who uses positive head nods in response to a student's comments will be perceived as friendly, concerned about the communication between teacher and student, and immediate" (Richmond 1991, 275). Accept that the only perfect example is the one that helps your students learn. Above all else, enjoy yourself. What would you rather teach: a class that you've memorized and that never changes, or one that changes with every new group of students? From which teaching experience do you have more to gain, and from which will you receive more material upon which to reflect?

The session concluded with small-group discussions of workshops the participants had recently taught, and how encouraging feedback could further develop those classes, as well as questions from session participants. One librarian indicated that she had taught a class on chemistry resources, and that the majority of her students were not comfortable participating. This is a very real scenario that every teaching librarian will face at some point in their career, and the only way to address it is to be prepared for it to happen. Always prepare carefully for your classes by trying to ascertain if they are a group who are normally comfortable with interactive classes; if they are at all familiar with performing small-group work, and perhaps even their demographic characteristics—for example, men and women do communicate differently, and it can be very useful to know whether your class will consist primarily of male or female students, or an equal mix of both. Knowledge of your audience might also help you to formulate back-up plans; if your questions are not being answered, have a sample answer ready and ask the class to respond to it in small groups. Any number of different classroom scenarios exist, but you have to be ready to create any of them at a moment's notice. Another question involved methods of giving positive reinforcement to all participating students; the most effective way to develop that habit is to maintain your enthusiasm for the subject matter, and to recognize that a good teacher can relate any student's response in a useful way to the subject at hand. This also becomes easier with practice, especially once the speaker realizes that every minute the students spend talking is one less minute they have to fill.

Facing your classes with the intent of letting their feedback immediately dictate the course and content of the session can be one of the most liberating experiences a teaching librarian can have. Always take a step back and consider ways in which you can immediately reflect upon and react to student feedback in order to increase your own immediacy behaviors. Plan an active response from your students, be ready to use their questions and answers in your teaching, and study current communication and education theory to further develop your ability to facilitate discussion and participation. It may not make for a coherent conference paper (this hour-long breakout session consisted of a five-sentence outline, and was otherwise created on the spot using participant feedback, responses, and questions) but it can be a lot of fun, for you and your students. It can also lead to the telling of great jokes like: "Why did the elephant paint his toenails red? So he could hide in the strawberry patch!"

REFERENCES

Christophel, D.M. "The Relationship Among Teacher Immediacy Behaviors, Student Motivation, and Learning." *Communication Education* 39 (1990): 323-340.

DeVito, Joseph A. *The Interpersonal Communication Book*. New York: Harper & Row, 1976.

McKeachie, Wilbert J. *Mckeachie's Teaching Tips: Strategies, Research, and Theory for College and University Teachers*. 9th ed. Lexington, MA: D.C. Heath, 1994.

Richmond, Virginia P., James C. McCroskey, and Steven K. Payne. *Nonverbal Behavior in Interpersonal Relations*. 2nd ed. Englewood Cliffs, NJ: Prentice Hall, 1991.

Rowe, Mary Budd. "Wait-Time and Rewards as Instructional Variables, Their Influence on Language, Logic, and Fate Control: Part One." *Journal of Research in Science Teaching* 11, no. 2 (1974): 81-94.

Shannon, Claude E., and Warren Weaver. *The Mathematical Theory of Communication*. Urbana, IL: University of Illinois Press, 1949.

SUGGESTED RESOURCES

Baringer, Doreen K., and James C. McCroskey. "Immediacy in the Classroom: Student Immediacy." *Communication Education* 49, no. 2 (2000): 178-186.

Billson, Janet Mancini, and Richard G. Tiberius. "Effective Social Arrangements for Teaching and Learning." *New Directions for Teaching and Learning* 45 (1991): 67-86.

Dimitrius, Jo-Ellan, and Mark Mazzarella. *Reading People*. New York: Ballantine Books, 1998.

Fatt, James P. T. "It's Not What You Say, It's How You Say It." *Communication World* 16, no. 6 (1999): 37-40.

Mehrabian, Albert. *Nonverbal Communication*. Chicago: Aldine Atherton, 1972.

—SARAH STATZ—

GET "REAL": PARKER PALMER, BLOOMBERG, CAMTASIA AND ME

Sally Weston

Get "Real"!

Q: What does it mean to get "real"?
A: To be "authentically myself" as an instructor.

Why be "Authentic"?

Author Parker J. Palmer writes: "My ability to connect with my students and to connect them to my subject depends less on the methods I use than the degree to which I know and trust my selfhood, and am willing to make it available and vulnerable in the service of learning." Palmer's book, *The Courage to Teach* advocates authenticity, i.e., "selfhood" in the classroom. *Identity* and *integrity* are components of selfhood. Identity can be defined as "an evolving nexus where all the forces that constitute my life converge in the mystery of self, including: my genetic makeup, the culture I was raised in, and my life experiences and relationships." Integrity consists of "whatever wholeness I am able to find in that nexus as its vectors form and reform the pattern of my life."

Stories are the best way to portray these realities, according to Palmer. His book includes a story of two teachers with vastly different relationships to their own "selfhood". One is comfortable and authentic; the other feels disconnected and alienated. The story helps to illustrate these elusive concepts.

Weston is Head of Instruction at Kresge Business Administration Library, University of Michigan Business School, Ann Arbor, MI.

The "Downside" of Authenticity

Authenticity (as defined by Palmer) in the classroom involves risk. This kind of vulnerability is scary; it's easier to distance yourself. After all, you can't control everything that might go wrong, and it's hard to relax and be authentic under these conditions. Examples of "variables" include: students; technology glitches; format/software (e.g., Web-based training (WBT)); and complex, constantly changing databases, to name but a few.

Think About It

What does it mean to rely on your selfhood rather than methods? What fears do you have about making your selfhood available and vulnerable? How have these fears led you to disconnect from your students or subjects in various ways? (This question, and other "thought" questions in this paper, are taken from *The Courage to Teach, a Guide for Reflection and Renewal*, by Rachel C. Livsey and Parker J. Palmer.)

Obstacles I've Personally Experienced to My Own Authenticity as an Instructor

An example of the kinds of challenging databases we deal with every day would be *Bloomberg*, a vast financial database which is used by Wall Street traders to trade stocks. This database can be difficult to learn and difficult to teach, thereby causing nervousness and anxiety. Our new state-of-the-art Tozzi Financial Center is a bit intimidating with all of its high tech equipment that can be used to simulate an actual stock exchange. I've had to teach in the center without a microphone—a daunting task in a large room that looks like the bridge of the Starship Enterprise!

Web-based training has also been a "bugaboo" for me at times. I had one project in the summer of 2001 that ruined a friendship with a coworker in computing services and took the whole summer to do. Unfortunately, it was obsolete nine months later. I was trying to create a library instruction unit with a multimedia screen using HTML headings, a video window, a window with scrolling text, and another window with still images (screen dumps). The software we used, *ePublisher*, did not live up to our expectations. My reference to *Camtasia* (think "Fantasia") reflects my difficulties that summer learning and using at least four different types of software, up to and including a film editing program called *Premiere*, which should only be used by Steven Spielberg, and others of his ilk. Finally, the file size of the "almost" finished project was too big to load on many student machines, even though we were supposed to be able to make it a reasonable file size.

All of these various problems, which recur over and over again in different guises, have challenged me to stay "real" as an instructor, instead of retreating behind a distant "safe" facade. The embarrassment of not knowing something, not being able to get something to work, and/or being surprised (in front of a class) by a sudden change in a database all tax one's ability to be "real." I don't know how to bring my authenticity to Web-based training, exactly, but I do know that trying to become an overnight expert in Web design software and graphics is NOT the way for me to do it.

Thought Question

What methods have **you** used to try to connect to your students with your subject? Which ones were effective? Which ones were ineffective? What do you learn about your identity and integrity as a teacher from knowing which methods do and do not work for you?

Getting "Real": What Can Help

(From a presentation by Anne Harrington, faculty at the University of Michigan Business School.)

First, figure out your "Social Style as a Speaker." There are four types, Amiable, Driver, Analytic, and Expressive. This helps because once you know your own strengths and weaknesses as a speaker you will be able to feel more confident interacting with the other three types, and will have some idea how to address them most effectively, given your style.

The Four Social Styles as Speakers

Amiable Style?
- Cooperative, agreeable, responsive, supportive
- Patient, caring, empathic, connection-oriented

Analytic Style?
- Logical, organized, systematic, thoughtful
- Reserved, serious

Driver Style?
- Direct, candid
- Forceful, decisive, strong-willed, results oriented

Expressive Style?
- Energetic, enthusiastic, dynamic, dramatic
- Visionary, spontaneous, outgoing

(See Merrill, David W. *Personal Styles and Effective Performance* for more detail.)

Accommodate all Four "Social Styles" Types

Analytics? Give 'em deductive reasoning with emphasis on details, objective two-sided arguments, explicit logical framework, articulated reasoning and methods (e.g., HANDOUTS.)

Drivers? Give 'em a deductive approach with conclusions clearly stated, simple structure, progress toward goal. (Make a POINT.)

Expressives? Give 'em an inductive approach, vision, creativity, intuition, overall organization subordinate to ideas and creativity. (Make it FUN.)

Amiables? Give 'em deductive reasoning with emphasis on connections, big picture, systemic relations, framework, models (Make EYE CONTACT and SMILE.)

More Help: *Creativity at Work*

University of Michigan Business School (UMBS) faculty member Jeff DeGraff and Ph.D Student Katharine Lawrence wrote the book, (literally.) To get comfortable with your own creativity, you need to figure out:

- When am I creative?
- What am I doing or not doing when I'm most creative?
- Where am I? A noisy or quiet place?

—SALLY WESTON—

- What time of day? Morning or night?

Learn Your Pattern of Creativity

Are you most creative when you are collaborating with others, or alone?

What gives you the most energy? What saps it? (Uh…I think we already know some answers to "What saps it!")

Use this knowledge to make your life easier. Arrange your teaching schedule, if you can. Do your Web-pages or WBT when you're "on." Go with **your** flow. It helps make work more fun, so you can be more relaxed, and more authentic.

Simplify: How We Do WBT Right Now

Ahhh…relief. I do the content, and our systems librarian does the Web design. Right now we're using Dreamweaver and Fireworks. (Complete title of software: Macromedia Studio MX which includes Dreamweaver MX and Fireworks MX) and it's working well. I write the text in Word and create screen dumps in Photoshop 5.0, and our systems librarian puts it all into Fireworks in a streamlined process. We plan to do several Web tutorials this way over the summer 2003.

My Own Tips for "Getting Real" and Staying There

(Based on 13 years of teaching in academic libraries, plus 2 years of storytelling)

- Remember: you are simply the "vessel." Think of it as the material comes **through** you—it helps get the focus off of you and onto the material. You are "translating" the content for the audience.
- If nothing (technology) works, cancel the class and offer to meet with them later one-on-one. Hand out your cards.
- Have them jot questions on your cards during class, and then follow-up and email them later.
- Have a sign up sheet, and take roll if you're waiting out a glitch. Everyone loves to hear their name. They will listen better if you know their name.
- Give them a handout! Should be obvious, but…some librarians withhold handouts!
- If it (technology) breaks down, say "talk amongst yourselves."
- Always ask for a separate mouse on laptops, especially if you're not that coordinated (like me.)
- Admit ignorance, it's refreshing.
- Praise their superior knowledge if need be, and skip ahead in your agenda—let them out early!
- NEVER, NEVER, NEVER go **over** your time! You will lose their trust for next time.

Advanced Authenticity: Bob Quinn's Life Statement

Bob Quinn is another fantastic faculty member at UMBS. His books include *Letters to Garrett*, *Deep Change*, and *Change the World*. Bob has a life statement which he continually revises He asks himself many questions; here are some of them to consider for yourself:

- To specify your life mission: List the ten best and ten worst things that ever happened to you, and then ask, *What has life prepared me to do that no one else can do*?
- Specify your daily life-strategy checklist. Indicate those daily routines that give you creative energy when you do them and cause you to suffer when you don't do them.
- Specify your professional life mission. What are the fundamental assumptions of your work-life? Why do you work? What is your professional purpose? See the book, *Letters to Garrett*, for more on life statements.

To Sum Up: Know Thyself

And laugh…you're **not** alone out there!

GET "REAL" BIBLIOGRAPHY

Adams, S. *Step One: Identify the Problem Dilbert 2003 Block Calendar*. CA: Andrews McMeel Publishing, 2003.

Alessandra, T. *People Smarts: Bending the Golden Rule to Give Others What They Want*. San Diego: Pfeiffer & Co., 1994.

Alessandra, T. *The Platinum Rule: Discover the Four Basic Business Personalities - And How They Can

Lead You to Success. NY: Warner Books, 1998.

Benson, H. *The Breakout Principle: How to Activate the Natural Trigger That Maximizes Creativity, Athletic Performance, Productivity and Personal Well-Being*. NY: Charles Scribner, 2003.

Bolton, R. *Social Style/Management Style: Developing Productive Work Relationships*. NY: AMACOM, 1984.

DeGraff, J., and Katherine A. Lawrence. *Creativity at Work: Developing the Right Practices to Make Innovation Happen*. San Francisco: Jossey-Bass, 2002.

Field, J. *A Life of One's Own*. London: Virago, 1986.

Hirsh, S. *Life Types*. NY: Warner Books, 1989.

Keirsey, D. *Please Understand Me: Character and Temperament Types*. Del Mar, CA: Prometheus Nemesis Book Co, 1984.

Levoy, G. M. *Callings: Finding and Following an Authentic Life*. NY: Three Rivers Press, 1998.

Livsey, R. C. and Parker Palmer. *The Courage to Teach: a Guide for Reflection and Renewal*. San Francisco: Jossey-Bass, 1999.

Merrill, D.W. and R.H. Reid. *Personal Styles & Effective Performance: Make Your Style Work for You*.

Radnor, PA: Chilton Book Co., 1981.

Palmer, P. *To Know As We Are Known*. New York, NY: HarperCollins, 1993.

Palmer, P. *The Courage to Teach*. San Francisco: Jossey-Bass, 1998.

Quinn, R. E. *Deep Change: Discovering the Leader Within*. San Francisco: Jossey-Bass, 1996

Quinn, R. E. *Change the World: How Ordinary People Can Achieve Extraordinary Results*. San Francisco: Jossey-Bass, 2000.

Quinn, R. E. *Letters to Garrett*. San Francisco: Jossey-Bass, 2002.

Ruge, K. *Where Do I Go From Here? An Inspiration Guide to Making Career and Life Choices*. New York: McGraw-Hill, 1998.

Tieger, P.D. *Do What You Are: Discover the Perfect Career Path for You Through the Secrets of Personality Type*. Boston: Little, Brown and Company, 1995.

Tolle, E. *The Power of Now: A Guide to Spiritual Enlightenment*. Novato, CA: New World Library, 1999.

KNOW THY USERS, FOR THEY ARE NOT YOU

Jerilyn Veldof and Melissa Kalpin

We are seeing a unique generation of young people at our colleges and universities today using, or sometimes not using, our libraries. This paper describes this generation's values, culture, lifestyles, academic behaviors and challenges. It addresses some implications for libraries and how we might connect libraries with this group in more meaningful ways. Even though some of the characteristics, behaviors, and beliefs described may not pertain to every unique member of this generation, current research and our own focus group studies show they are fairly widespread and dominant.

What exactly do we call this new generation? After analyzing results from a 1997 poll conducted by abc.com, news anchor, Peter Jennings, reported:

> Several thousand people sent suggestions to abcnews.com. Some thought that gen.com would be a good idea. Others said Generation Y, Generation Whatever; Gen-D was one; The Boomlets; The Prozac Generation. When everyone got talking about it online, the second-largest number thought there should be no label at all, and the greatest interest was in the Millennium Generation, or the Millennials.[1]

The second most popular identifier, "Don't Label Us," clearly makes a statement about this generation. They do not want to be boxed in, categorized, or labeled. They see themselves as unique individuals and

---

Veldof is Director of Undergraduate Initiatives and *Kalpin* is Reference and Instruction Services Librarian at the University of Minnesota, Minneapolis, MN.

considerably different from the generations before them. Since the late nineties, in addition to the term, "Millennials," the term "Gen Y'ers" is also widely used.

The Millennial Generation is the group of people born between 1977 and 1994. They are currently aged 9-26. They are 71 million strong, the largest teen population in U.S. history. They account for 26% of the total population, with Baby Boomers at 28%.[2]

They are a very diverse group, and their diversity is rising. According to *The Condition of Education 2002 Indicator on Undergraduate Diversity*, "minority students represented nearly a third of all undergraduates in 1999-2000, up from about a quarter in 1989-90."[3]

The Millennials are also a global generation. Travel, study abroad programs, and the Internet introduce them to and connect them with other cultures. They are the first high-tech generation, having grown up with computers, the Internet, laser surgery, and genetic engineering.[4] Technology is what *connects* them to the world and to each other. It is a very integral part of their lives. As 17 year-old Tanner Rouse says:

> I think the most important invention during my lifetime was the cell phone. I just got one for Christmas. I got like 7,000 calls a day because I have the easiest number to remember of all my friends. Everyone calls to find out what's going on.[5]

They have a very fast-paced lifestyle as well. These young people are working, going to school, making time for friends and family, and participating in sports and other extra curricular activities. They literally use palm pilots to schedule their lives. This fast-paced lifestyle is exemplified by the characteristics of MTV. Demographer, Susan Mitchell, describes the MTV visual style as speaking "specifically and effectively to Gen Ys" by using "loud graphics, rapid edits, moving cameras," and the like. She says, "That MTV style of editing is impossible for adults to follow, but I suspect that there's some difference in today's kids' hard wiring now because they've had this rich, rapid visual growing up."[6] These students are excellent multi-taskers and have twitch speed, hypertext minds.[7]

Gen Y'ers are high achievers. Their parents train them to be doers; they earn college credits in high school and practice for the SATs as early as the sixth grade. This is apparent in recent headlines from the early 2000s: "Packing Courses Instead of a Lunch," "Stressed Out Kids Aiming for Top Colleges, " "Freshman's Internet Use a Way of Life," "Palm Pilots Now Get Handed Out in Class," and "Sleepless in America."[8] But while students are striving to score high on achievement and entrance exams in high school, they're often times not prepared for the transition to college life and college academics. Students, themselves, describe this transition on a CD-ROM issued to incoming undergraduates at the University of Minnesota:

> I went to school thinking: "oh, I'm going to be fine; you know, this is great; I can't wait to go to college." I got there, and I sat in my room, and you seriously think "OK, so now what? My stuff's unpacked; um, now what am I going to do?"

> It was a big change—a very big change. I mean, I went from a graduating class of 42 [students] to an incoming freshman class of close to 5,000.

> I think my first quarter I could have maybe used some harder advice....I was so unprepared. My first quarter ended up being a total disaster.

> It's real important to have enough going on and you're not just consumed in your schoolwork, because that's not the whole college experience, you know. And I think trying to find a way that you can, you know, feel like you fit in—you fit and you do things on the campus really helps—so to have some sort of balance with social stuff.[9]

The students have expectations of college as well. In a presentation on Generation Y, Stephen Merritt describes the following student perceptions. They see education as a commodity—they are paying big money for their education and expect their professors to teach effectively and to be available to them outside of class. They expect clear investment outcomes such as a job and graduate school. They expect value-added courses and experiences. They expect enhanced personal support including one-on-one advising and counseling, faculty connection, and one person to stay with them throughout their college careers. They expect diversity in the classroom and through study abroad opportunities. They expect access to global information 24/7. They expect to be provided with integrated information technology with easy access, high speed, reliability, and with a user orientation.[10]

In late winter of 2003 the University of Minnesota Libraries launched an Undergraduate Services Initiatives project.[11] The Council for this project conducted student focus groups to try to uncover what issues students are facing on the U of M-Twin Cities campus and how the libraries might address these issues. Undergraduates spoke of three main problems: time management is extremely challenging (balancing work, life, and school), academic preparation is poor (what they learn in high school doesn't match or transfer directly to the expectations they face in college), and academic expectations are unclear. Here are student comments regarding academic expectations and making time to study, as transcribed from the CD-ROM mentioned above:

> My senior year in high school was...[well], I came out of high school having straight As. My first semester in college was a big surprise to me because I didn't realize how much work you had to do. I think I had two Bs and two As—and it had been a long time since I had a B—and I was very surprised about what I had to do. That's when I realized the work that I had to put into it, and just realizing what I had to do with my day to make sure that I reached that goal.

> Actually, one of my friends [who] came from my home town was probably the one that I knew had the biggest problem with it. He came to college, you know—he was a really smart kid in high school and everything—and he discovered in college that "hey, I'm on my own and I can do what I want to do," and everything. He had some roommates who were just like him in that respect,

—JERILYN VELDOF AND MELISSA KALPIN—

and so they really didn't go to class too much; usually most of the time they were drinking or doing something else during the week instead of studying. But, yeah, he missed a few tests and he just slid by, actually, for this next semester, and so, yeah, he did it. Now he really regrets what he did. I mean, he kind of learned from it, and now, once you have your GPA—I mean, once you drop your GPA—it's very hard to get it [back] up.

I think my first quarter I could have maybe used some harder advice about maybe keeping things under control, with like my grades and like, maybe telling me to take school more seriously, because my first quarter ended up being a total disaster. Definitely just telling [me]—I needed someone there to tell me that I needed to study more often, I think.

In the library focus groups, students said:

I just don't have any time for anything and I don't have any money so I'm, like trying to work and I don't have any time to study and I'm trying to go out and it's just, like, I don't have any time to sleep.

It's just difficult when you've got extra-curriculars you want to do and work that you have to go to and all the classes you have to take if you're a full-time student. So it's...work to put all that together and make it fit into a week and then go to the next week and just keep plugging through.

But students do find or make time for studying and they certainly have their own habits and preferences:

Coffee shops are always a popular place. I go to this place in Uptown—French Meadow Bakery—a cool place.

You know, the Bio-Medical Library in Diehl Hall, right off the Superblock, is a good, quiet place. My freshman year especially, it was close to the dorms. I could walk right across the street and you're there. Nice place to write a paper.

...In the springtime, usually there's a lot of open area—like on the [Northrop] mall there's a lot of grass—[and] you can sit around and study for a while.

...and sometimes when I need to, I'll just, you know, be in my room and shut everything off.

[I like a place] that just kind of puts you at ease. For me, [it's] a nice cushion on the seat [and] I like a lower table and good lighting.

Students also face unclear expectations from their instructors. In the focus groups, one student expressed that "teachers are really inconsistent across the board...as far as papers go." And another said:

I think one of the toughest things is...to understand what exactly your professor wants in the paper because everybody has their definition of what an academic or research-type paper is supposed to be like.

They also want clear and focused instructions. One student expressed:

I think everyone's already nervous or scared anyways so even when the professor tells them exactly what to do they're still going to question everything like I know I do. I need to hear something from them like 8 times or see it in paper to know *for sure* that that's what I need to do.

So what do the students say about libraries? Many do visit libraries as a place to study, as indicated in the student interviews, but some of the focus group comments were less than encouraging in regard to library resources:

The majority of students, given the option, would rather sit in their room...and look something up online where they don't have to leave, than to go out, especially in the cold, and go to the library.

I still don't know the library system. I don't ever use them. I use my own resources and the Internet, mostly.

Another student comment reflected many others we heard: "You need to do something to show that libraries aren't obsolete in the face of the Internet."

Clearly, what undergraduate Gen Y'ers think about the research process and the library is quite different from that of librarians. In a 1998-99 study conducted at the University of Minnesota-Twin Cities, undergraduates participated in several rounds of usability studies and their instructors of English Composition contributed in two focus groups. Veldof and Beavers discovered that there are distinct differences between the mental models of undergraduates and librarians. Undergraduates think of research as merely a means to a good grade and think it is—or should be—fast and easy and not something you have to learn to do. Librarians, on the other hand, often think of research as an end in and of itself and value the research itself. Librarians think research is complicated and needs to be learned as a special process with a special body of knowledge. These are two very different mental models of the research process; librarians are not our users.[12]

Given these fundamental differences, what can libraries do to reach out to this group of students, capture their attention, and offer them libraries that meet their needs and respond to their academic and life challenges? In the rest of this paper we'll look at the power of branding, brand identities in businesses and finally examine brand identities for libraries. Good brand management can be a powerful way to reach out and bring Gen Y'ers into our virtual and physical libraries.

A good brand is more than a name and a slogan. A brand is a personality and an identity.[13] To be successful, it doesn't necessarily have to be a blinking, moving, in-your-face, just-off-the-street kind of identity. None of the 20 brands most recognized by teens worldwide (out of 75 brand logos tested)[14] are new and fresh (see Appendix A). These are all tried and true, trusted and familiar brands to youth. GenY'ers have an emotional connection they have attached to these logos. They don't just see a certain type of font, they feel emotions and make assumptions about the product based on the brand identity of the product or company. How do you react to the logos in Appendix A?

Winning brands synthesize emotional projections with knowledge and beliefs about the brand. You don't just "know" that McDonald's is a happy and friendly place to go, you believe it and you project your own happy childhood memories onto McDonald's. A winning brand also makes you feel good about the choice you made to use the product or to buy it. It has a certain personality—Phillips 66 looks solid and masculine while MTV looks cool and unpredictable. A winning brand also gives you a feeling of product security. Every time you pop open a Coke you know you're going to get the same good product. Your trip to Disney World was just as great as your neighbor's trip. Ultimately however, it is your emotional responses that are key to making a brand a winning brand.

A brand—winning or not—says something about who a GenY'er is. Their brands encompass their entire lifestyle.[15] Choosing between Skechers sneakers and Adidas, for example, communicates to a Gen Y peer who they are and what they are like. Wearing a t-shirt with the words "Abercrombie & Fitch" scrawled across the front is not an intention to give away free advertising, but rather a form of social expression that announces that this person is an Abercrombie kind of person.

Take a look at the brand logos you use every day. What kind of brand identity do these logos create? For example, the Vicks cough drop logo uses a deep color combination of blue and green. Just the logo alone looks soothing and deep, as if it will be sure to cure what ails you. Sun Light is a dish cleaning detergent with a very bright, clean, and cheery brand logo that creates an emotional confidence that this product will surely get your glasses sparkling clean. Speed Stick has a very masculine and firm logo, but the sense of movement makes it seem like you'd get somewhere if you used the product and that it would be able to keep up with you.

These brands are very valuable and very expensive commodities. Even universities carefully control their logos. Take a look, for example, at Carnegie Mellon's "brand strategy and identity system: http://www.cmu.edu/identity/id_history.html. They do not allow even subtle changes to their brand logo.

The University of Minnesota-Twin Cities is also very aware of the power of branding. They are trying to distinguish themselves from their many local competitors. Why should a student choose the U of MN over St. Thomas University, Macalester College, the College of St Catherine, St. Cloud State, and the many other choices within a manageable driving radius? Instead of allowing students to create their own brand identity (such as "it's too overwhelming and we get lost in the bureaucracy") they have hired a firm to create the kind of identity the U of MN wants to project. So far the proposal is "Welcome to the Big Time!" This reflects the U's unique niche in the academic community: there are no other research universities in the state (aside from some of the small coordinate campuses of the Twin Cities).

What about the library? GenY'ers now have many information choices. They can often, for a lower level course paper, use Google to find articles and information and use their local bookstore where they can browse the latest trade books and sip coffee at the same time. They can use Infotrac or the "other" basic index they used in high school through their public library and access that book collection. They can also use a variety of computer labs on campus and a variety of study areas. It's conceivable that a Gen Y'er could go through all four or five years of college without using a college library at all, even to study in, as a science faculty member pointed out to us in a recent focus group[15].

So, if students have information options and if they in general choose products and services whose brand identity is aligned with their lifestyle and personal identities, what are they saying about themselves if they align with the academic library? Do you have a brand identity that appeals to GenY'ers or are you letting them develop their own brand identity of the library in contrast to your competitors'? For example, if it's cool to hang out in Barnes & Noble and study there, are they not as cool if they study in the library? If it's quick and easy to use Google, are they wasting their time using the library? If it feels friendly and homey to use their public library, do they perceive using your library as isolating and uncomfortable?

Have you let the GenY'ers decide who your library is going to be for them? Have you helped them create an emotional projection onto the library that is going to get them to use it? Or have you spent time and money (like we have) branding our library to faculty and graduates, to the exclusion of the Gen Y undergraduates?

Take a look at these brand logos from the University of Minnesota-Twin Cities Libraries.

Based on these logos, who do you think the Libraries are? For whom is this brand identity developed? Based on these logos, participants in the audience at LOEX described the University Libraries as being old-fashioned, stilted, formal, rigid, heavy and stuck. This looked fine for faculty and graduate students, they said, but not for undergraduates.

Have a look at your "competition's" logos; Google, your public library, the academic bookstore, the local bookstore/café (such as Borders). Who are they being? For whom is their brand identity developed? Just as businesses actively create an

identity for their target markets, we need to choose the identity we want for our libraries in terms of this new generation of users. To get the right formula, we need to integrate the current personality of the student body, the library, and the campus, with what we know about Gen Y'ers.

First, we need to take notice of the general personality or identity of the student body. Are your students party types and mostly concerned with having fun and getting in "face time"? Or are they academic types with high levels of perfectionism and performance expectations? Are they juggling school, work, and families and mostly concerned with speed and no hassle service?

What about your library? Is your library built with columns and beautiful lofty ceilings and does it elicit a feeling of intellectualism and scholarship? Or is it brand new, glassy and modern and exude a sense of being slick, edgy, and wired? Or perhaps is it Barnes & Noble chic with a coffee shop? Does it have a lot of deep, dark wood and have a cozy, comfortable, "home away from home" feel?

And finally, what about your college or university? Does it take risks and experiment or is it conservative? Does it take itself very seriously or is it fun and colorful? What overall tone is it trying to create in its recruitment materials and in its own identity look and feel?

Brand identities need to be communicated in many ways. The most obvious way is through the ubiquitous use of brand logos. The library logo should be on walls, on signage, on handouts, on the side of the building, on business cards, etc. But brand identity is also communicated in more subtle ways—the colors and art you choose for the walls, the types of furniture and the fabrics on them, the fonts that you choose to put on your handouts, the design of your web pages and the kinds of clothes your public service people wear. Brand infiltration needs to happen everywhere. We are competing against businesses with billion dollar budgets designed to lure GenY'ers into using or buying their brands.

Our closing advice is to keep your eye on the trends. "Out" is truly out.[16] Don't get caught being out of date (unless that's your "look"). Constantly monitor events and ask what opportunities can this event or trend possibly have for your brand? When the University began shifting its focus to improving the undergraduate experience, this was a key change about which the libraries needed to be proactive. Also, recreate your brand for the next generation; do not get complacent and think that your brand will be timeless.

And finally, "know thy users." Have regular focus groups and interviews with them. Survey them. Find out what their lives are like, what their greatest challenges are, and what they think about the library and about research.

ENDNOTES

1. Neil Howe and William Strauss, *Millennials Rising: The Next Great Generation* (New York: Vintage Books, 2000), 6.

2. Susan Mitchell, *American Generations: Who They Are. How They Live. What They Think* (Ithaca, NY: New Strategist Publications, 2000), 5-6.

3. U.S. Department of Education, National Center for Education Statistics, *The Condition of Education 2002, NCES 2002-025* (Washington, DC: U.S. Government Printing Office, 2002), 99.

4. Mitchell, *American Generations*, 5.

5. Pamela Paul, "Getting Inside Gen Y," *American Demographics* (Sept. 2001): 45.

6. Paul, 47.

7. Mark Prensky, *Digital Game-Based Learning* (New York: McGraw-Hill, 2001), 44.

8. Stephen R. Merritt, "Generation Y: A Perspective on America's Next Generation and Their Impact on Higher Education," ed. Shelley Neville, *The Serials Librarian* 42, no. ½ (2002): 48.

9. University of Minnesota, Division of Epidemiology, School of Public Health, *Freshman Survival Skills: Stories From Those Who've Been There* [CD-ROM] (Minneapolis, MN: University of Minnesota, 2002).

Excerpts from transcripts of student interviews, presented as video clips on the CD-ROM.

10. Merritt, "Generation Y," 49.

11. University of Minnesota Libraries, *Undergraduate Initiatives Focus Group Report, 20* May 2003. Internet on-line <http://staff.lib.umn.edu/ug/uicd-na.phtml>. [22 May 2003].

12. Jerilyn Veldof and Karen Beavers, "Going Mental: Tackling Mental Models for the Online Library Tutorial," *Research Strategies* 18 (2001): 3-20.

13. Peter Cheverton, *If You're So Brilliant... How Come your Brand Isn't Working Hard Enough? The Essential Guide to Brand Management* (CT: Kogan Page US, 2002).

14. Elissa Moses, *The $100 Billion Allowance: Accessing the Global Teen Market* (New York: John Wiley & Sons, Inc, 2000), 11-12.

15. Cheverton, *If You're So Brilliant*, 15-16.

16. University of Minnesota Libraries, *Undergraduate Initiatives Focus Group Report*.

17. Marc Gobe, *Emotional Branding: The New Paradigm for Connecting Brands to People* (New York: Allworth Press, 2001), 21-22.

—JERILYN VELDOF AND MELISSA KALPIN—

Appendix A

THE NERD, THE MESSIAH, AND THE CLASSROOM: PERSONALITY TYPES AND REFLECTIVE TEACHING

Jeanine Akers and **Wendy Crist**

Introduction

At Arkansas State University, librarians are involved in teaching First Year Experience (FYE) courses that offer an extended orientation to the university and its resources. These courses endeavor to raise student success and retention rates. An integral part of the First Year Experience course involves having each student take a personality test, the Myers-Briggs Type Indicator Instrument® (MBTI®)[1], to assist them in making appropriate career decisions and to foster understanding of how their personality type affects their learning experience and relationships. Two librarian instructors, having taken the Myers-Briggs test along with their students, discovered that reflecting on personality types increased their ability to connect with their students and also improved their teaching styles.

The instructors, a web services librarian and a reference librarian, have some similarities in their Myers-Briggs personality types. However, the two instructors vary in two significant areas: thinking versus feeling and judging versus perceiving. As the two librarians began reflecting on their teaching experiences and began to collaboratively create and revise assignments, they learned practical tips for using personality types to enhance teaching.

Akers is Instruction Services Librarian at the University of Memphis, Memphis, TN; *Crist* is Web Services Librarian at Arkansas State University, State University, AR.

Students at Arkansas State University and the First Year Experience Program

Arkansas State University (ASU) is located in Jonesboro, AR (about 60 miles northwest of Memphis, TN). In 2002, the full-time equivalent student enrollment was 8,518 and the vast of majority of students (88%) at ASU are from the state Arkansas. The remaining majority (9%) of students come from closely neighboring states such as Missouri, Tennessee, Texas, and Mississippi. International students account for only 1.5% of the total enrollment.[2]

In an effort to improve student retention and success, the First Year Experience (FYE) program at ASU was launched in the fall of 1999. In 2002, there were a total of 1,477 new freshmen at ASU and 318 of those were enrolled in a FYE course. An additional 380 freshmen were enrolled in a "Strategies for College Success" course which is quite similar to FYE, but aimed at students who scored lower on their ACT tests. In other words, nearly half of all incoming freshmen are enrolled in some kind of extended orientation course.[3]

Librarians first became involved in teaching sections of FYE (a semester-long, 2 credit course) because instructors were needed and it was seen as an opportunity to bring information literacy to a greater number of students. The sections of FYE taught by librarians are arranged so that the first half of the semester is devoted to traditional extended orientation topics such as time management, study skills, and critical thinking. The second half of the semester is set aside entirely for library orientation, evaluating web resources, and term paper development.

Myers-Briggs Testing

The Myers-Briggs Type Indicator® Instrument is routinely given during the first week of classes to all freshmen enrolled in a FYE course. Instructors take the test along with students and the test results are used to discuss career options for students, choosing a major, and relationships. There are 16 MBTI® types consisting of 4 letters each. Characteristics of each type are compared in table 1.[4]

Extroverts	Introverts
-More outgoing and comfortable in social situations -Work well in groups -Get their energy from people and/or objects	-Feel comfortable working alone -Enjoy introspection -Draw their energy from within and/or ideas or concepts
Sensing	**Intuitive**
-Realistic and practical -Use senses to obtain information -Want clear, step-by-step directions	-Imaginative and creative -See beyond the facts, go with gut -Like open-ended instructions
Thinking	**Feeling**
-Logical, analytical -Place a high value on competence	-Empathetic, sensitive -Place a high value on relationships
Judging	**Perceiving**
-Prefer organization, structure -Find comfort in rules	-Prefer flexibility and spontaneity -Find rules limiting

TABLE 1. MYERS-BRIGGS CHARACTERISTICS EXAMINED

Various authors and organizations have given a descriptive label to each of the sixteen types. Type labels from the book *Please Understand Me II* are provided in table 2,[5] along with humorous (and less flattering) labels which were found on the personal homepage of Hal Dendurent.[6]

Type	*Please Understand Me* Label	Humorous Label
ENFJ	Teacher	"Busybody"
INFJ	Counselor	"Messiah"
ENFP	Champion	"Muckraker"
INFP	Healer	"Fanatic"
ENTJ	Field Marshall	"Tyrant"
INTJ	Mastermind	"Crackpot"
ENTP	Inventor	"Frankenstein"
INTP	Architect	"Nerd"
ESTJ	Supervisor	"Stuffed Shirt"
ISTJ	Inspector	"Bean Counter"
ESFJ	Provider	"Gossip"
ISFJ	Protector	"Sidekick"
ESTP	Promoter	"Beer Drinker"
ESFP	Performer	"Clown"
ISTP	Operator	"Assassin"
ISFP	Composer	"Snob"

TABLE 2. SIXTEEN MYERS-BRIGGS TYPES AND DESCRIPTIVE LABELS

—JEANINE AKERS AND WENDY CRIST—

Librarians and MBTI Type

Recent studies of the library profession have shown that a significant change in the personality types of librarians has occurred in the last couple of decades. Studies done in the 1970s and 1980s found that the majority of librarians were ISFJ types, or "protectors." A study completed by the Center for the Applications of Psychological Type (CAPT), determined that 19% of librarians generally fit the stereotypical "quiet, conscientious, serious, and unassuming" character often associated with the librarian persona. However, a nationwide study of librarians' personalities conducted by Mary Jane Scherdin in 1992 uncovered that as little as 8% of the 1,600 librarians tested were actually ISFJs.[7]

Scherdin hypothesized that a great range of personality type preferences exists in the profession and that the preferences are related to library and job type. The resultant article, "Shattering Our Stereotypes: Librarians' New Image," co-authored by Scherdin and Anne K. Beaubien in the July 1995 *Library Journal,* explains that more librarians prefer introversion (63%), intuition (60%), thinking (61%), and judging (66%). The most frequent MBTI® types for librarians involved in this study are the ISTJ (inspector) at 17% and the INTJ (mastermind) at 12%. Furthermore, the INTJ type was found to be most associated with librarians who had been in the profession for less than five years. Scherdin and Beaubien propose that this shift in type may be attributed to new job duties for librarians and the transfer of many of the "practical tasks" to library support staff.[8]

Education and MBTI

There are a variety of personality differences between librarians and college students, which help explain some of the communication difficulties that exist between the two groups. According to CAPT, the majority of people in the United States have extrovert and sensing preferences. The same is true for college freshmen. However, college and university faculty and librarians strongly lean toward introversion and intuitive preferences. Not surprisingly then, introverted, intuitive students have an academic advantage and generally make better grades in college.[9] It is also true, however, that the number of extroverted and introverted students becomes more evenly distributed after the freshman year, evincing either that extroverted students leave college by the end of the first year or acquire introverted preferences as they proceed through their college careers.

CAPT reports indicate that the thinking/feeling preferences are divided by gender, with the majority of

females as feelers (65-70%) and males as thinkers (60-65%). Although there is no evidence of significant academic achievement based on thinking or feeling preferences, university faculty and librarians tend to be thinkers.[10] Interestingly, female librarians are twice as likely to have a thinking preference than women in the general population.[11] This could potentially aggravate communication between students who expect female instructors to behave and respond in ways characteristic of "feelers".

The majority of people in the United States have a preference for judgment over perception and it is in this dimension that college students, teaching faculty and librarians all share the majority preference. CAPT reports indicate that judging types do make better grades, but perceiving types generally make higher scores on aptitude tests.[12]

The Nerd and the Messiah Reflect on Teaching

During the Fall 2002 semester at Arkansas State University, Wendy, the INTP, or "nerd" instructor, noted the personality types of her students after FYE classroom discussions became increasingly chaotic. Examination of the 16 students' personality types revealed that there were 12 extroverts (the majority types were ENFJ and ESFJ) and only 4 introverts (2 INTJs and 2 INFPs). The "nerd" instructor faced a semester of total chaos during which the strongly extroverted students dominated class discussions, competed for attention, and left little opportunity for introverted students to participate in the class. In addition, Wendy realized that sensing (S) students frequently misinterpreted assignment instructions and could not intuit the assignment objectives.

At this point, Wendy and Jeanine began to collaborate and together examined the effects of personality on teaching and learning. Several questions came to mind: How can we teach students with varying personality types? When do we adjust our own personality style to foster better communication and when is it appropriate to impose our style the students? And, lastly, how can assignments and instructions be altered so that students with differing styles have equal opportunities for success?

A popular assignment among FYE instructors is that of weekly journal writings. Jeanine, an INFJ, or "feeler" instructor, integrated the weekly journal assignments into her syllabus with ease, even adding three personal conferences with each student. In contrast, Wendy, a thinker instructor, felt uncomfortable with journal assignments and personal interviews, choosing not to include them in the course plan. When we looked at our syllabi side by side, we began to notice that the ways in which our course plans differed could be directly correlated to our differences in personality styles. For example, Jeanine's syllabus showed emphasis on making personal connections with each student and developing skills to ease the emotional transition from high school to college. Wendy, on the other hand, put a strong emphasis on critical thinking assignments, even using a note taking exercise as an opportunity to have students read and take notes from a chapter dealing with critical thought.

Reflecting on Feeling vs. Thinking

Though it is true that behaviors consistent with feeling personality types do indeed have merit in the classroom, there are several aspects of feeling behavior that may pose difficulties for librarian instructors. Above all, there is the issue of time. Most academic librarians have a variety of roles in their institutions that need continuous attention. When personal relationships are emphasized in the classroom, less time is available for other, more traditional librarian duties. Grading journals in a thoughtful way requires a great deal of time and often multiple readings to ensure that useful feedback is given. Personal conferences also opened up a great dialogue between Jeanine and her students, but on many days she felt that her loyalties were divided between conversing with homesick or otherwise troubled students and fixing database problems or working on an electronic journal project that would increase access to materials for the entire campus community.

When instructors allow feeling behaviors to enter into their teaching, they must also be aware of how their relationships with students affect their grading. Feeling instructors may be more sensitive to students' behavior and feel as though the more friendly and personable students are most interested in the class. Also, feeling instructors are likely to be responsive to students' emotional outbursts, which may put them in a situation where some students can potentially manipulate the instructor.

Feeler instructors should also make certain that they show themselves to be competent as well as feeling, so as not to lose the trust of students with thinking preferences. This can be particularly difficult for instructors who are both introverted and feeling, since self-promotion does not come as naturally to them. Furthermore, it is important to realize that not all topics lend themselves easily to a feeler approach and sometimes it is necessary to adjust preferences to ensure the best possible teaching scenario.

Thinker instructors, on the other hand, must be willing to adjust to more of a feeler approach when the nature of the course or needs of the students require it.

For example, upon reflection Wendy realized that assigning her students even a small number of journal writings might have been an excellent way to ensure that the introverted students were getting the opportunity to communicate with the instructor. In essence, the "thinker" may have to accept some discomfort and adopt some "feeler" skills in order to ensure a better learning environment for all students.

Just as Wendy can see the benefits of adjusting her thinking preference to a feeling one so that she can provide the best possible learning environment for her introverted students, Jeanine has realized that she teaches best when she can make personal connections with her students, which forces her towards more extroverted behavior.

Asking Our Students to Reflect

Information literacy is a meta-cognitive process and many instructor librarians assign journals, research logs, I-search papers and other assignments that require students to reflect on their research processes. However, many instructors may not consider how their personality preferences affect the design of their assignments and ultimately students' success. Susan Callahan, Associate Professor of English at Northern Illinois University, explored the relationship between MBTI® and students' reflective writing. Her article, "Responding to the Invisible Student," published in *Assessing Writing*, provides useful guidance for librarians who assign reflective work to their students.[13]

Taking each dimension of the MBTI into consideration can enhance the overall design of reflective research assignments. It is important to create assignments that allow for students' success regardless of preference in each dimension. To reach both introverted and extroverted students, it is necessary to provide sufficient models and explanations, develop questions that ask students to reflect both outward and inward, and provide opportunities for both written and oral reflection. To ensure that the assignment communicates to both sensing and intuitive students, instructors should ask students to examine relationships that may seem obvious and list specific elements that they might discuss. Also, avoid assuming that good writing and effective use of metaphor is evidence of higher-level reflection.[14] Allowing for success of both thinking and feeling students can be difficult, particularly because we often place a greater emphasis on logical, objective thinking in higher education. Reflective research assignments that ask for both a logical and an emotional response can result in better reflection from students with both preferences. It is also important to provide feedback that speaks to thinking and feeling students so they too can see that they managed to communicate their ideas.[15] Finally, when dealing with judging students, it may be necessary to ask them to stretch their reflection and consider alternatives, while we should also be patient with the imperfect writing from perceiving students who might provide us with new perspectives on the assignment, curriculum, or course.[16]

While it is important to consider the relationship between personality type and assignment design, we realized that it is sometimes beneficial to ask students to use their less-preferred behaviors. For example, a critical thinking exercise developed by Wendy, the INTP instructor, requires students to analyze a suspect email message to determine whether the email is a hoax or trustworthy information. The premise of the exercise requires all students to approach the assignment as an "intuitive thinker" (NT). Though students may initially meet such an assignment with discomfort or confusion, forcing this new way of thinking on the students can result in a more effective, if uncomfortable, learning experience.

Conclusion

Upon study of the personality types of the instructors and students in the First Year Experience course, it became clear that the course could be improved by reflecting on the effects of personality on learning. We discovered strategies for introverts teaching in an extrovert-dominant classroom as well as practical tips for communicating with students of differing personalities. The "thinker" instructor learned from "the feeler" instructor about building student-teacher relationships and "the feeler" discovered that feeling behaviors need to be incorporated into the classroom with some degree of caution. Together, we were able to reconsider curricula, assignments, and teaching methods in ways that increased student success, accepting that some discomfort entering into the classroom may be the key to better teaching.

NOTES

1. The Myers-Briggs Type Indicator®, Myers Briggs®, and MBTI® are trademarks or registered trademarks of the Myers-Briggs Type Indicator Trust in the United States and other countries.

2. The Office of Institutional Research & Planning, Arkansas State University, *The Arkansas State University 2002-2003 Factbook* (State University, Ark.: Arkansas State University, 2003), 39-45.

3. Paula Bradberry, "The First Year Experience at ASU," 16 May 2003, personal e-mail, (16 May 2003).

4. "CAPT: The MBTI Instrument," *Center for the Applications of Psychological Type.* Internet on-line. Available from < http://www.capt.org/The_MBTI_Instrument/Overview.cfm > . [22 May 2003]. Jung's Theory of Psychological Types and the MBTI Instrument.

5. David Mark Keirsey, "The Sixteen Types," *Kiersey Temperament and Character Web Site.* Internet on-line. Available from http://soli.inav.net/~catalyst/Humor/mbtihaha.htm. [22 May 2003].

6. Hal Dendurent, "MBTI Type Descriptions (Funny)," *Hal Dendurent, Catalyst.* Internet on-line. Available from http://soli.inav.net/~catalyst/Humor/mbtihaha.htm. [22 May 2003].

7. Mary Jane Scherdin and Anne K. Beaubien, "Shattering Our Stereotype: Librarians New Image," *Library Journal* 120, no. 12 (1995): 35-36.

8. Scherdin and Beaubien, "Shattering Our Stereotype," 36.

9. Mary H. McCaulley, "CAPT Using Type: Education," *Center for the Applications of Psychological Type.* Internet on-line. Available from < http://www.capt.org/Using_Type/education.cfm > . [22 May 2003].

10. McCaulley, "CAPT Using Type: Education."

11. Scherdin and Beaubien, "Shattering Our Stereotype," 37.

12. McCaulley, "CAPT Using Type: Education."

13. Susan Callahan, "Responding to the Invisible Student," *Assessing Writing* 7, no. 1 (2000): 57-77.

14. Susan Callahan, "Responding to the Invisible Student," 71.

15. Susan Callahan, "Responding to the Invisible Student," 71-73.

16. Susan Callahan, "Responding to the Invisible Student," 73.

REFLECTIVE PRACTICE THROUGH SCHOLARSHIP: INITIATIVES FOR SCHOLARLY TEACHING AND SCHOLARSHIP ON TEACHING

Lisa Janicke Hinchliffe and Robert Burger

Initiatives to integrate teaching and research offer librarians opportunities to re-energize their teaching while building their tenure and promotion dossiers through scholarship activities. Such initiatives are already underway at many institutions of higher education though librarians may or may not be aware of or involved with them—likely depending upon the status librarians have at given institutions. Regardless, librarians can both take advantage of the lessons learned from such initiatives and seek the benefits they offer as well as starting or joining existing initiatives at their own institutions.

This paper presents two models of integrating teaching and research—scholarly teaching and scholarship on teaching—in the context of the broader issue of reflective professional practice and then discusses two related professional development initiatives at Library of the University of Illinois at Urbana–Champaign (UIUC) as well as future plans.

Context: Reflective Professional Practice

Donald Schön's works such as *The Reflective Practitioner* and *Educating the Reflective Practitioner* provide a general framework for considering reflective professional practice, particularly his discussion of "knowing-in-action" and "reflection-in-action." As summarized by Joan

---

Janicke Hinchliffe is the Coordinator for Information Literacy Services and Instruction and *Burger* is the Associate University Librarian for Services at the University of Illinois at Urbana-Champaign, Urbana, IL.

Ferraro, "Schön recommended reflective practice as a way for beginners in a discipline to recognize cognizance between their own individual practices and those of successful practitioners ... reflective practice involves thoughtfully considering one's own experience in applying knowledge to practice while being coached by professionals in the discipline."

Similarly, writings about evidence-based practice emphasize a scholarly approach to professional activity. Andrew Booth, for example, defines evidence-based librarianship as "an approach to information science that promotes the collection, interpretation and integration of valid, important and applicable user-reported, librarian observed, and research-derived evidence. The best available evidence, moderated by user needs and preferences, is applied to improve the quality of professional judgements[sic]."

Integrating Teaching and Research

Programs to help faculty better integrate teaching and research attempt to create coherence among faculty's various roles and are usually also aimed at improving student learning through improved teaching. An additional purpose in some cases is to elevate the status of teaching on campus and the relative merit faculty members receive for their teaching efforts. The national initiative to integrate research and teaching is the Carnegie Academy for the Scholarship of Teaching and Learning, also known as CASTL, which has three components: Carnegie Scholars Program, Campus Program, and Scholarly and Professional Societies Program(http://www.carnegiefoundation.org/CASTL).

CASTL, as do many of the institutional-level initiatives, builds upon Ernest Boyer's work *Scholarship Reconsidered: Priorities of the Professoriate*. Boyer's work detailed four types of scholarship that can be briefly described as follows:

- The Scholarship of Discovery—traditional conceptualization of research, investigation and creation of new knowledge and understanding
- The Scholarship of Integration—making connections within and among fields of knowledge through synthesis, analysis and interpretation
- The Scholarship of Application—intersection of theory and practice; applying knowledge to individual, group, and institutional problems
- The Scholarship of Teaching—well-informed and intellectually engaged instructors effectively communicating knowledge to students

Efforts in the scholarship of teaching have developed along two distinct but related paths: scholarly teaching and scholarship on teaching.

"Scholarly teaching" is an approach to teaching activities and is similar to Boyer's original description of The Scholarship of Teaching. Scholarly teachers not only develop their content knowledge and continue developing it during their teaching years after their formal schooling experiences end, but also seek to develop their understanding of teaching and learning through professional reading, attendance at workshops, and classroom activities aimed at better understanding students and their learning. In essence, scholarly teachers actively pursue the development, not only of general teaching techniques, but also of pedagogical content knowledge that "underlies effective teaching... [it] includes information about typical difficulties that students encounter as they learn about a set of topics; typical paths students must traverse in order to achieve understanding; and sets of potential strategies for helping students overcome the difficulties that they encounter ... teaching strategies differ across disciplines" (Bransford, Brown, and Cocking, 1999, p. 33). Kathleen McKinney points out that scholarly teaching is closely related to notions of reflective practice.

Scholarship on teaching has come to be understood, generally speaking, as scholarship that takes teaching, and learning, as the topic of scholarship. Such scholarship on the topic of teaching can employ scholarly approaches that can be categorized as the scholarship of discovery, integration, and application (McKinney, *in press*). The CASTL program put forward a definition of the scholarship of teaching as "problem posing about an issue of teaching or learning, study of the problem through methods appropriate to disciplinary epistemologies, application of results to practice, communication of results, self-reflection, and peer review" for discussion at institutions participating in its Campus Program (see, for example, http://www.aahe.org/teaching/Carnegie/instruct1.htm). Institutions were invited to adopt the CASTL definition or to create their own. During its participation in the Campus Program, Illinois State University developed a definition of the scholarship of teaching and learning that has since been adopted at other institutions as well: "systematic reflection on teaching and learning made public" (http://www.cat.ilstu.edu/sotl/). This definition captures the essence of the scholarship of teaching and learning.

For faculty new to the scholarship of teaching and learning, *Classroom Research: Implementing the Scholarship of Teaching* by K. Patricia Cross and Mimi Harris Steadman is an excellent handbook for gaining understanding of this type of scholarship and for preparing to engage in a classroom research project. The *Research Agenda for Library Instruction and Information Literacy* developed by the Research and Scholarship Committee, Instruction Section, Association of College and Research Libraries provides a framework for thinking about scholarship on teaching and learning within academic librarianship. The *Research Agenda* details potential research questions in four areas: Learners, Teaching, Organizational Context, and Assessment.

Initiatives at the UIUC Library

The UIUC Library has two initiatives related to the themes discussed above: scholarly teaching and scholarship development.

The scholarly teaching initiative is a partnership program with the Graduate School of Library and Information Science and is named the GSLIS-Library Teaching Alliance. Founded in fall semester of 2001, the Teaching Alliance provides professional development opportunities focusing on teaching and learning and has been funded in part by grants from the Provost's Initiative on Teaching Advancement. Program topics have included: Learning Styles, Peer Observation, Teaching in the Electronic Classroom, Effective Lecturing, Who Are Our Students?, Internet and College Life, Developmental Theories of Learning, Diversity in the Classroom, and Teaching Portfolios. The Teaching Alliance is co-directed by two faculty members—one each from GSLIS and the Library—who are assisted by a graduate assistant. Program participants have included faculty from both units, library staff, GSLIS teaching assistants, and Library graduate assistants. Progress reports, program

—LISA JANICKE HINCHLIFFE AND ROBERT BURGER—

summaries, and other resources can be found on the Teaching Alliance website (http://leep.lis.uiuc.edu/seworkspace/teachingalliance/newhome.html).

The scholarship development initiative provides professional development opportunities related to scholarship and research methods. It is more organic in its organizational structure and is best understood in the larger context of librarian's faculty status. General professional development programming at the UIUC Library has been designed to help faculty members succeed in fulfilling the expectations for the three areas in which they are judged: librarianship, research and publication, and service. UIUC librarians have professorial rank and tenure and are expected to meet set standards in these three areas. For the past twenty five years this programming has been directed primarily at untenured faculty, in order to help them achieve tenure; however, many facets of the current scholarship development program, which has grown more intensive over the past three years, are available to all faculty members.

The present scholarship development program at UIUC was launched shortly after the arrival of Paula Kaufman, the University Librarian, in the fall of 1999. With both monetary support and collegial encouragement Kaufman directed one of the authors, Burger, to set up a professional development program that concentrated on untenured librarians, who by mid-2001 comprised approximately 40% of the Library faculty. Each year's set of individual events is collaboratively chosen by the untenured librarians so that it meets both immediate needs and contributes towards building a program that evolves over time. Over the past three years this program of scholarship development consisted of three types of sessions: informal social and culture-building events; presentations and short classes dealing specifically with research practice; and talks and panel discussions on presenting research at conferences and in publication as well as related professional activities such as national committee work.

The informal social and culture-building events include a fall and spring luncheon with the University Librarian and an all-library retreat in the spring. The second type, presentations and short classes about research practice, have included brown bag lunches where librarians present the results of current research, a short course on descriptive statistics and sampling, a session on using Excel for analyzing and presenting data, presentations on historical research methods and qualitative research methods, and structured seminars led by program officers and trainers from the Association of Research Libraries. The brown bag lunch seminars are useful in two major ways: the neophyte researcher has a "dry run" in presenting a research project, without the anxiety and expense of a major conference, and those attending learn other research techniques and methodologies. The third category, talks and panel discussions on the presentation of research at conferences and through publication, included panels on specific topics (e.g. "Games Publishers Plan and How You Can Win," and "Getting Involved in Campus and Professional Committees"), sessions that were directed at supervisory skills (e.g., "Basic Supervisory Skills" and "Managing the Challenging Employee"), and a presentation by the campus' Institutional Review Board about Human Subjects Research.

Future Plans at UIUC

Though the GSLIS-Library Teaching Alliance and the Library's scholarship development program will continue as distinct initiatives in the foreseeable future, the Teaching Alliance proposed focus for 2003-2004 draws upon the scholarly teaching emphasis from previous years as well as the efforts in the Library that focus more specifically on research skills and methodologies. The theme for the coming year's programming is *Scholarship of Teaching and Learning through Action Research*. As stated in the request for continued grant funding: "The direct intended outcome will be a greater awareness of teaching and learning practices as they relate specifically to the discipline of library and information science, as it is conveyed at the undergraduate level, while motivating faculty and staff to engage in action research."

BIBLIOGRAPHY

Boyer, Ernest L. *Scholarship Reconsidered: Priorities of the Professoriate*. San Francisco: Jossey-Bass, 1990.

Booth, Andrew. *Exceeding Expectations: Achieving Professional Excellence by Getting Research into Practice*. Paper presented at LIANZA 2000, Christchurch, New Zealand, 15-18 October 2000. Internet on-line. Available from: <http://www.shef.ac.uk/~scharr/eblib/Exceed.pdf>. [22 May 2003].

Bransford, John, Ann L. Brown, and Rodney R. Cocking, eds. *How People Learn: Brain, Mind, Experience, and School*. Washington, DC: National Academy Press, 1999. Also available from: <http://www.nap.edu/html/howpeople1/>.

Cross, K. Patricia, and Mimi Harris Steadman. *Classroom Research: Implementing the Scholarship of Teaching*. San Francisco: Jossey-Bass, 1996.

Ferraro, Joan M. *Reflective Practice and Professional Development*. ERIC Digest, 2000 Internet online. Available from: < http://www.eric facility.net/ericdigests/ed449120.html >. [22 May 2003].

Instruction Section, Association of College and Research Libraries. *Research Agenda for Library Instruction and Information Literacy*, 2003. Internet online. Available from: < http://www.ala. org/Content/ContentGroups/ACRL1/IS/ISCommittee s/Web_pages/Research/Research_Agenda_for_Librar y_Instruction_and_Information_Literacy.htm >. [22 May 2003].

McKinney, Kathleen. "The Scholarship of Teaching and Learning: Past Lessons, Current Challenges, and Future Visions." In *To Improve the Academy* (Vol. 22).In press.

Schön, Donald A. *The Reflective Practitioner: How Professionals Think in Action*. New York: Basic Books, 1983.

Schön, Donald A. *Educating the Reflective Practitioner: Toward a New Design for Teaching and Learning in the Professions*. San Francisco: Jossey-Bass, 1987.

CREATING STUDENT-CENTERED LEARNING: A CONSTRUCTIVIST APPROACH TO INFORMATION LITERACY INSTRUCTION

Pam Baker and Kathlene Hanson

As a concept, constructivism originated in philosophy and has been used to develop new paradigms in education, cognitive psychology, sociology and anthropology. When describing educational constructivism, the central tenet is that personal meaning is intimately connected with experience. Students are not seen as a blank slate waiting to be filled with information, but rather as individuals who come into a learning situation with their own preconceived knowledge and experiences, as well as a cognitive structure built upon those experiences. These preconceptions may be valid, invalid or incomplete, and a well-designed learning experience using constructivist ideas or techniques will help learners construct new knowledge and reformulate their existing knowledge framework based on new experiences and understanding. In other words, memorized facts unrelated to the learner's personal experience will be quickly forgotten.

Although faculty in the field of education may use or be familiar with this pedagogy, many instruction librarians may not. We were introduced to the idea of using constructivist pedagogy in the classroom during a conversation with an education faculty colleague from our institution. After discovering the characteristics of a constructivist classroom or learning experience, we realized that we had naturally incorporated several constructivist ideas in our library

Baker is the Coordinator of Library Instruction at California State University, Monterey Bay; *Hanson* is Electronic Resources Coordinator at California State University, Monterey Bay, Seaside, CA.

instruction sessions and particularly in our one-on-one teaching at reference desk interactions.

We felt that if we as instructors, were using these techniques without having a framework or vocabulary with which to understand them and that other teaching librarians might have similar reactions. This led us to organize a one-hour interactive session on constructivist approaches to information literacy instruction which we consciously designed using selected elements of constructivism.

We began the session with brief introductions and related how we had become aware of and interested in constructivist pedagogy. We then led the 66 participants in brainstorming, and recorded their ideas for later discussion. The first group brainstorm drew out the participants' prior knowledge on the basic ideas and techniques surrounding constructivist pedagogy. In the second group brainstorm the presenters summarized the previous ideas and used one or two of them to move into questions on what the participants wanted to know more about, i.e., "What would you like to know about some of the things listed in the first column?"

We demonstrated how these two brief group interactions had modeled the first two columns of a K-W-L chart—a commonly used constructivist learning tool that focuses on eliciting what students know, what they want to know and what they have learned about a particular topic or subject. Using this structured chart can help the learner to gather information, and think through a problem or define a research topic. Through a brief series of PowerPoint slides we then gave a short definition of the constructivist paradigm, an example of a complete K-W-L chart, and then listed the outcomes and elements of constructivist teaching as contrasted with "traditional" teaching.

As a central component of our session we then elaborated on the constructivist paradigm by giving some examples of how constructivist classrooms differ from traditional classrooms. In our discussion with the participants in forming the K-W-L chart, one participant talked about knowing that constructivism aims to build on "big concepts" rather than on skills. Another participant helped to focus our learning by asking us to further describe how constructivism can be used with different populations, in various settings and varying time constraints. Using examples from a chart in Jacqueline and Martin Brooks' *In Search of Understanding: The Case for Constructivist Classroom*, we focused on some of the elements of the constructivist classroom that help to shift focus to larger concepts and on the commonality of these elements in a variety of settings with a variety of populations.[1]

In their book, the Brooks' describe constructivist classrooms as environments where student questions are pursued, their point of view is sought to understand present conceptions, and they are valued as thinkers. The teacher in a constructivist classroom is an interactive facilitator and mediator. Assessment takes place during instructional activities. Rather than concentrate on student-centered group activity, the traditional classroom is one where students are seen as absorbers of information on a fixed curriculum provided by the teachers.

In addition to further defining constructivism through examples of a constructivist classroom or environment, we introduced a framework for designing a constructivist learning environment from Gagnon and Collay's *Designing for Learning: Six Elements in Constructivist Classroom*. One of our participants expressed concern that a constructivist classroom might be too "open-ended" or unstructured. Our intent in introducing a template for constructivist learning design was to focus our participants on some possible parameters for formulating a constructivist learning experience, and for giving the experience structure, while still focusing on building bridges between students' current knowledge, cognitive structures and learning outcomes.

Gagnon and Collay describe the six elements for constructivist learning design as *situation*, *groupings*, *bridge*, *questions*, *exhibit*, and *reflections*. In a constructivist situation the instructor frames the agenda and outlines goals and lesson format, concentrating on how students will be engaged in the activities. Groupings are an element because it is important to frame group activities and think about how students

will interact with each other. The bridge is a central piece of constructivist learning design because of its focus on building a learner-centered context from which new knowledge is created. Formulating types and content of questions is central in helping to focus the learning activity toward an outcome. An exhibit is a way for students to share the collective knowledge they have acquired. Finally, reflection is a way for students and instructors to articulate personal and collective learning.

In order to give the participants an opportunity to work on an example learning experience using the elements outlined above, we set a scenario for a group activity. In this scenario participants were asked to think about designing a learning session focused on working with educational psychology students to find two peer-reviewed journals articles to support a reflection paper. Using a handout (see Appendix 1 and 2) compiled from Gagnon and Collay's template and definitions[2] and including the scenario, the participants formed groups and discussed applications of the elements to the scenario provided.

Though we felt there was not adequate time to focus on this part of the session, we were able to get some ideas and feedback from the participants. One group suggested they might focus on building the "bridge" by having students in groups defining the vocabulary related to the learning session, such as "peer-review" "scholarly" etc.

The participants expressed a high level of interest in the session and we feel we learned much from them and from the experience of modeling a constructivist approach in our session. Some of the participants even commented that they appreciated us modeling a constructivist approach. To conclude the session, we asked the participants to fill out an evaluation that included a question asking the participants to list two things they had learned in the session. We asked the participants to see this evaluation as a tool for reflection and as a way of looking at the last column of the K-W-L chart, "What did you Learn?" Some of what the participants learned included how to use a K-W-L chart in their classrooms, how the constructivist approach is much like what we do during the reference interview, and how the constructivist approach is focused on student-centered learning and on concepts rather than skills. Below is a portion of the K-W-L chart that the participants created during the session.

—PAM BAKER AND KATHLENE HANSON—

What do you **Know**?	What do you **Want to know**?	What did you **Learn**?
• *Student-shaped*	• *Definition for constructivism*	• *Natural technique used in reference interview*
• *Instructor-facilitated*		
• *Build associations with prior learning*	• *How to adapt to different learning situations*	• *K-W-L chart*
		• *Students are not "blank*

In the evaluation, participants were also asked to what extent they might consider incorporating elements of the constructivist approach in their future instruction. Many indicated that they would make extensive use of constructivist approaches or that they already were using some of these approaches without having been aware that they were constructivist. Some of the participants indicated they would make selective use of constructivist approaches and none indicated that they would not use them at all. A few concerns about using constructivist approaches were also expressed. One participant was uncertain as to how bridges to new learning might be built for students of varying levels of experience, particularly those without much prior knowledge of the subject. Another participant indicated that faculty and supervisors often have rigid criteria established for a session that might make constructivist techniques difficult to incorporate.

As instructors who have used constructivist approaches, but who are fairly new to the concepts of the constructivist paradigm, we found it interesting to see that the participants had similar reactions about how they have been using some of these approaches without being aware that they were constructivist. At the same time, we certainly identified with some of the concerns about using constructivist approaches in

the classroom. We too are still working out how these approaches best fit into our information competency curriculum and look forward to future opportunities to interact with colleagues concerning this approach to teaching. Most of all, though, we feel that the student-centered, bridge-building experience of using constructivism in the classroom is something to strive toward and makes the classroom a more accepting, comfortable and encouraging environment for student learning. For us, the question is not whether to teach using constructivist approaches, but how to internalize the constructivist paradigm itself.

NOTES

1. Jacqueline Grennon Brooks and Martin G. Brooks, *In Search of Understanding: The Case for Constructivist Classrooms*. (Alexandria, VA: Association for Supervision and Curriculum Development, 1999), 17.

2. George W. Gagnon and Michelle Collay, *Designing for Learning: Six Elements in Constructivist Classrooms*. (Thousand Oaks, CA: Corwin Press, 2001), 7-10.

Appendix 1

Create a Learning Session Using a Constructivist Learning Design Template

Background: Students are undergraduates in an upper-division educational psychology course for their major. One of their assignments is to write a reflection paper that identifies their own cultural background and personal learning style and then relates these to the types of teaching approaches that best facilitate their learning. In this paper, students must identify two peer-reviewed journal articles that support their views on cultural identity and how it relates to learning.

Your job is to create a task for a one-hour class session that will enable students to find these two peer-reviewed articles.

CLD Template

Level: Upper-Division undergraduate students in their major **Subject**: Educational Psychology – cultural background, learning styles, teaching approaches **Title**:
Situation (What is the purpose of the exercise, which task to fulfill purpose, task description)
Groupings (What process to use for grouping students: random, intentional, teacher-selected, sets of materials)
Bridge (How to determine prior knowledge and hild a bridge between that knowledge and what they might learn from task)
Questions (To help students with task process, e.g. guiding, clarifying, anticipated, integrative questions)
Exhibit (How students demonstrate their thinking and what they've learned: written, verbal, etc.)
Reflections (How students think about what they've learned, as well as their thoughts and feelings about the process)

Adapted from, Gagnon. G.W. *Designing for Learning: Six Elements in Constructivist Classrooms.*
Thousand Oaks, CA: Corwin Press, 2001.

—PAM BAKER AND KATHLENE HANSON—

Appendix 2

A Brief Guide to Selected Resources on Constructivism

Black, J.B. and R.O. McClintock.. "An Interpretation Construction Approach to Constructivist Design." In *Constructivist Learning Environments*, ed. B. Wilson. Englewood Cliffs, NJ: Educational Technology Publications, 1995. Internet on-line. Available from <http://www.ilt.columbia.edu/publications/papers/icon.html>. [28 April 2003].

This article focuses on the construction of Study Support Environments (SSEs) and on Interpretation Construction (ICON) Design Model as constructivist learning design principles.

Brooks, Jacqueline Grennon and Martin G. Brooks. *In Search of Understanding: The Case for Constructivist Classrooms*. Alexandria, VA: Association for Supervision and Curriculum Development, 1999.

This book is a reprint of one originally published in 1995 and is considered a core work in building the case for constructivist pedagogy.

Gagnon, George W. and Michelle Collay. *Designing for Learning: Six Elements in Constructivist Classrooms*. Thousand Oaks, CA: Corwin Press, 2001.

This book details elements of constructivist learning design that assist teachers in organizing their curricula around student-centered learning.

North Carolina State University. *Teacher Resource Room K-W-L Chart*. Internet on-line. Available from < http://www.ncsu.edu/midlink/KWL.chart.html>. [25 April 2003].

This page from *Midlink Magazine* contains a sample K-W-L Chart in a printer-friendly format.

Ryder, Martin. *Constructivism*. Internet on-line. Available from <http://carbon.cudenver.edu/~mryder/itc_data/constructivism.html>. [2 May 2003].

This page, compiled by martin Ryder from the University of Colorado Denver School of Education, provides a number of useful links to resources and readings on constructivism.

Thirteen Ed Online and Disney Learning Partnership. *Constructivism as a Paradigm for Teaching and Learning*. Internet on-line. Available from <http://www.thirteen.org/edonline/concept2class/month2/index.html>. [15 April 2003].

This link leads to a free workshop on constructivism provided by "Concept to Classroom," a collaboration between Thirteen Ed Online and the Disney Learning Partnership.

Southwest Educational Development Laboratory. *Building an Understanding of Constructivism*, 1995. Internet on-line. Available from <http://www.sedl.org/scimath/compass/v01n03/2.html>. [20 April 2003].

From the online publication "Classroom Compass," this article provides a brief definition and overview of constructivism.

ENHANCED STAFF DEVELOPMENT PROGRAMS: STRENGTHENING THE PERSONAL THROUGH COLLEGIAL REFLECTION

Trisha Mileham and Ruth Connell

Valparaiso University (VU) is a private, four year liberal arts university located in northwest Indiana, about 45 miles east of Chicago. Our campus is home to about 3600 FTE students. Moellering Library is the current main library, and in fall 2004, we are scheduled to move into our new facility, the Christopher Center for Library and Information Resources. Eight librarians have varied primary duties with seven of us participating in instruction and reference services. We average 5-10 students working in reference services and 1-3 students working in instruction.

While our jobs often overlap, this particular collaboration grew from work on a common publishing project that opened our eyes to our similar needs and opportunities: we both had issues with training and supporting our respective staff members. The collegiality we've modeled through working with and supporting one another in these endeavors has seemingly pervaded our staff as well, assuring us that in the areas of staff development, we are doing the right things at the right times.

Mileham and *Connell* are Instruction and Reference Services Librarians at Valparaiso University, Valparaiso, IN.

Instruction Services Staff Development Program

Our Environment

Moellering Library has formally supported a library instruction program since the mid 1980s. Currently, there are eight members of the instruction team, seven librarians and our interlibrary loan manager. Of those eight, five of us serve as primary instructors. In the classroom, we are team-based, with four possible roles: lead instructor, co-instructor, facilitator, and assistant/observer. This model allows participation at a level comfortable for those not in the classroom as often as others. We teach course-integrated, assignment-specific sessions, creating hands-on assignments for class use when appropriate. Our program structure is a subject-liaison based model, arising from our collection development subject areas.

Our library supports two hands-on classrooms, providing 21 workstations for attendee use. We reach between 1500-1800 attendees per academic year through up to 168 sessions. In the new library, three classrooms offer seating for 90, 39, and 24 attendees at individual workstations. Campus enrollment is projected to increase in the upcoming years as well.

While our program has been active for years, very few of us have had any formal education in instruction and there is currently little chance to attend education instruction opportunities outside our immediate area. With a growing program, a small staff, and an increasing enrollment, staff support and burnout prevention have become primary concerns. As we began our work last summer, it seemed like the perfect time to also investigate the possibility of creating an instruction staff development program.

Development of the Program

Preparation for this program involved the usual suspects: a literature review, gathering of conference ideas, and interaction with colleagues, on-and off-campus. These steps may seem obvious but their worth should not be taken lightly. While no one instruction program situation directly matches another, the variety of resources available allows for appropriate comparison and consideration.

As this experience progressed and four categories began to take shape, it was decided that they were to act as the cornerstones for the program's development. While they are listed here in an order, the process is much more circular, with revisions and revelations calling attention to previous steps.

FIRST CORNERSTONE: Identify and Meet Immediate Needs

We needed some immediate help in certain areas but we didn't want that to drive the program. Three needs were found that became primary focuses for this cornerstone. We needed materials of all types on instruction: the how-to, the why, the practical, the theoretical, the reflective. We needed personal interaction about instruction issues, with one another and with other teachers on campus. Finally, we needed ongoing, programmatic support, from our university librarian, our campus Teaching Resource Center, and appropriate campus faculty committees.

SECOND CORNERSTONE: Determine Goals and Objectives

Why here? Why not first? Based on prior experience, we arrived at the conclusion that it's only after immediate needs are met that the view can become clear enough to consider the long-term situation. For example, one of the goals is to increase staff confidence in their teaching. To do this, resources and materials were identified to share (ILI-L items, LOEX News, LOEX Currents, LIRT News, IS Newsletter, authors of note, etc.). The availability of

these items needed to be made known while keeping cognizant of the time needed to thoughtfully consider them (i.e., e-mail small bits of information rather than the entire day's digest posting of ILI-L). The third step was to identify, and now create, interaction opportunities for the staff with other campus teachers, such as those who have won our VU "Caterpillar Award for Excellence in Teaching." Had the staff's immediate needs not been taken care of first, it is doubtful that the goals would be as cohesive and attainable as they are now.

THIRD CORNERSTONE: Create a Program Plan

We learned the need to keep a reasonable implementation schedule for the program. Even though we didn't want things to drag on and on, we also needed to remember how slowly things can change on an academic campus. From the start last fall, the staff knew the layout of the program plan; this helped them to feel more involved and perhaps increased their buy-in to the program from the start. Resource management is another key area. Some crucial factors to consider here are: what are the selection criteria, how to gather materials, where to collect the materials, and how to provide access to them.

FOURTH CORNERSTONE: Keep Staff Involved

Staff involvement is essential; not only is this program for them but it can be BY them as well. During the academic year, we have monthly User Services meetings, addressing current issues in that service area but also liaison-based "show and tell" of new, intriguing, or hard-to-use resources. The instruction staff development program purposely appeared at two of these meetings each semester, each focusing on a theme supported by an article everyone read. Last year's themes were: who are we teaching, the paradigm shift from teaching to learning, instructor burnout issues, and "we the teachers." This summer, we're keeping the monthly meetings and adding four topic-focused two-hour sessions (from suggestions by the staff): teaching portfolios, learning styles, classroom activities, and a get-outside-your-comfort-zone.

Results

Overall, the instruction staff is pleased with the development program and they are anticipating the

—TRISHA MILEHAM AND RUTH CONNELL—

topic-specific summer sessions. Our disciplinary faculty have remarked positively on the changes in the classroom activities; we feel more freedom to reflect and consider class content rather than just react to the assignments. The article-reading activity was useful but follow-up was hampered when our discussion time-lines changed. This fall, a few reflective questions will be provided along with each article and will keep the discussion time-lines in place. We will bring in the reference quizzes as refresher tools (more about these quizzes in the second half of this article).

Future Considerations

We need to further personalize the program to encourage the instruction staff to identify their individual needs and how these needs can be met. The library's Intranet site, StaffWeb, will be the online repository for any resources, citations, tips, and guides that we discover or create as well as the summer's topic-focused sessions' content. Our university librarian is working with us in consideration of a full-blown retreat or workshop for our staff and possibly other area instruction librarians. On a smaller scale, we plan to model this program for all of our public services support staff, especially those who are on the spot when we are in the classroom.

Reference Services Student Assistant Development Program

Background

Valparaiso University's Moellering Library reference student-training program slowly began to take shape in the fall of 2000. Developing a strong training program was of paramount importance since the reference department's students actually answer reference questions when on duty. That first semester, there were 8 students working in reference. Except for late evenings and Saturday shifts, the students worked under the supervision of a librarian, who could step in if a question was beyond their abilities. However, sixteen hours a week, student assistants answered actual reference questions on their own—not just ready-reference questions. They needed a strong knowledge of reference sources and research techniques. The students had to be confident in this knowledge so that they could teach patrons how to research, use databases, and find materials. Therefore, the training program had to be comprehensive, and provide students the knowledge

they needed to perform their jobs well.

Our Needs

Unfortunately, that first year, there was almost no training program for reference student assistants. At that time, the greatest needs for the reference department were documenting and developing reference procedures and policies and secondly, creating a training program to teach this information to student employees. The first year, we talked with returning students about how things had operated in reference before fall 2000. Using this information, we documented procedures that had been practiced but not written down. In addition, policies were written, as well as directions for frequently performed procedures (processing new reference books, using the scanner, etc.)

The second year, the training program consisted of sharing these policies, procedures and tasks with students; followed by a several hour research training session. Upon completing this multi-day training, students were given a post-training quiz to test their retention of information. When changes to policies and databases occurred, as well as when timely issues arose, student assistants were e-mailed to keep them up to date.

In early January 2002, an e-mail went out to the students to remind them that tax season was fast approaching and let them know where to locate tax forms. A couple weeks later, an assistant mentioned that a patron wanted tax forms, and asked whether we had them. After helping the patron, the student was asked if she had read the e-mail on tax forms. Appearing confused, she said she did not remember what it had said. It was clear that an ongoing training program with checks and balances was needed.

Development of Reference Intranet

As part of the training program, it was important to place the documented procedures and policies online. Many students took the paper copies they received during their initial training home, and did not have access to this information when they needed it. Thus, a reference Intranet site was created. Directions for processing new books, instructions on how to process pamphlet file materials, tasks for students to perform when they come on duty, printing and guest login policies, student assistant schedule and subbing information, and shelf-reading instructions were all included on the Intranet site.

Development of Quizzes

Once the Intranet site was developed, the next step was to develop the training quizzes. The quizzes would test the students' knowledge of material they should know, as well as expose them to new information. In other words, they would encounter questions and sources they had no background or experience with, and the quizzes would cause them to explore new information; it would serve as their teaching tool. In developing the quizzes, many sources were culled for question ideas. A review of the literature proved very useful. For example, an article by Chris Neuhaus entitled "Flexibility and Feedback: a New Approach to Ongoing Training for Reference Student Assistants" provided many examples of quiz questions and themes. The article relates how in the late 1990s, the University of Northern Iowa began a training program that included biweekly worksheets for reference student assistants. Their program was larger than ours was, but many ideas from the article could be adapted and used immediately in our program. For example, students who missed questions received one-on-one assistance from more advanced students or reference librarians.[1] This feedback provided the personal attention to help make their program a success; therefore, this aspect was incorporated into our reference-training program.

Another great source of question ideas was course material from Professor Terry Weech's reference class at the University of Illinois. He gave challenging reference assignments that we wanted to emulate with the reference quizzes. His questions were not used verbatim, but rather for the concepts behind the questions. For example, Professor Weech had a question where he gave the last line of a poem, with one word altered, and asked students to find the author and the title of the poem. The first time the students worked on a last line question, we did not alter a word in the last line, and many of them just did a Web search for the answer. The second time they tackled such a question, we altered a word which prevented doing a Web search for the answer, and the students were tested on their knowledge of the reference source in question, Kline's Last Lines.

Other ideas for questions came from timely issues (e.g. the location of tax forms) and questions asked at the reference desk. If a patron asked an interesting reference question that would challenge the reference students, it was noted and the question was used later.

Originally, the intention was to give quizzes every other week. However, due to time constraints, only nine quizzes were given during the 2002-2003 academic year—about once a month. It took about half a day to develop a quiz, and then after each student completed a quiz we would go over the answers with him or her individually. This time of mentoring after the quizzes created quite a few teachable moments. We talked about things they had done well; other sources they could have used to better answer questions; and when they were completely wrong, covered sources or methods they should have used.

Surprisingly, most of the student assistants really enjoyed the challenge of the quizzes. In fact, at the end of the first semester of the quiz program, a student asked if the they could make up their own questions and have a "student challenge" quiz. Although taking the quiz was not optional, submitting questions for the quiz was, and six out of seven students chose to participate. Most students really enjoyed this exercise, and worked hard to come up with questions that would challenge their fellow assistants.

Training Program: Student Opinion

At the end of the fall 2002 semester, the students were surveyed to find out how they felt about the training program. Six out of seven students agreed or strongly agreed that the quizzes had improved their researching skills. All students felt their skills had improved as a result of their initial training. In addition, six out of seven students felt their skills had improved from the time of their initial training to the time they took the survey. Many students had comments: good, bad and bizarre. One student said, "I can't even begin to fully explain how much more use I have received from the library after my training. I find researching to be much easier and I am always eager to help friends out as well. My training has made being a history major less daunting as far as the amount of research required." At the other end of the spectrum, one student responded, "not really", to a question about whether his training has impacted his library use as a student. Another question on the survey asked students to reflect on areas that were not adequately covered during training. One student's bizarre and humorous response was, "tax law, I really don't recall covering this subject at all."

Training Program: Student Performance

After the quiz program began, there was a noticeable difference in students' performance on the reference desk. For example, for the past few years a professor from the college of business has given his students an assignment where they were required to research a brand name and its company. After the reference student assistants took the business quiz, they felt much more confident helping these business students. They referred fewer questions, and said they felt more comfortable with business sources (Standard and Poor, Hoovers, Directory of Corporate Affiliations, etc.)

Training Program: Student Retention

In order to get more quantifiable results; students were given a cumulative end-of-the-year quiz. The quiz was designed using questions that most students had missed the first time around. At the time the cumulative quiz was given, only five students were working in reference. One had been hired mid-year, and had only taken three of the nine quizzes given during the 2002-2003 academic year. The new student had worked in the library for several years, but was new to reference, although she proved to be a quick learner. Despite this, she scored several points lower (5 correct out of 11 questions) than any of the students that had taken all nine quizzes. Most of the questions she missed were harvested from quizzes she had not taken. Everyone else did fairly well, most getting 8 or 9 correct questions out of 11. The cumulative quiz demonstrated that students did learn from the quizzes, and managed to retain most of the information they learned.

Future Considerations

For the future, several goals have been set for the reference-training program. The first will be to implement some student suggestions. One student suggested that new hires shadow more experienced students during their first few shifts. This suggestion will be implemented this fall. Secondly, more feedback from the other librarians would be helpful, especially from those who work in the reference department. This could provide ideas for topics to cover and questions to include. Finally, several user-services departments (circulation, reference and interlibrary loan) would like to cross-train our students. This would enable us to maximize student power, by shifting students around to where they could be most useful.

Our Collaboration

The collegiality formed by recognizing common goals of similar projects has been but one of the rewards of our project. Keeping our staffs involved added to their respective buy-ins of the programs, heightening each person's engagement without threatening anyone working at a different level. The student assistants enjoy the sense of ownership and legacy they are instilling in their work. We feel our reference desk staffing quality is higher than ever and more evenly distributed. This success feeds itself, for as the classroom instruction improves, it supports improved reference work and student contact, which leads to more comfort in the classroom, and so on. This model also instills continuous reflection, renewal, and professional support, even with limited staff and no funding, in areas of library work that are often known for burnout and high stress.

For more information, a complete bibliography, and audience comments, please visit our Web site at http://www.valpo.edu/library/pd/loex03.

NOTES

1. Chris Neuhaus, "Flexibility and Feedback: A New Approach to Ongoing Training for Reference Student Assistants," *Reference Services Review* 29, no. 1 (2001): 53-64.

Fanning the Flames: Strategies for Combating Burnout and Reinvigorating Instruction

Lisa Barnett, Melissa Browne, and Katherine Harris

Introduction

The repetitive nature of many tasks associated with bibliographic instruction produces tedium that can lead to burnout. The result is often ineffectual instruction sessions that are boring for the students and unfulfilling for the librarians. This paper outlines strategies including self-reflection, collaboration and evaluation that provide librarians with tools to combat burnout and reinvigorate instruction sessions.

Burnout Defined

The term burnout began appearing in the professional literature in the 1970s, and since that time numerous definitions have been proposed. Christina Maslach, a social psychologist, characterized burnout as a three dimensional syndrome encompassing symptoms of emotional exhaustion, depersonalization, and reduced feelings of personal accomplishment. She explained burnout as "...a response to the chronic emotional strain of dealing extensively with other human beings, particularly when they are troubled or having problems."Maslach's definition grew out of her research into people-oriented, helping professions such as health care, social services and education; her definition also applies to the public service aspects of librarianship, especially instruction and reference.

Barnett, *Browne* and *Harris* are Information Services Librarians at Ball State University, Muncie, IN.

Symptoms of Burnout

The symptoms of burnout are complex and multifaceted, and have physical, mental, emotional and social consequences.[1] Often people are unaware or even unwilling to acknowledge these symptoms, leading to compounded and magnified affects. In order to combat burnout librarians must be able to identify warning signs in themselves.

Mild physical symptoms include backaches, headaches, nausea, weight gain or loss and insomnia or hypersomnia. If left unchecked these symptoms cause serious health problems such as elevated blood pressure, coronary heart disease, poor immune responses, increased occurrences of illness and physical exhaustion. Physical signs of burnout are often overlooked because they may originate from outside activities as well as from work-related issues.

Mental symptoms may include depression, mental exhaustion, a growing concern for self over others and a dread of teaching. A change in professional goals resulting in lowered job expectations and standards is another manifestation of burnout. In addition, burned-out employees may no longer find their jobs mentally stimulating or challenging and experience a psychological withdrawal from work. As with physical symptoms, mental symptoms are not confined to the work environment, but may create a negative attitude towards life in general.

Emotional symptoms of burnout include emotional exhaustion or detachment, which translate into a reduced ability to empathize with patrons. A tendency to blame students for their inability to understand concepts or tools in the classroom is another indicator. The emotional cost of burnout also includes feelings of reduced personal accomplishment and loss of professional fulfillment. Thus, emotionally taxed librarians often turn to non-work pursuits for meaning and stimulation.

Social symptoms include feelings of isolation from colleagues or the profession. This is especially damaging for teaching librarians who like collaborative environments in and out of the classroom. Other signs include rudeness, irritability or impatience with patrons and a lack of time for colleagues or activities. Librarians experiencing burnout often exhibit an unwillingness to help students. Depersonalization, the grouping of students together rather than viewing them as individuals, is also a symptom of social burnout.

Causes of Burnout

Recognizing the symptoms is one key to combating burnout; another key is recognizing the causes. Librarians in the Information Services unit at the Ball State University Libraries experiencing symptoms of burnout sought to identify causes in order to combat negative feelings and experiences within the unit. They grouped the causes into four categories: personal, professional, organizational and societal.[2]

Individual beliefs and work habits shape personal causes of burnout. Unrealistic job expectations and poor interpersonal relations are two major factors and if left unchecked manifest in high turnover rates. The one hundred percent turnover in the last two years in the Information Services unit has exacerbated job stress and feelings of burnout.

Professional causes are associated with job duties and responsibilities. Chronic work overload is a main factor. In addition to teaching, Information Services librarians staff the reference desk, participate in collection development, serve on library and university committees and maintain various web pages. Position cuts in the unit have led to a decreased number of staff on hand to cope with an increased number of classes. Compounding this situation is the jump in freshmen enrollment at Ball State University, which translates into more freshmen composition classes requesting library instruction.

The lack of feedback received from students and faculty is another factor contributing to professional causes of burnout. At Ball State most library instruction classes are one-shots, and post-session contact with students and faculty is limited. Thus, librarians are often unsure of their instructional effectiveness, which contributes to feelings of reduced personal accomplishment and low job satisfaction.

Organizational sources stem from workplace characteristics such as management practices and physical surroundings. At Ball State, librarians are adjusting to a new administration with different communication styles and priorities. Within the Information Services unit, the lack of an instruction coordinator has caused a vacuum in the decision-making structure. This has led to unit members taking on additional responsibilities, contributing to increased levels of job stress and burnout.

The physical environment is another source of organizational strain. Excessive noise levels, a lack of privacy, inadequate lighting and temperature fluctuations can cause discomfort and interfere with job performance. Ergonomically incorrect office furniture may also intensify the physical symptoms of burnout.

Societal sources of burnout include factors in academia and extend to society in general. While these sources impact librarians less directly, they produce negative feelings that influence job performance. Teaching faculty often have stereotypical perceptions of librarians. This contributes to feelings of role ambiguity among librarians and raises questions about job functions and responsibilities. Negative societal attitudes and failure to recognize the value of libraries result in decreased professional satisfaction and low self-esteem.

Combating Burnout at Ball State

The complex nature of burnout may be overwhelming. By taking proactive measures to combat the syndrome, librarians can reinvigorate their teaching and regain a sense of control over the situation. Information Services librarians at Ball State use personal, collaborative and institutional approaches to combat burnout.

Personal strategies include humor, self-reflection, developing new teaching techniques, reading articles or books and pursuing outside interests. Humor, especially the willingness to laugh at the irony of a situation, is important. Even gallows humor serves to release tension.

Self-reflection is an important tool to combat burnout. Information Services librarians use instruction data sheets[3] to keep records of their classroom experiences. The data sheets include basic information about a class as well as reflections from librarians regarding their teaching strategies. Another reflective technique involves keeping a teaching log or journal to record new ideas and approaches as well as methods that need improvement. However, it is important to remember not to be too critical when using self-reflective techniques.

Employing new teaching techniques is an additional strategy to combat burnout. Using different

—LISA BARNETT, MELISSA BROWNE, AND KATHERINE HARRIS—

activities to teach concepts, teaching through games and altering the order of material presented in instruction sessions are all helpful. These make classes more enjoyable for the librarian, which positively influences student learning.

Reading articles and books, either about burnout, teaching or general interests may help alleviate stress. Also, pursuing outside interests relieves tension. Examples include exercise like yoga or walking, community involvement and hobbies such as gardening or pottery. However, librarians must ensure that these outside pursuits do not replace professional fulfillment.

The success of collaborative strategies hinges on a solid support network. Discussing problems or issues with colleagues is important to relieve stress and prevent feelings of isolation associated with burnout. Collaborative strategies in the classroom include team teaching, trading instruction responsibilities, conducting workshops and implementing peer observation, while group projects extend these strategies beyond the classroom

Team teaching is useful both in terms of reducing preparation time and refining teaching methods. A variation on team teaching involves trading instruction responsibilities, which is an excellent way to gain exposure to new resources and subject areas. Conducting drop-in workshops are rewarding because librarians control content and topic, and the audience is self-selected. Attendance at workshops may be increased by partnering with other service areas on campus such as writing or career centers. While initially intimidating, peer observation is another beneficial strategy to foster reflection and professional growth.

Group projects are the professional equivalent of cooperative learning since employees work together to accomplish a common objective. Group goals cultivate perseverance and motivation and enhance employee morale. Examples include developing tutorials, creating class materials, publishing articles and presenting at conferences.

While institutional strategies are often difficult to influence or control, they directly impact job performance and satisfaction. Conducting formal assessments of all or portions of the instruction program is one method to gauge teaching effectiveness and measure student learning. Organizational support for attending conferences is important in order to explore new teaching techniques and cultivate a professional support network. Enhancing the instruction environment by creating bulletin boards or altering the arrangement of student stations may alleviate feelings of stagnation and boredom among both teaching librarians and students. Participation in

decision-making whenever possible empowers librarians and provides a degree of control over policies that may impact job responsibilities and duties.

Institutional strategies are most effective when they involve library managers or instruction program coordinators. Managers and coordinators create an atmosphere that minimizes job stress among teaching librarians by setting realistic goals and outlining job expectations. By establishing clear lines of authority and fostering open lines of communication, managers build trust and avoid situations that cause role ambiguity and job dissatisfaction that lead to burnout.[4] Effective management practice necessitates being sensitive to employee morale and monitoring working conditions.

Conclusion

Personal, collaborative and institutional techniques help Information Services librarians combat burnout and reinvigorate teaching. Viktor Frankl, Holocaust survivor and psychotherapist, stated, "What is to give light must endure burning."[5] Librarianship is a stressful occupation, especially for teaching librarians who struggle with burnout due to characteristics inherent in their work. While burnout is a constant issue, through combative techniques librarians may rediscover meaning and fulfillment.

ENDNOTES

1. Wilmar B. Schaufeli, Christina Maslach, and Tadeusz Marek, eds. *Professional Burnout: Recent Developments in Theory and Research* (Washington, DC: Taylor and Francis, 1993), 20-21.

2. Karen A. Becker, "The Characteristics of Bibliographic Instruction in Relation to the Causes and Symptoms of Burnout," *RQ* 32, no. 3 (Spring 1993): 351.

3. Janette S. Caputo, *Stress and Burnout in Library Service* (Phoenix: Oryx Press, 1991), 28 ff. Barbara L. Brock and Marilyn L. Grady, *Rekindling the Flame: Principles Combating Teacher Burnout* (Thousand Oaks, CA: Corwin Press, 2000), 4-8.

4. Brock and Grady, 124.

5. See Instruction Session Data sheet, Appendix 1.

6. Caputo, 133 ff.

7. M. Scott Peck, *Abounding Grace: An Anthology of Wisdom* (Kansas City, Mo: Andrews McMeel, 2000), 69.

Suggested Readings

Becker, Karen A. " The Characteristics of Bibliographic Instruction in Relation to the Causes and Symptoms of Burnout." *RQ* 32, no. 3 (Spring 1993): 436-457.

Brock, Barbara L., and Marilyn L. Grady. *Rekindling the Flame: Principles Combating Teacher Burnout.* Thousand Oaks, CA: Corwin Press, 2000.

Caputo, Janette S. *Stress and Burnout in Library Service.* Phoenix: Oryx Press, 1991.

Russo, Michelle Cash. "Recovering from Bibliographic Instruction Blahs." *RQ* 32, no. 2 (Winter 1992): 178-183.

Schaufeli, Wilmar B., Christina Maslach, and Tadeusz Marek, eds. *Professional Burnout: Recent Developments in Theory and Research.* Washington DC: Taylor and Francis, 1993.

Seale Osborne, Nancy and Andrea Wyman. "The Forest and the Trees: A Modest Proposal on Bibliographic Burnout." *Research Strategies* 9, no. 2 (Spring 1991): 101-103.

Sheesley, Deborah F. "Burnout and the Academic Teaching Librarian: An Examination of the Problem and Suggested Solutions." *The Journal of Academic Librarianship* 27, no. 6 (November 2001): 447-451 .

Sheridan, Jean. "The Reflective Librarian: Some Observations on Bibliographic Instruction in the Academic Library." *The Journal of Academic Librarianship* 16, no. 1 (March 1990): 22-26.

Westbrook, Lynn. "Getting in Gear: A Short-Term Program to Revitalize Your BI Staff." *Research Strategies* 6, no. 4 (Fall 1988): 177-184.

—LISA BARNETT, MELISSA BROWNE, AND KATHERINE HARRIS—

INSTRUCTION SESSION DATASHEET

Library Instructor		Class Instructor	
Course		Department	
Date of Session(s)		Room number	
Estimated Attendance		Actual Attendance	

Course Topic (if applicable)	

Type of Presentation: ☐ Lecture ☐ Orientation ☐ Workshop ☐ Interactive

Materials Used

Handouts	
Overheads/Elmo	
Print Sources	
Electronic Databases Demonstrated	

Instructors: *Please furnish Instructional Services with the following information about any instruction you complete. Also, attach originals of any printouts or specialized handouts used as well as outlines of searches used or copies of the class assignment.*

About the CLASS:

Did the class come to the library instruction session with a specific assignment or task?	
Give a brief description of the assignment:	
Other comments:	

About the INSTRUCTOR:

Was the instructor present for the library instruction session?	
If NO, who attended in the instructor's place?	

The instructor participated in the instruction session by: (check all that apply)

☐ making comments relevant to the instruction session.

☐ answering student questions.

☐ assisting student with topic-related searching.

☐ Other:

Additional comments, which could be helpful for future classes:

```

```

Form created 11/01 Instr. Svcs.
Revised 1/02

—LISA BARNETT, MELISSA BROWNE AND KATHERINE HARRIS—

TEACHING AS A LIVE ENCOUNTER: SHARING OUR AUTHENTIC SELF INVITES STUDENT LEARNING

Elizabeth O. Hutchins

Effective teaching involves live encounters between students and teachers. When teachers take the risk of being fully, authentically engaged, students risk exploring questions that have meaning for themselves. Such a trusting relationship is at the core of teaching and learning.

Libraries are ideal places for these live encounters, yet a paradox is embedded in the student-teacher relationship in libraries. We want students to come to us with questions; however, the formality of libraries and academia may be precisely what inhibits them from doing so. It takes courage to voice questions that by their very essence admit one's vulnerability of not knowing, but students' questions play an integral role in our work in classes, at the reference desk, and with tutorials. When we continue to hear that students fear asking questions in the library, we are called to work even harder to create open and hospitable places of intentional listening where it is safe to share fears, thoughts, and stories.

Such sharing is at the heart of learning. Being fully present and engaged in deep intentional listening is at the heart of passionate, authentic teaching. This calls us to be in touch with our own stories, grounded in our inner landscape. Storytelling offers us "a way of being present in the world" and making meaning of our lives.[2] Storytelling offers us a key to being truly authentic in teaching's live encounters.

Hutchins is Reference/Instruction Librarian at St. Olaf College, Northfield, MN.

Taking the Risk: The Story of a Passionate Paddler

Parker Palmer, author of *The Courage to Teach*, is noted for saying, "We teach who we are."[3] I am a passionate paddler who each summer leaves the library for wilderness waters. To be honest, I doubt whether the students and my colleagues would want me back in the fall, if I didn't get myself to these waters. I haven't, however, always renewed in this fashion. For a long time, I would regularly take a workshop or course that would enhance my professional practice. In 1988, I did the same, but it was a different kind of course in a very different setting.

At that time, I was running a high school library in Cambridge, Massachusetts and was professionally very successful. But personally, for whatever reason, I found myself drying up without energy or dreams. Some might call this burn out. As a person who believes in dreams, it was disheartening—to say the least. So, I applied for and received a grant to take a wilderness skills course with the National Outdoor Leadership School. Without really understanding what compelled me to do so, I was destined to be kayaking for two weeks above the Arctic Circle on the Sheenjek River in Alaska's Brooks Range. Had I ever kayaked before? No. Had I ever actually done any wilderness camping? No. Was I particularly athletic? No. Did I know why I wanted to take this trip on my own? No. Did I have a clear sense, as my mother consistently asked me, what a wilderness skills course above the Arctic Circle had to do with leadership skills in a highly academic secondary school? No. Thank goodness, then, that the principal of my school did have the wisdom to know that whatever difference this trip would make in my professional career, it could well be significant.

So, one late July day in 1988, I enthusiastically and somewhat blithely left my family and wended my way north. And wasn't I surprised on the flight from Seattle to Fairbanks to find myself second-guessing this entire idea. My anxiety level rose as one fit, tan, Alaskan after another walked past my seat down the aisle. Add to this, a heavy duffel, too much gear, and an unknown city, and my devil-may-care attitude of the previous 40+ years seemed to wane rapidly. I had 24 hrs before trip participants were to gather and spent most of it reflecting on potential lower back pain, my lack of paddling skills, and the absence of any emergency evacuation which would be needed when I inevitably would let my trip colleagues down. Consequently, I—whom many friends would have deemed an extrovert—arrived at our meeting place the following day virtually catatonic with apprehension. Nor did it help to have the first person I saw be another extremely fit, deeply tanned, confident man whom only later I discovered was one of the guides!

Why share this story, a variation of which many of you could also tell? Because it didn't stop with me being in speechless anxiety over my lack of skills and a large looming unknown. In fact, the course was a life-changing event for me precisely because I found myself in a state of extreme vulnerability supported by a group of caring, skilled people who offered me a safe place to learn competencies with which I travel today. As a participant I was privileged to be the recipient of extraordinary mentoring, authentic listening, and compassion. So skilled were our guides that first night and throughout the trip that all participants embraced our gifts, excelled beyond our own expectations, and entered new places of leadership. What does this story have to do with libraries and teaching? For me....everything. As a result, I opened the library's first staff meeting the following fall saying, "Never underestimate the terror which may lie behind a student's brave smile as she or he approaches the reference desk saying, 'I know this may be a stupid question but could you help me?'" Also, never underestimate the value of providing a safe place in which students can risk asking a question and acquiring competency.

Libraries as Safe Spaces of Hospitality

In her *Chronicle of Higher Education* article, "Fear of Reference," Barbara Fister reminds us that students continue to be fearful when approaching the reference desk and at times "speechless with anxiety." [4] Asking a question and admitting that one doesn't know leaves one extraordinarily vulnerable. Frequently our real questions lie deep within our hearts and are silenced because it's too risky to ask. For our students to risk voicing their questions, their views, and their passions, they need to have access to safe spaces that offer hospitality in its truest sense.

The Dutch theologian, Henry Nouwen, one of my favorite authors, probes the meaning of such hospitality. He says, "Hospitality is not to change people, but to offer them space where change can take place. It is not to bring men and women over to our side, but to offer freedom not disturbed by dividing lines....It is not an educated intimidation with good books, good stories and good works, but the liberation of fearful hearts so that words can find roots and bear ample fruit...." [5]

Libraries are actually ideal settings for offering just such hospitality, for while they are traditionally viewed as places to which our students and faculty come to get answers and find resources, I propose that their most important function may be to offer a place where questions matter. Fister notes that the reference desk is "the perfect place to ask dumb questions—dumb only in the sense of being unvoiced." [6] Often in asking, it isn't so much an answer that is sought as it is the opportunity to ask and define the question. In fact, the student may not know, without being offered a safe place and compassionate listening, why the question even matters to them. Librarians, as keen listeners are called to help others hone questions profoundly important to them. We are privileged to hear and mentor students and colleagues so that through having their questions honored they can connect with a passion and find a voice deep within themselves; a voice that leaves them hungry to keep searching.

Voices on Behalf of Deep Listening

I am in good company when I talk about deep listening. Nelle Morton, in her book *The Journey is Home* coined the phrase of "hearing one another to speech." [7] Parker Palmer in *The Courage to Teach* says, "Behind their fearful silence, our students want to find their voices, speak their voices, have their voices heard. A good teacher is one who listens to those voices even before they are spoken." [8]

Students hunger for such "deep listening." However, as Mary Rose O'Reilly (English professor at St. Thomas University) observes, listening in an academic culture is most often critical listening where even as some students speak their thoughts others are rapidly developing counter-arguments or critiquing a supposed hidden agenda. "Seldom," she says, "is there a deep, openhearted, unjudging reception of the other.

—ELIZABETH O. HUTCHINS—

By contrast, if someone truly listens to me, my spirit begins to expand."[9] Such intentional listening calls others into existence.

Richard Light notes throughout his now well-known book, *Making the Most of College,* that students consistently refer to the many ways in which relationships, connection, and trust with faculty have been at the heart of their positive college experience.[10]

University of Chicago professors, Anthony Bryk and Barbara Schneider, in their research on reform in Chicago public schools discovered that "the 'missing ingredient' without which schools stand little chance of improving" is a relationship of trust that, in turn, reduces vulnerability and allows risk-taking.[11] When we offer a relationship of trust to students, we are frequently rewarded by their sharing a deep engagement with projects that touch their hearts. Listening to that voice before it is spoken, "means entering emphatically into the student's world so that he or she perceives you as someone who has the promise of being able to hear another person's truth."[12] Such intentional listening is based on our being authentically present.

Authenticity

So the challenge is how to be "someone who has the promise of being able to hear another person's truth." It has been my experience that it is only in taking the risk of sharing our authentic self that we create a safe space where others can discover theirs. To do this we need to be in touch with both our outer professional self, what we might call our "role," and our inner self that some refer to as "soul." As Parker Palmer has repeatedly discovered in his work with teachers, our authenticity is grounded in rejoining our inner and outer self and is, I believe, what invites student learning.

Being in touch with our inner self is a challenge in academia. We all know that there is a dominant culture, sometimes one of considerable stoicism. Scholars subscribe to disciplinary perspectives that hone how they see themselves and the world, they jump through tenure track hoops, they promote the objective (rather than subjective) voice, they initiate students into disciplinary boot camp first through foundational and then more advanced courses, and they pay deep homage to disciplinary discourses and credentials often at the expense of themselves. Of course, as Gloria Leckie and Anne Fullerton noted in their 1999 ACRL talk, "counter faculty discourses"[13] exist but faculty, in deference to external authorities, may opt to hold their own passions and inner self in abeyance. In addition, there is often an innate or learned modesty that inhibits any acknowledgment of

our gifts independent of the external criteria of scholarly achievement and/or status of title and position. Parker Palmer describes this climate as a "Culture of Fear" in which "it is easy to revert to the dominant pedagogy, even if it has little relation to who we are."[14] If we revert, we are silencing who we truly are; this is the gift we bring to our students, and we are sending them a message.

A Totally Subjective Case Study

So let me offer another case study of personal experience:

Just over 10 years ago, after being a secondary school library director for a number of years, I returned to graduate school to study feminist liberation theology. The time came to write a thesis. After considerable research in women's studies and theology exploring issues of patriarchy, power construction, and alternative models of decision-making, I decided that my thesis would weave these themes together. With eagerness I met with my advisor and presented an outline of the project that would take a full year of further research. I quoted authorities, presented some ideas for case studies and models, and identified my methodology. The room was filled with words, many words, my words. Then when I drew a breath, my advisor quietly asked, "Where is this coming from, Elizabeth?" to which I responded, "John, I had an experience in Alaska which changed my life and encouraged me to explore new territory. This is the territory." He asked me to tell him about this experience, the tale about the time I almost lost my life as a result of a capsize in 42 degree waters and was saved by the community of persons around me. His response was "Elizabeth, that is the story you are to tell. That story needs to begin your thesis." "But, John," I said, "One can not use "I" in a scholarly thesis. You know that it needs to be completely objective and research based!" "Elizabeth, you must. This is where your passion lies. This is where your questioning is grounded and voiced." And so I did.

Why am I sharing this story with you? Because, *we are our stories.* My advisor detected that I was in danger of betraying myself; of being a fraud; of playing the role of objective, scholar while silencing my inner voice. My words lacked authenticity. Students are pros at detecting fraud, when our words and messages float in front of us but are not ones with which we are truly engaged.

Students need to know, as I did, that their stories are as important as scholarly texts.[15] In his research, Richard Light heard repeatedly that any professor who "simultaneously invites [students] to make connections between abstract ideas and their own real lives, becomes an unforgettable professor. The learning that takes place in such a class transcends....purely academic learning, and is really seared into our consciousness."[16] Our subjective self matters. The "I" matters. Students' "I," my "I," and your "I" are at the heart of teaching. It is in this live encounter of "I"s that learning is invited and evoked.

We Teach Who We Are

It is truly quite simple for as Parker Palmer says, "We teach who we are."[17] When we teach well, we possess a "capacity for connectedness."[18] To hear students' questions, to hear them into speech, we need to be in touch with our own questions. What is integral to my selfhood? Who am I when I am real? When we find and embrace the answers to these questions, we connect with an inner self that is fully present and engaged.

This deepest, most original self, is "[The teacher] whom we knew when we were children but lost touch with as we grew into adulthood...."[19] Reclaiming a relationship with our inner self enables us to reclaim a relationship with ourselves as passionate teachers who invite student learning in live encounters.[20]

END NOTES

1. The author recognizes that there is a grammatical disconnect between the plural "our" and the singular "self." However, she wishes to focus on the first-person narrative, so has intentionally left it without proper agreement.

2. Mary Rose O'Reilley, *Radical Presence: Teaching as a Contemplative Practice* (Portsmouth, NH: Boynton/Cook Publishers, 1998), 25. See also, Jerome Bruner, *Acts of Meaning* (Cambridge: Harvard University Press, 1990) in which he explores the ways in which we strive to make meaning through our stories, and Howard Thorsheim and Bruce Roberts, *I Remember When: Activity Ideas to Help People Reminisce* (Forest Knolls, CA: Elder Books, 2000).

3. The author's commitment to passionate teaching and being authentically present with students has been significantly influenced by Parker J. Palmer's work. *In The Courage to Teach: Exploring the Inner Landscape of a Teacher's Life* (San Francisco: Jossey-Bass Publishers, 1998), Palmer explores the premise that "we teach who we are." He also examines the essence of live encounters in chapter 4 of *The Active Life: Wisdom for Work, Creativity, and Caring* (San

Fransicso: Harper & Row, 1990; reprint, San Francisco: HarperCollins paperback ed., 1991).

4. Barbara Fister, "Fear of Reference," *Chronicle of Higher Education* 48, no. 40 (14 June 2002): B20.

5. Henri J.M. Nouwen, *Reaching Out: The Three Movements of Spiritual Life* (Garden City, NY: Doubleday & Co., Inc., 1975), 51.

6. Fister, B20.

7. Nelle Morton, *The Journey is Home* (Boston: Beacon Press, 1985), 55.

8. Palmer, *The Courage to Teach*, 46.

9. O'Reilley, 19.

10. Richard Light, *Making the Most of College* (Cambridge, MA: Harvard University Press, 2001).

11. Anthony S. Bryk and Barbara L. Schneider, Trust in Schools: A Core Resource for Improvement (New York: Russell Sage Foundation, 2002); quoted in Catherine Gewertz, "'Trusting' School Community Linked to Student Gains," *Education Week* 22, no. 7 (16 October, 2002): 8.

12. Palmer, *The Courage to Teach,* 69-70.

13. Light, 113.

14. Palmer, *The Courage to Teach,* 69-70.

15. Palmer, 69. See also, Parker J. Palmer, "Evoking the Spirit," *Educational Leadership* 56, no. 4 (December 1998/January 1999): 6-11.

16. Light, 113.

17. Palmer, *The Courage to Teach*, 1.

18. Marcy Jackson and Rick Jackson, "Courage to Teach: A Retreat Program of Personal and Professional Renewal for Educators," in *Stories of the Courage to Teach: Honoring the Teacher's Heart,* S.M. Intrator (San Francisco: Jossey-Bass, 2002), 283-308.

19. Parker J. Palmer, "The Heart of a Teacher: Identity and Integrity," *Change* 29, no. 6 (November/December 1997): 19.

20. Two breakout sessions followed this talk. The first

—ELIZABETH O. HUTCHINS—

one focused on childhood stories and the second on a group poetry reading of and reflections on Marge Piercy's poem, "The seven of pentacles." Marge Piercy, "The seven of pentacles." *Circles on the Water: Selected Poems of Marge Piercy*. (New York: Alfred A. Knopf, 1982), 128.

WORKS CITED

Bruner, Jerome. *Acts of Meaning*. Cambridge: Harvard University Press, 1990.

Bryk, Anthony S and Barbara L. Schneider. Trust in Schools: A Core Resource for Improvement. New York: Russell Sage Foundation, 2002. Quoted in Catherine Gewertz. "'Trusting' School Community Linked to Student Gains." *Education Week* 22, no. 7 (16 October, 2002): 8.

Fister, Barbara. "Fear of Reference." *Chronicle of Higher Education* 48, no. 40 (14 June 2002): B20.

Jackson, Marcy, and Rick Jackson. "Courage to Teach: A Retreat Program of Personal and Professional Renewal for Educators." In *Stories of the Courage to Teach: Honoring the Teacher's Heart,* S. M. Intrator, 283-308. San Francisco: Jossey-Bass, 2002,

Leckie, Gloria, and Anne Fullerton. "The Roles of Academic Librarians in Fostering a Pedagogy for Information Literacy." In *Racing Toward Tomorrow, Proceedings of the Ninth National Conference of the Association of College and Research Libraries, April 8-11, 1999,* ed. Hugh A. Thompson, Chicago: The Association, 1999. Internet on-line. Available from < http://www.ala.org/Content/NavigationMenu/AC RL/Events_and_Conferences/leckie99.pdf >. [5 May 2003].

Light, Richard. *Making the Most of College.* Cambridge, MA: Harvard University Press, 2001.

Morton, Nelle. *The Journey is Home.* Boston: Beacon Press, 1985.

Nouwen, Henri J.M. *Reaching Out: The Three Movements of Spiritual Life.* Garden City, NY: Doubleday & Co., Inc., 1975.

O'Reilley, Mary Rose. *Radical Presence: Teaching as a Contemplative Practice.* Portsmouth, NH: Boynton/Cook Publishers, 1998.

Palmer, Parker J. *The Active Life: Wisdom for Work, Creativity, and Caring.* San Francisco: Harper & Row, 1990. Reprint, San Francisco: HarperCollins paperback ed., 1991.

_____. *The Courage to Teach.* San Francisco: Jossey-Bass, 1998.

_____. "Evoking the Spirit." *Educational Leadership* 56, no. 4 (December 1998/January 1999): 6-11.

_____. "The Heart of a Teacher: Identity and Integrity." *Change* 29, no.6 (November/December 1997): 15-21.

Piercy, Marge. "The seven of pentacles." *Circles on the Water: Selected Poems of Marge Piercy.* New York: Alfred A. Knopf, 1982.

Thorsheim, Howard, and Bruce Roberts. *I Remember When: Activity Ideas to Help People Reminisce,* Forest Knolls, CA : Elder Books, 2000.

WORDS, MUSIC, AND MOVEMENT: MEDIA'S EFFECT ON LEARNING

Angela Megaw

Introduction

How do you learn about the world? The answer to that question is both simple and complex. The simple answer is through your senses: hearing, seeing, touching, tasting and smelling. Psychologists and educators debate the complexity of this question throughout the literature. In my personal experience, the one commonality I have found is that everyone has their own individual learning style and strategies. How then do we adapt library instruction to meet the wide spectrum of our learners? One solution is using media. The activity outlined here asks participants to reflect and explore the emotional impact (*affect*) of various formats of media as well as the *effect* of media on their learning and teaching.

Media Literacy

What is media? It is the plural of the word medium and according to the *Oxford English Dictionary* is, "any intervening substance through which a force acts on objects at a distance or through which impressions are conveyed to the senses." Media can be a wide variety of things from cave paintings to television. The National Communication Association describes media literacy as:

Being a critical and reflective consumer of communication requires an understanding of how words, images, graphics, and sounds work together in ways that are both subtle and profound. Mass media such as radio, television,

and film and electronic media such the telephone, the Internet, and computer conferencing influence the way meanings are created and shared in contemporary society. So great is this impact that in choosing how to send a message and evaluate its effect, communicators need to be aware of the distinctive characteristics of each medium. (Baran 2002, 51)

We as educators need to be media literate and have an obligation to instill in our students these evaluative skills as well.

The Activity

According to W. James Potter, a media researcher, there are four dimensions in which we interact with media: cognitive, emotional, aesthetic, and moral (Baran 2002, 59-60). This activity attempts to probe each of those dimensions but focuses most on the first two: the mental processes and feelings produced by media. The activity consists of three elements. It is up to you to determine how much time you give each one of these parts. It can be completely done in an hour session or broken up over several days. The first element is a multi-media presentation that reflects a variety of media. Element two is evaluating your participants learning styles. The final element is reflection that leads to application.

The first element, the multi-media presentation, does take some time and thought to create. The amount of time you have decided to dedicate to this activity will determine the length of this part of the exercise. You should allow at least 25 minutes. Begin the presentation with a short summary of the development of media from oral histories, to the creation of the written alphabet, to the development of

---

Megaw is the Reference/Instruction Librarian at Gainesville College, Gainesville, GA.

the printing press to today's use of telephones, movies and the Internet. The presentation should consist of examples of these varied formats centered on a theme. Your theme can be anything your audience can relate to on an emotional basis and that you can find an appropriate selection of media to use. Examples I've used are war, the American flag and motherhood.

The presentation takes place in five stages. Stage one is reading aloud poetry or a short story. This provides an example of an oral verbal format. The second stage is a demonstration of a verbal/visual format. Provide each participant a handout of the material you just read aloud. You many also choose to include a new piece. Allow a few minutes for them to read silently. When it appears that most are finished move to stage three, listening to music clips. The clips should contain both instrumental and vocal pieces. Stage four focuses on visual images using a timed PowerPoint presentation (12-15 seconds per slide). This portion of the presentation should be as diverse a selection of images that you can find. Be sure to include clipart, photos, paintings, and vary the use of color and black and white images. The fifth stage is to show a clip from a motion picture that incorporates visual images with sound and movement.

Keep in mind the ideals of media literacy in your selection process. Create a balance of different points of view. For example, in using the theme of war, one would want to incorporate patriotic music and images along with images of anti-war protestors and slogans. Also remember that the presentation needs to be "legal" in terms of following all copyright guidelines. Finally, keep in mind the digital quality of your images and sounds. I've found the Library of Congress's *American Memory Collection* <http:// memory .loc.gov> to be a useful source of material. Provide your audience with a short summary of the stages before beginning the presentation to prepare them for the experience. Ask them to jot down any thoughts or emotions they feel during each stage. Below are some suggestions you might offer them to fuel their thinking:

- Is there a different impact in using color vs. black and white photos? Instrumental music vs. music that includes vocals? Written vs. spoken word?
- Different combinations of multimedia (eg: What kind of impact would adding a musical score to the PowerPoint slides have?)
- When is it appropriate to use what media?
- Would a scary movie be so scary with the volume muted?
- Do learning styles react/affect/influences use of media? If so, how?

For the learning styles portion of this activity there are a variety of models and theories about learning you could use. For example, it can be approached from a personal learning theory model such as the *Myers-Briggs Type Indicator* or from a social learning point of view such as *Reichmann's and Grasha's Learning Styles Scale* (Giles, Prite & Womack, 2003). For the purpose of this activity I use *A Learning Style Survey for College* developed by Catherine Jester of Diablo Valley College. This quick and simple survey can be found online at <http://www.metamath.com/multiple/multiple_choi ce_questions.cgi>. It is free and provides immediate feedback to the user.

The third part, reflection, can be orchestrated in a variety of ways and you might choose to allow participants to express their reflection according to their learning style. Begin the activity by expressing to your participants the goals of the activity and sharing with them the definitions of media and media literacy. Begin the reflection process by asking them to share various forms of media they use in everyday life listing them on the board. Reflection should continue with the journaling of emotions during the media presentation and in taking the learning styles survey however, the goal of this exercise would be lost if one isn't given the opportunity to synthesize those two experiences into reflective statements. If you are attempting to do this activity in one session, a group discussion format can be used to encourage participants to share with one another. The drawback to this approach is an open class discussion of how something emotional impacts you—makes you venerable. Some of your participants may not feel comfortable sharing or may not have had enough mental processing time to ingest their experiences in a way that can be expressed. Another approach might be asking participants to write a reflection paper. If your participants are teachers you might also ask them to adapt an existing lesson plan to incorporate a new form of media or explain how a lesson plan that uses media reaches various learning styles.

Using Media in Library Instruction

So how can I effectively use this experience and use media in my classroom? A good starting place would be to explore Tim Boyle's book *Design for Multimedia Learning*. It provides good background on instructional design theory with practical application steps without using a lot of educational or "techie" jargon. Here's an example of one of the more creative ideas a colleague shared with me. At her institution they are creating "Library Ads" (using contemporary music, text and images) to play as

—Angela Megaw—

students enter the instruction classroom and wait for class to begin (like the ads you see before a movie starts in the theatre). This idea is a great way to capture students' attention as well as promote services you might not have time to cover in your session. Remember: think outside of the box.

Conclusion

I've conducted this activity with library colleagues and with students. It always amazes me the variety of responses and actions that are generated from it. Media is powerful. We can use it as a tool in our instruction sessions to not only enhance learning but to have fun! I encourage you to take a moment to reflect on your teaching and learning experiences to see how words, music or movement can improve your classroom experience.

REFERENCES

Baran, S. J. *Introduction to Mass Communication: Media Literacy and Culture*, 2d ed. Boston: McGraw-Hill, 2002.

Boyle, T. *Design for Multimedia*. New York: Prentice Hall, 1997.

Giles, E., S. Pitre, and S. Woman, S. "Multiple Intelligences and Learning Styles." *In Emerging Perspectives on Learning, Teaching, and Technology*, ed. Michael Orey, 2003. Internet on-line. <http://itstudio.coe.uga.edu/ebook>. [5 May 2003].

Jester, C. A *Learning Style Survey for College*. January 1998. Internet on-line. <http://www.metamath.com/multiple/multiple_choice_questions.cgi>. [5 May 2003].

Library of Congress. *American Memory: Historical Collections for the National Digital Library*. 2003. Internet on-line. <http://memory.loc.gov>. [5 May 2003].

Making the Teaching Library an Institutional Priority: Academic Readiness, Retention and Information Literacy

Miriam Laskin and Lucinda R. Zoe

Academic libraries play an integral and significant role in the academic enterprise. Faculty status for librarians in academic libraries is now more common that not, with libraries considered academic departments and library faculty doing a great deal of teaching (Jackson 2000). Academic libraries and the library faculty can, and should, take the lead in making the library's teaching agenda an institutional priority. This article presents strategies for making the library a visible and critical partner in the college's teaching and learning mission. It will offer methods of reaching faculty and administrators, suggestions to increase visibility, a program for re-tooling library staff, and approaches to developing library objectives and activities to address college-wide goals. The article will use the experience gained at the City University of New York's (CUNY) Hostos Community College in the South Bronx as a model of one college library's path to navigating the road to a place on the institutional agenda.

Multi-level Curriculum Integrated Information Literacy Mandate

Evidence of a curriculum integrated information literacy (IL) program is a recent addition to the Middle States Commission on Higher Education standards and guidelines. Two years ago Hostos Community College was undergoing the Middle States review process for accreditation, and since the previous review mandated the college to address information literacy, college administration was receptive to new programming ideas. Thus, the stage was set for progress and cooperation, as it was in the best interest of the institution to support a new IL initiative. Armed with the Middle States Report recommendations, the library at Hostos was able to hire new staff, develop an information literacy program, and promote a new library curriculum. When the college began work on a new Liberal Arts Core Curriculum a year later, the library was ready with a program, a plan and the support needed to get information literacy in the new core.

To this end, the library department worked with the faculty who teach the freshman orientation course to integrate information literacy skills into this freshman course that is now required for all liberal arts students. Information literacy basics are introduced and taught in the student's first semester through the library's introductory three-class sequence curriculum. As students progress through the liberal arts curriculum, more advanced skills are taught through course-integrated classes in each "cluster" in the liberal arts core. Thus, the library department has gradually come to be recognized as the academic department that it is, with a teaching agenda of its own that is now reflected through proactive curriculum development. The Middle States review and the

---

Laskin is Head of Instruction and *Zoe* is Chief Librarian at Hostos Community College, Bronx, NY.

accreditation standards presented a golden opportunity to advocate for the library as an academic department and put forward a new, more dynamic image of library faculty—that of educator and faculty partner. If we do not define ourselves, our mission and our profession, our academic colleagues will surely do it for us (Jackson 2000). A teaching library will become an institutional priority when that library can demonstrate it can speak the same language and identify and serve institutional priorities.

Strategies for Reaching Faculty and Administrators

Academic libraries need to recognize their politically influential constituents, study their priorities and take a proactive approach to programming. Stebelman and others noted in an article on improving relations with faculty and administrators that "one of the most important activities of any library is to recognize its most powerful and influential constituents" (Stebelman and others 1999, 121)—which in this case would be faculty and administrators. Patricia Iannuzzi promulgates this idea in an article on faculty development and information literacy, when she directs librarians to identify the most important initiatives on their campus and work to demonstrate how the library department supports those initiatives (Iannuzzi 1998). This will not only get the attention of administrators, but their support and encouragement as well. Moreover, organizational culture theorists submit that organizational culture is by and large defined from the top down, and any sort of major change in the culture will demand support of top administrators (Schein 1985).

Identify administrative priorities and major campus initiatives, such as retention, recruitment, academic integrity and writing across the curriculum, as is the case at Hostos, and strategize on ways that the library's teaching agenda can support these programs and priorities. Then take a proactive approach to presenting the library's programmatic offerings, rather than our traditionally more comfortable, reactive approach where we wait around to be asked to do something, then are thrilled to drop everything at a moment's notice to respond to last minute request for a tour or a workshop. In fact, this image of the reactive, self-deprecating, "shusher" is not only inaccurate and counter-productive, but it is dangerous as such a low profile can contribute to a loss of funds and low library usage (Jackson 2000). Library faculty must present themselves as the invaluable teaching

partners they are, with unique expertise in the information technologies that are so critical to the success of our students and faculty.

Changing the image and role of librarians on your campus will, in many cases, involve a major change in the institutional culture. Know this and be prepared to be diligent and patient. It is important to speak the language of faculty and administrators and understand their priorities. When you sense a change in the air or see a new initiative coming to the forefront, be prepared with an agenda. Times of change present great opportunities for those with a clear plan and agenda. Take every opportunity to advocate for the library as an academic, teaching department. And if your campus does not have faculty status for librarians, think in terms of "teaching partners," collaborators in the academic mission of the college. Reaffirming and defining ourselves professionally in the academic environment couldn't be more important.

Design and Promote a Library Curriculum

In the spring of 2001, we designed our still-evolving curriculum integrated, multi-level information literacy program. We actively promote it. An important part of promoting information literacy programs is incrementally changing faculty culture (Hardesty 1995; Jackson 2000). Since our IL program is only two years old, many Hostos faculty remain unclear about or unconcerned with our IL curriculum; nor do they always see librarians as their peers and colleagues. But this is changing. We market our curriculum and ourselves, showing that as library faculty, we use our information technology and literacy expertise, pedagogic skills and enthusiasm for collaboration, to contribute significantly to Hostos' mission. On a simple level of terminology, we take every opportunity with students, administration and faculty to refer to ourselves as "professor" and to stress that we have a "curriculum." Over time it becomes clear to all that we are faculty, who have to meet the same tenure and promotion requirements as other teaching faculty.

We created a Web site that supports our IL curriculum with online information competency and information technology tutorials, handouts, subject guides and guidelines for designing more effective library assignments, among other resources. We regularly publish a newsletter that promotes our IL program and other events and programs such as our new incentive-based laptop loan program, which is

—MIRIAM LASKIN AND LUCINDA R. ZOE—

tied to our IL initiative.

Build Strategic Partnerships

As noted above, our first strategic partnership was with faculty who teach SSD1000, the college orientation course. The goal of SSD1000 is to increase students' academic readiness and positively affect student retention rates. SSD1000 is thus a natural place to introduce information literacy. When we structured our IL program, a big selling point for the SSC1000 faculty was that students take the workshops outside of regular class times as required assignments.

Library faculty are also collaborating with faculty who are working with the new Hostos Honors Program students. We created a new office in the library that will be used by honors students to study, write and do research. Other collaborations are taking place, both on the departmental and the individual faculty level. Two of our IL workshops were created through these collaborations, one of which addresses the issues of academic integrity, plagiarism and citation instruction. Other close working partnerships with individual faculty members have led to course-related IL workshops and the creation of Internet pathfinders for specific courses.

Identify Potential Contributions to Academic Priorities

When library faculty seek to identify their institution's "hot initiatives" (Iannuzzi 1998, 98-99), they can then make significant contributions and gain widespread support from administration and faculty. Besides supporting retention and academic readiness initiatives through collaboration with SSD1000 faculty, the library recognized the importance of the CUNY Writing Across the Curriculum (WAC) program and took the initiative to demonstrate that a librarian's participation in the campus WAC committee is beneficial, when our faculty proposal was one of a few that were selected for participation in the CUNY-wide symposia. We took the lead here and made the library an important part of this program. The library supports WAC by providing faculty resources for redesigning course curricula to include writing, and by being a proactive presence in the work of the WAC committee. Additionally, we have shown the administration and faculty that our IL program supports CUNY's Proficiency Exam (CPE), which all CUNY students must pass in order to receive a degree or to transfer to one of CUNY's four-year colleges. Critical thinking

skills are closely aligned with information literacy skills and the library has an important educational contribution to make when its IL curriculum is used to reinforce the progressive mastery of critical thinking skills.

Train and Re-Tool Faculty and Staff

If you are committed to making the teaching library a priority, then be prepared to invest some resources in faculty and staff training and professional development. Every member of the library, from faculty to clerks to student aides should develop their expertise in basic information technology skills. As we were developing our IL program and preparing for the accreditation review, a case was made to hire an instructional designer to work with the library faculty and staff on the new technologies. A *Technology Training Program for Library Faculty and Staff* was developed and took place over a summer and into the fall. It included sessions that all staff were required to attend on using MS Word, Excel, PowerPoint, and e-mail for library applications. All handouts, session materials and self-guided tutorials were mounted on the network drive for future access and reference. Additional sessions were developed for library faculty on "Using MS Word to Build Web-based Subject Guides" and "Developing Instructional Materials: Product Guides, Pathfinders and Subject Guides." Give the faculty and staff the training and support they need to succeed.

This was an excellent method of revitalizing faculty and staff who had been here for many years and for insuring that all staff have the skills needed to fulfill the duties required of a teaching library. Moreover, any and all sorts of professional development opportunities, both on and off campus, were encouraged. Library administration made it a clear priority to support both faculty and staff in seeking out opportunities to increase their skill set. As a result, the staff began to feel a renewed sense of the job and their own self-worth as they learned new skills, which led to increased enthusiasm and creativity in the workplace. In most cases allowing for increased professional development was more a matter of time than additional funds—granting a morning or a day off to attend training. In cases where fees were required, the library covered the cost.

It is equally important to commit resources to teacher training. As all academic librarians are well aware, very few of us were trained as teachers, yet ended up in the classroom. It may come as a surprise, but most other teaching faculty were not trained as teachers either. They were trained in their disciplines and learned to teach on the job. With a new library curriculum being presented and marketed, it is critical to make learning how to teach a priority. This means providing every possible professional development opportunity for faculty, creating an environment where sharing classroom ideas is encouraged, purchasing relevant materials on teaching, pedagogy, active learning, and providing clear class modules and support material for each session so that new teachers feel they have a framework and some guidance. Encourage observation, sharing of ideas and classroom activities. Make learning how to teach, teaching and improving teaching, a priority and support it.

Increasing Visibility

We have tried to be creative and proactive in finding ways to increase the library's visibility as well as our own. Librarians' images and relationship with other faculty has been studied and analyzed (Hardesty 1995; Jackson 2000). Hostos library faculty have tried to use all opportunities to participate in the life of the campus as an academic partner. In addition to our liaison program and the library Web site, we sponsor a variety of educational and extracurricular programs and events each semester. The head of instructional services acted on her interest in spoken word performance competitions—poetry slams—to organize a slam series sponsored by the library that attracted the attention of administration, faculty, and students from both the college and a high school that shares our space. Demand is high for the slams to continue. Another benefit of this series is that it aids in college recruitment efforts, since it is through shared programs such as the slams that the high school students become more interested in enrolling in our college.

The library is also involved in an annual *Children's Multicultural Literature Festival* held at Hostos for educators, librarians and students. We produce film series for Black History and Women's History months and have co-sponsored an essay-writing contest for Women's History month. This past year we started publishing a Hostos literary magazine for students.

Library Objectives and Activities Should Address College-Wide Goals

Align your goals and objectives with that of college administration. This goes back to identifying

institutional priorities and thinking strategically about the role the teaching library plays in each initiative. Look to the college's primary documents for guidance—the mission statement, strategic plan, and goals for the college. Examine each goal carefully and write specific library objectives and activities that address the goals. Do not wait to be asked to do it; do it now; be ready to present it when the occasion arises or, better yet, find an opportunity to present it to your provost, dean or president. As noted earlier, look for change and when and where you see it; be standing right there with an agenda, a plan and a clear set of objectives and activities that address the goals of the initiative or program. For instance, if it is a *goal* of the college to facilitate the growth and development of the instructional staff, then you make it clear that one of the library's *objectives* is to provide and promote professional development opportunities for all instructional staff. The library then meets these objectives by providing *activities* such as a professional development training program on information technology tools to faculty and providing online faculty development support materials in the form of Web-based faculty guides to plagiarism and ideas for library related course assignments.

Librarians as Teaching Faculty: Changing our Image

If academic librarians are to be recognized as faculty, it is important to become involved in the life of the college on as many levels as possible. Lobby, or volunteer, for committee assignments, especially committees that are engaged in major decision and policy making such as the Curriculum Committee, the Outcome Assessment Committee, and the Personnel and Budget Committee. Further, make sure you assign representation on those committees to those who are willing to work, who clearly understand the library's goals and who are committed to working collaboratively to promote the library's teaching agenda. Be engaged as faculty, as a teaching department with a curriculum and a plan that moves the mission of the college forward. If we are faculty, we need to act like faculty and become involved in our discipline and contribute to it.

Library administrators need to support and encourage research and scholarship in the library department. Help with grants, brainstorm with faculty on ideas for research, look for the research component in your daily work that could be written up and shared. Explore options for providing library faculty

—MIRIAM LASKIN AND LUCINDA R. ZOE—

with more time for research both on and off the job, like flextime. The more we publish and contribute to the literature of our field, the more respect we will get from our teaching colleagues and administrators. It's true that many faculty, and even administrators, do not realize that we have a discipline or do research. It is our job to change that erroneous impression.

Make the Teaching Library an Administrative Priority

Changes in the organizational culture will require support from senior administrators, so be prepared to make your case to them. It will take time, clever strategies, networking, patience and continually working to build new partnerships, but it can be done with a good plan and a willing faculty and staff. You can put the library on the college agenda by finding the information component in every campus initiative and making sure the library participates in strategic planning efforts. Find a way to insert library programs and initiatives into every major campus document. This often means being in the right place at the right time, but it also means taking a proactive lead to seek out these documents and keeping your ear to the ground for word of new initiatives. It means being present and remembering that during times of change, having a clear agenda ready can make your library an indispensable partner in the mission of the college.

REFERENCES

Donnelly, Kimberly M. "Building the Learning Library: Where Do We Start?" *College & Undergraduate Libraries* 6, no 2 (2000): 59-75.

Hardesty, Larry. "Faculty Culture and Bibliographic Instruction: An Exploratory Analysis." *Library Trends* 44, no. 2 (Fall 1995): 339-368.

Haynes, Evelyn. B. "Library-Faculty Partnerships in Instruction." *Advances in Librarianship* 20 (1996): 191-221.

Iannuzzi, Patricia. "Faculty Development and Information Literacy: Establishing Campus Partnerships." *Reference Services Review* (Fall/Winter 1998): 97-116.

Jackson, Michael Gordon. "Image and Status: Academic Librarians and the New Professionalism." *Advances in Librarianship* 23 (2000): 93-115.

Laskin, Miriam. "Bilingual Information Literacy and Academic Readiness: Reading, Writing and Retention." *Academic Exchange Quarterly* 6, no. 4 (Winter 2002): 41 - 45.

Schein, Edgar H. *Organizational Culture and Leadership*. San Francisco: Jossey-Bass, 1985.

Stebelman, Scott., Jack A. Siggins, and David J. Nutty. "Improving Library Relations with the Faculty and University Administrators: The Role of the Faculty Outreach Librarian at George Washington University." *College & Research Libraries* 60, no. 2 (1999): 121-130.

BE A (ROLE) MODEL! OR JUST TEACH LIKE ONE: CONNECTING EVALUATION, ASSESSMENT AND REFLECTIVE PRACTICE IN THE INFORMATION COMPETENCY CLASSROOM

Kyzyl Fenno-Smith

Introduction

The ability to reflect about oneself, community, and the larger world is central to acquiring information literacy as well as to learning, teaching, and scholarship in higher education. This paper discusses the use of reflective practices in information literacy curricula and proposes making *reflection* integral to research processes through instructional design and teaching orientation. This pedagogical orientation uses student reflection and self, peer, and classroom evaluations as primary sites of learning. Student-generated reflective texts are also the basis of on-going evaluation of the curricula, instructional design and pedagogy employed. These texts provide both evidence of student learning and eye-witness or informant accounts of teacher strategies. The use of students' reflective texts as the basis for evaluation privileges student development and agency before teacher impressions, providing authentic evidence of both learning and instructional efficacy.[1]

In this discussion *evaluation* refers to those internal processes used by students and teachers to understand the influence of their own values, practices, and habits of mind on the quality of their work—that is the quality of learning, teaching and research. In this context *assessments* are those formal practices tied directly to departmental, disciplinary, or institutional requirements and are defined by both in-ternal and external values. One purpose of this method is to bring about a closer interaction between evaluation processes used by students and teachers and broader assessment practices by using and articulating student and teacher values in the definition of quality work.[2]

Although my conference the presentation relied heavily on students' own words to illustrate and analyze methods used, this paper will focus on the curricula itself. What follows is a description of the reflective practices employed and discussion of the theory and philosophies informing the instructional design and pedagogy.[3]

The student texts presented were generated in undergraduate information literacy credit courses taught at two public institutions, one urban and the other in a metropolitan suburb.[4] Both are master's level institutions with comprehensive general education programs for undergraduates. The courses were either single credit sections in a block-scheduled cluster program required of incoming freshman or sections of a three-credit course required of some social science majors, but open to any student, which attracted a mix of academically disadvantaged freshman and other undergraduates including many juniors and seniors. Additional material came from a curriculum delivered in two sessions to first year students in block-scheduled English composition courses as part of a first-year experience program.

Journaling

Journaling techniques have long been used in composition and creative writing courses. Laboratory

Fenno-Smith is the Education/Instruction Librarian at California State University, Hayward, Hayward, CA.

and natural science researchers document experiments and research in notebooks, as do field researchers in the social sciences, who compile observations and interviews for analysis. Many disciplines that include information literacy in their curricula use process logs to record and organize research. Learning to observe oneself in the act of research and becoming familiar with one's own preferences and stumbling blocks, are important aspects of developing a critical orientation to research and the process of creating knowledge.

Student' are introduced to reflective practices in a class discussion regarding the purposes of weekly journaling. Two weekly journals are required, a course journal which is due (via e-mail) within 24 hours of the class meeting, and a research process journal turned in with each week's work. The course journal is a record of what happened in the face-to-face meeting, it includes a description of materials distributed in class,
a strategy for completing the weekly assignment, and researched responses to or definitions of new ideas, questions, or unfamiliar terms which arise in class. These journal assignments may include definitions for the terms *information* and *knowledge* or an entry describing the student's usual method of research and an analysis of the strengths and weaknesses of the method. In the research process journal students record how they completed the work for the week, including their thoughts and questions as well as the details and mechanics of their research. Research process journals may also contain discussions of the purpose of specific assignments or readings and their relation to the learning objectives for the course.

Journaling helps students become more aware of their own habits of mind and methods of research. One of the stated purposes of journaling in the course context is to slow the researcher by imposing a pause for formal reflection about what has occurred (in class or in their research), what they are in the process of doing, and the purposes of their work. Students observe themselves, especially their own decision-making and evaluation techniques, during the research process, describing how they frame their inquiry, select or reject sources, and why they have made these choices.

Topic Development

Topic development processes prepare students to begin their research and can deepen their orientation to inquiry at either an initial or later stage. Pausing to think or re-think the question(s) one is pursuing is another important reflective technique for the researcher.

Initial brainstorming serves to get everything the students know about their topics into written form. A rather long series of questions (in a format of *what, who, where, why, and how*) are posed to help students access their current knowledge, assumptions, and biases and to frame their topic (by time, place, population, issue, etc.). The same process can be used in the classroom with students interviewing each other in pairs, or as a take-home assignment. In either case a follow-up class discussion and/or one-on-one conferences provide opportunities for the instructor to model thought processes and behaviors which connect the student's ideas to the larger context in which information is produced, organized and accessed.[5]

A related topic development practice is the *best source* essay. In a brief essay, which can be used either in-class or as a take home writing assignment, students describe the attributes of a 'good' source for their research project. This source can be the 'best source' found so far or an ideal source they are still seeking. The essay can also be assigned by course faculty in advance of a library instruction session to help students focus their topics.

Information Producers

The information producer concept is central to a philosophy and pedagogy that emphasizes ideas and questions rather than specific information resources. This theory developed out of a common and somewhat problematic question students ask, "How do I know when my research is finished?" Rejecting strategies that rely on specific library collections or sets of tools to frame an answer, the information producers theory prompts researchers to identify and consult (usually through publications) any person or group who has something to say about their topic. This approach asks students to find out what has been said about their area of research from a multiplicity of perspectives, is not bound to particular sets of resources, and works to include information produced outside of academe and mass media outlets. It has some similarities to stakeholder analysis and action research models and is designed to help students develop their own sense of how to frame and complete their inquiry.

Peer Evaluation

Peer evaluation helps students understand what "good'" work is by developing and applying criteria in the evaluation of each other's work. The process begins by generating criteria of "good" work from a whole class discussion. Questions about how a peer evaluator will know if the researcher has done a good job prompted the discussion. The criteria are recorded as suggested by the class and are projected on a screen for everyone to see. A print version is then supplied to student evaluators so that they can become familiar with the criteria in advance of the peer evaluation session. When developing evaluation criteria for the oral presentation of a group research project, students often emphasize the public speaking aspects first showing their concern over having to speak in front of the class. Then, with some guidance, they move on to how to identify and evaluate evidence of research in the presentations. The criteria developed in class are fairly consistent from term to term and, not surprisingly, incorporate the major themes of the course.

Presentation evaluation criteria usually include:

- Presenters should answer obvious questions and leave the audience thinking "hmmm, interesting ..." and not "what were they talking about?"
- The various information producers should be identified and their perspectives and biases described.
- The topic itself and the scope of the research should be framed in an introduction. Presenters should be able to respond thoughtfully to additional questions from the audience about their research.

Students often spontaneously connect this process of developing criteria for evaluating the presentations to evaluating information in general and frequently make a specific connection to the broadcast media and how to analyze the research (or lack thereof) behind news reports.

Self-Evaluation

How do students know when their research is finished, and when their work is of "good" quality? These can be very difficult questions for undergraduates—or anyone—to answer. Framing the parameters of one's own work and life, the act of defining oneself, is a developmental milestone for both young adults and college students. Yet many of the educational processes students are exposed to, in both secondary and higher education, assign the task of definition solely to the expert who is most often the teacher. Students are seldom explicitly asked to define the purpose, rationale, and scope of a question or project, although they may be expected to display these sophisticated abilities in finished papers or projects. Self-evaluation processes can help students develop their own strategies and methods for defining, organizing and evaluating their work.

Although a final portfolio and self-evaluation project provide synthesis for the course, students are encouraged to develop and practice self-evaluation throughout the term. Research process journals often include the students' own rationale for the work they did, the choices they made in research and their interpretation of teacher instructions or assignments. The emphasis is on the students' definitions of how the work should be done and their articulation of why this is appropriate and an exemplar of "good" work.

The final self-evaluation is an essay, which displays students' understanding of the course objectives through a review of all work in the course. Students describe their understanding of the objectives through explicit examples from their class discussions, journals, assignments, and research projects. If a particular piece of evidence shows an incomplete understanding of an objective, students may then explain why the example from their work is not correct and how their understanding has developed since. Students also describe their "best" work in the course by synthesizing all of the course objectives in an analysis of a specific sample of work. Finally, students assign themselves a numerical grade in accordance with the assessment system used at the institution, in most cases this becomes their course grade. Individual evaluation conferences provide an opportunity to discuss the portfolio and self-evaluation, and (after the course grade has been determined) the students critique of the course itself.

Conclusion

The reflective methods described here provide rich learning opportunities for both students and teachers. Student generated texts contain much useful information for the reflective teacher about the impact of the curriculum, instructional design, and pedagogy on students' learning. Students have the opportunity to record and reflect on the efficacy of their own methods and habits of mind, and learn to articulate and apply their own definition of "good" work.

Both students and teachers benefit from these processes of reflection and definition that generate alternative and authentic values for learning and teaching information literacy. The work of teaching and evaluating information literacy can become an important part of the formal research record and influence larger curricular and assessment agendas through classroom research.[6] Classroom research and the broader scholarship of teaching movement provide opportunities for reflective teachers to use their classrooms as sites of research from which to define and evaluate "good" practices in learning and teaching information literacy.

NOTES & ADDITIONAL READING

1. For more on the use of students texts in evaluation and assessment see: Angelo, Thomas A. and K. Patricia Cross. *Classroom Assessment Techniques: A Handbook for College Teachers*, 2nd ed. San Francisco: Jossey-Bass, 1993.

2. For a discussion of the relationship between evaluation practices and broader assessment initiatives see: Banta, Trudy, ed. *Building a Scholarship of Assessment*. San Francisco: Jossey-Bass, 2002.

3. For an overview of reflective practices and their uses (albeit in the K-12 environment) see: McEntee, Grace Hall, ed. *At the Heart of Teaching: A Guide to Reflective Practice*. New York: Teachers College Press, 2003.

4. The curricula presented here was originally developed and co-taught with Olga François. I also owe a debt of gratitude to my colleagues at Baruch College for inspiration in faculty development and curricular work.

5. For the connection between faculty research behaviors and student information literacy see: Neely, Teresa Y. "Aspects of Information Literacy: A Sociological and Psychological Study." Ph.D. diss., University of Pittsburgh, 2000.

6. For more on using classroom texts and teaching as the basis for research see: Cross, K. Patricia and Mimi Harris Steadman. *Classroom Research: Implementing the Scholarship of Teaching*. San Francisco: Jossey-Bass, 1996.

—KYZYL FENNO-SMITH—

Make It More Than "Just" 50 Minutes: Improving Instruction Through Peer Mentoring

Pam Kessinger

Introduction

Portland Community College (Oregon) is a large college, with three separate campuses, each with its own library and eight librarians (seven FTE). We do not have a freshman seminar, and as yet for-credit information literacy courses are not offered. We use the resources we have, typically the 50-minute instruction session. Our 'standard 50 minute one shot', though, is far from the traditional lecture-demo.

We not only tailor our instruction to particular curricula, but also to the needs of each group of students. Each session can be unique if:

- We establish learning outcomes with each instructor
- We assess the skills levels of the students during the instruction session
- We present material in a learning environment enhanced by active learning techniques.

To do this well–as we meet with each class usually only the one time–we must have flexibility and courage: the librarians must be willing to take risks, to be open and teach in a student-centered way.

Each of us does that to a varying degree, and we all can learn to do more. My focus here starts with using performance criteria to provide informative feedback to a mentee, in the belief that good teaching involves much more than performance or techniques. It requires sharing yourself. You can do that in a single session, and it is worth it.

Kessinger is Reference Librarian and Reference Faculty Chair at Portland Community College, Portland, OR.

Learning from your Peers

Why initiate a peer-mentoring process? What justifies the effort or expense? Consider the attention now given to accountability for student performance, and the correlative necessity to demonstrate the achievement of student learning outcomes, especially for college accreditation. If there was ever a time to improve librarians' teaching, this is it.

Teaching is a remarkably complex process; it can only be learned by doing it, and by observing others. Peer-mentoring gives us the window to see how other librarians share themselves in their teaching.

Peer-Mentoring

It is not easy to have a colleague come in to observe your instruction. So often, observation may be viewed as a negative experience, only associated with a summative evaluation process. It is a 'necessary evil', suffered through for tenure or to satisfy contract terms. Mathew Richardson illustrates the resistance faculty displayed when he requested a chance to observe their teaching. Some had outright hostility to the idea.[1]

The structure of this program provides a mechanism through which we learn how to mentor and how to be mentored effectively. Through this mutuality in the process, where each librarian is assigned to be a mentor and then to be also a mentee, we can mitigate some of that initial fear or hostility. The purposes are simple:

- Building confidence in each other

- Renewing focus on student learning outcomes
- Recognizing excellence
- Learning what makes teaching fun.

Moving from Summative to Formative

As Faculty Chair, I have been charged with identifying areas of improvement for the part-time and probationary full-time librarians. I designed an evaluation process that included some formative elements. I would observe an instruction session, then meet with the librarian to discuss what I had observed —both positive and negative.

I wrote a play-by-play narrative with evaluative comments, based on specific performance criteria. I required the librarian to write a reflection, and then together we would identify the key areas of improvement and goals to submit to the library director. We would also identify areas of excellence. I refrained from commenting on teaching style. I focused on how connected the students were, and whether the librarian could determine if they had achieved the learning outcomes for the session.

As I observed my colleagues teaching, I saw things that surprised or inspired me. I found techniques and strategies that informed my teaching, and I wanted to have others share in these rewards. I began the peer mentoring process in addition to our more formal summative evaluations. All of the librarians participate, including me. As Faculty Chair I must be scrupulous about keeping my observations confidential: for this system to work, there must be a high level of trust.

I started with one-to-one meetings with each librarian to talk about my expectations. We reviewed the forms used, discussing the parameters, such as how much detail was to be in the written observations, and how to give suggestions for improvement. It can be just as difficult to provide critical feedback to a colleague as it is to be observed.

Peer-to-Peer and Confidential

The peer mentoring process can provide identification of improvement areas, of course, but only for personal goal setting. Any improvement areas are reportable only voluntarily. This is a feedback cycle that creates dialogue. With a spirit of sharing we look for excellence as well as opportunities to improve. Both mentor and mentee can find strategies and techniques to improve student learning outcomes. And among the misperceptions we needed to counter

are that only bad teachers needed mentors or that only the best teachers could be mentors. As we became equal participants in both roles we learned to be both keener observers and also role models.

Round-Robin Pairing

Confidentiality is what builds trust. If something goes wrong during an instruction session, there is to be no reporting of it. The mentor's responsibility is to help the teacher learn what they can do better. Through round-robin pairing, we will each get the chance to discover who our most helpful mentor might be. That may not be the person we'd expect. It could be someone quite different, either in personality or teaching style.

Round-robin pairing is fairest in the long run because it creates an atmosphere of equality. The one concession I made initially was to try and match librarians' schedules where possible. Beyond that, I cross-paired people, matching up part-time with full-time librarians. A very useful strategy was deliberately linking librarians at different campuses, thus increasing college-wide communication.

	Mentees	Schola	Jane	Torie	Alan	Michael	Flora	Len	Pam
Mentors									
Pam		X							
Len			X						
Alan				X					
Jane					X				
Flora						X			
Schola							X		
Michael								X	
Torie									X

Portland Community College Peer Mentoring 2002-2003

Mentors and Mentees

Quick turnaround times are the key to success. This must be done while the impressions and ideas are fresh in each person's mind. Each pair was required to schedule their in-class observations on their own. They were then required to:

- Write and share their observation within one week
- Meet to discuss the observation
- Receive the mentee's reflections shared one

—PAM KESSINGER—

week after the discussion
- Meet again to discuss the reflection, if necessary.

Face-to-face discussions are best, though logistically this was not always possible. A phone consultation can also work. The most important aspect is to have undivided time for the conversation.

Program Costs

Peer mentoring can be a relatively low-cost program. It requires administrative support for Faculty Chair hours to set up and monitor the process, and perhaps inter-campus travel time. The main cost is in the release from reference-desk hours for the librarians to do in-class observations. Time away from the desk is also necessary to write up observations and reflections.

Participants need to be prepared to invest time and effort. To be effective, they should have a preliminary conversation to identify particular areas for the mentor to focus on. To provide useful feedback, mentors will also need to be familiar with performance-skills criteria and pedagogical issues.

Effective Mentors

Learning to teach well and to be an effective mentor is a recursive process. It takes practice as well as time to reflect. The main qualities a mentor should possess include:

- Experience/interest in student-centered learning
- Familiarity with performance skills criteria
- Willingness to provide honest criticism
- Willingness to share time
- Good communication skills
- Active and open listening.

Effective Mentees

Mentoring won't work unless the mentee is ready to be mentored. It takes an open mind and the willingness to trust that a colleague will be ready to help you. Qualities that an effective mentee should possess:

- Being open to critical feedback
- An interest in improving performance
- Being willing to be reflective about their teaching

- A sense of humor
- The ability to listen.

Beginning the Peer Mentoring Process

Use the Performance Skills chart (Appendix 1) for data collection during the in-class observation. As you take notes, consider first the areas that the mentee wants to have assessed. The Performance Skills chart is not a score sheet. You don't need to assign points, nor account for every single subcategory. Use it to guide your observation.

The details of this chart may seem like nit-picking, but keep in mind that it's less a matter of finding fault than one of finding specific things to help a teacher to improve.

As you look at the details in this chart, think of examples of common problems exhibited for each subcategory. For example, for "Organization", what's the use of purposeful transitions? For "Presentation Style", what do constant filler words indicate?

Next, consider the consequences and relative importance of each subcategory. What traits do you think are the most critical for students to achieve the learning outcomes? What would be the most distracting? For "Audience Reactions," what would be indicators that the class is disengaged? Why would that be important?

Are there instructional methods or models that you'd be looking for here? For example, how much will having students discover the answers help?

Observation

Using the Performance Skills chart to guide you, your purpose is two-fold: to track problems evident in performance and to note examples of where something worked well. As you write your observation, think of techniques and tips for your mentee. It is also advantageous to consider strategies for improving their pedagogy. You are trying to enhance your mentee's instructional effectiveness. Think about what would be the number one thing that you must point out to him/her?

Remember, being mismatched is okay. You may be mentoring someone with a lot more experience; or less interest in student-centered learning. Keep in mind that even very experienced teachers can learn something new. In addition, assuming that your mentee enjoys teaching, you are there to observe why. You will also be able to see who they are and how they share their selves as they teach.

Evaluation

A lot can be accomplished in a page or two. You need to provide specific points that can be discussed together (Appendix 2). A good observation is detailed and thoughtful but also concise. The mentor needs to be open to ideas and have the ability to write in an interested and supportive tone. They should focus on the areas where the mentee has identified they want to improve; mentors should also be as objective as possible.

Sharing Critical Comments in a Formative Way

Use the Performance Skills criteria to gather specific examples, and use the written observation to begin a conversation. You can have fun – you should have fun! If you can get the other person to laugh, they will be able to listen to you.

To avoid making a mentee defensive:

- Tailor your evaluation to the mentee's stated needs
- Cast a positive light on what you can
- Identify what you have learned for yourself
- Keep your comments within the context of assessing student-centered learning.

Effective Reflection

Reading a detailed observation can give a teacher some sleepless hours. It may take a couple of days to process the information, while thinking deeply about the implications. Writing a reflection may be difficult and time-consuming. But you should take the time. Think about what your mentor has observed, and reflect on their suggestions. Consider also what you thought was effective during the instruction session, mentioning those points as well (Appendix 3). Reflections should:

- Be individualized and personal
- Be thoughtful
- Acknowledge opportunities for improvement
- Add further insights.

Conversations

A peer mentoring process renews focus on student learning outcomes because that is the crux of our conversations, based on our observations and reflections. It provides a unique opportunity to share experience and enliven instruction, as we see how others share themselves in their teaching. It opens a professional and personally rewarding dialogue.

All of the Portland Community College librarians found that the mentoring process was very helpful to them. They agreed that doing it once per year would be optimal. Half of them indicated interest in doing it for other faculty, which would certainly raise teaching faculty awareness of the librarians' teaching expertise. All liked the concept of rotating the pairs each year, to learn different things from different librarians.

NOTES

1. Mathew O. Richardson. "Peer Observation: Learning From One Another," *Thought and Action: The NEA Higher Education Journal* 16.1 (Summer 2000): 9-20.

SELECTED SOURCES

Bess, James L. *Teaching Alone, Teaching Together: Transforming the Structure of Teams for Teaching.* San Francisco: Jossey Bass Inc., 2000.

Lundin, Stephen C. *Fish! A Remarkable Way to Boost Morale and Improve Results.* New York: Hyperion, 2000.

Palmer, Parker J. *Courage to Teach: Exploring the Inner Landscape of a Teacher's Life.* San Francisco: Jossey-Bass Inc., 1998.

Shea, Gordon F. *Making the Most of Being Mentored: How to Grow From a Mentoring Partnership.* Menlo Park, CA: Crisp Publications, Inc., 1999.

Zachary, Lois J. *The Mentor's Guide: Facilitating Effective Learning Relationships.* San Francisco: Jossey-Bass Inc., 2000.

APPENDIX 1

ORGANIZATION	PRESENTATION STYLE	AUDIENCE REACTIONS	ACTIVE LEARNING TECHNIQUES	TECHNOLOGY	ROOM
Introduction	**Attitude** Enthusiastic? Non-enthused?	**Participation** Responses: Class disengaged?	**Reviewing strategies** Used: Where needed:	**Online services** Facility with: Problems with:	**Lighting**
Use of examples Class centered? Clear?	**Energy** Ex. High: Ex. Low:	**Body Language** Active listening: Distancing, distracted:	**Discovery Strategies** Ex. Used: Ex. Where needed:	**Computer**	**Layout**

PCC LIBRARY INSTRUCTION SESSION PERFORMANCE SKILLS

Transitions	Eye Contact	Questions	Student Self-Assessment	Screen	Temperature
Effective:	Scanning class?	Clarifications?	How demonstrate learning: Where needed:		
Where needed:	Focus in one place?	New topics?			
Jargon Ex. Clear: Ex. Unclear:	**Voice** Volume: Tone:	**Emotions** Interested? Bored? Angry?		**Projector**	**Noise**
Conclusion	**Physical/Verbal Mannerisms**			**Software**	
	Gestures				
	Space Move through class? Stationary?				
	Pauses Worked: Too short:				

PCC LIBRARY INSTRUCTION SESSION PERFORMANCE SKILLS (continued)

Portland Community College Library
Peer Assessment Observation [SAMPLE]

Questions to
discuss with
mentee:

Peer Assessment for: Miss Information

Session Observed: Literature 240

Date: Monday, April 6 2003, 8:30 am Rock Creek

Observer: Pam Kessinger

She could have
developed learning
outcomes from the
Instruction
Request Form.

Miss Information started the class right on time. She introduced herself; she

told the class that she welcomed questions. She referred to the Instruction

Request form, acknowledging the name of the class and the purpose of their

library research project.

Was her answer
helpful? Did the
student understand?

The students were to find literary criticism of contemporary authors. It was

evident that they had chosen which authors they wanted to research—one

student persistently raised her hand to ask Miss Information how to find

literary criticism on Amiri Baraka.

Rapport with the
class? Were they
ready to answer
this question?

Miss Information did try the reviewing strategy of asking the class how to use

the online catalog to determine the location of books in the library. She waited

for several seconds to get a reply. Several students offered answers. The

student who finally said the correct answer sounded impatient, though.

It took several minutes for Miss Information to work her way through the example of searching the online catalog. This was justified, she said, because so much information is still available in books, and it is authoritative and reliable. She used "physics" as her subject term.

> Did she notice they had relevant authors to use as examples?

The class was attentive at first. Several students raised their hands to ask questions. One student persisted in his questioning about what was on the catalog record. She acknowledged his question and pointed out the answer a couple of times, though very quickly, on the screen. Her focus though, was on the monitor, rather than on the students. It was sometimes difficult to hear her at the back of the room.

> How many times did she look at the students? What were they doing?

Two students had audible conversations using a cell phone. One student fell asleep. Towards the end of the instruction session, Miss Information had to nearly shout over the noise of students talking. They appeared concerned about completing their assignment, and I heard one student say that they would have rather have used the time to do library research than to be in the instruction session.

> Harsh criticism; the trick will be to have her recognize she's responsible for it.

She made a clear transition to the topic of searching an online magazine index. She used Hemingway as her example. The students questioned this; one said they did not know who Hemingway was. She searched by Subject, and was about to show relevant examples but ran out of time. The class ended abruptly, without a conclusion.

Miss Information was organized in her presentation. She worked through it systematically. Active learning techniques could be use more effectively, to engage the attention of the class and to help the students learn the tools they'll need to start using right away.

> Did she assess the skill levels of the students? Did she know what they needed?

Portland Community College Libraries
Peer Assessment Reflection [SAMPLE]

Subject: RE: Assessment/Observation of Writing 90

I really appreciate the opportunity to "see my teaching through your eyes." You know the kind of respect I have for you because of the opportunity we had to work closely together at [   ]. The thoroughness and thoughtfulness of the narrative and observations indicate a real commitment to this peer process and a strong personal and professional commitment to me as a colleague. Thanks.

As I reflect on the lesson and on the observations you make, I share the frustration that [the instructor] did not stay with the class. This is the first time I have had this occur with her since she has had me instruct her class.... Perhaps the fact that she had been out sick over the previous couple of days and another instructor had "left" her class with us made her think it was okay in this instance. I will clarify in the future with [the instructor] and other instructors that we need to be both in the room and to emphasize the learning and partnership aspects of library instruction.

I was particularly interested in your wondering whether the small size of the class enhanced the "control and attention" factors with the students and whether a similar attention-holding result would occur with a larger class. As you experience too, we often have larger classes, sometimes exceeding 25 students. I have found that the moving around and positioning myself near each row and table throughout the class has so far resulted in fairly consistent attention-giving behaviors by students. I also use the one-on-one contracting with students relative to seeking their agreement to ask for assistance. I find this is an interaction and demand that students initially find surprising and unusual; however, in the long run I have found that then students do come in, almost always say "Hi," and feel enabled to ask for help. I struggle with being "imposing", yet not "threatening" in my teacher-student relationships, particularly as class size increases. After 35 years of teaching I am tolerant of "off-task" student behavior, and I call it out to the specific student(s) if it occurs. Unlike high school teaching, this is rarely necessary.

I'm especially appreciative of your noticing the topics I did not cover, e.g. subject-specific databases. I, as you and all our colleagues, face the dilemma of time limitations set by the instructor and content expectations also often established by the instructor. I have begun to be much more assertive with faculty since I came to [certain campus] to set limits on the amount of content that is appropriate for a given amount of time. I have begun to unbundle the classic Library Orientation class into more manageable and higher level components, i.e. Intro to the online catalog & online magazine index...browsers and Google; Walk and Talk [library tour]. I have found some instructors more open to this micro-unit approach than others.

Thank you again.

VITAL CONNECTIONS: PORTRAIT OF THE POET AS A LIBRARIAN

Priscilla Atkins

Introduction & Questionnaire

I want to begin by welcoming all you brave souls for attending a session with the word "poet" in the title. During the past day and a half of the conference, several people approached me and asked, "So, what exactly is your session going to be about?" One time I replied, "It's going to be about passion." Another time I reassured someone, "It's not going to be just about poetry."

Let me say that when I sent in my proposal to the LOEX planning committee, I suggested "Vital Connections: Portrait of the Poet as a Librarian," as an alternative to the more banal, "Vital Connections: Building Relationships In and Out of the Classroom." I think the committee may have gone with the former title because it's more interesting. At any rate, I'm glad so many of you found your way to this room.

Before I show the video, I wanted to see if I could get a glimpse of who you are. When I was planning our time together, I wasn't sure what this room we were going to be in would look like, and I see that it might not be that easy for you to write. I have a very brief questionnaire that will take about a minute or so to fill out, so if you would indulge me and do this, I would appreciate it.

Quick Survey (participants completed at their seats)

1) Why did you come to this session?
a) the others were full,
b) I was curious about the

---

topic,
c) I love poetry . . . ,
d) other (explain, if possible).

2) I have a strong working relationship with faculty/students in the following departments? (i.e., Nursing, Political Science, English)

3) If I could give a new instruction librarian one piece of advice for how to connect with classroom faculty, it would be:

4) I saw *Austin Powers: International Man of Mystery* (the first in the series) and
a) loved it,
b) hated it,
c) I didn't see it, and why are you asking this question?,
d) None of the above.

Video

Perhaps ideally, I could best shared my life as poet/librarian by bringing faculty and students from Hope College here to the conference. But, due to logistics and scheduling, I knew early on that that would be impossible. In late January, I decided to look into working with Video Services at Hope College to make a video that involved a "sample" faculty member and students. I wanted you to be able to see and hear what they might say about the experience of working with a poet/librarian work. I decided to choose an English professor with whom I worked with during a summer workshop. The class where we collaborated was one of her poetry writing

---

Atkins is a Reference Librarian at Hope College in Holland, MI.

classes. I think the video will show how and where the collaboration went.

The nine minute video begins with me reading a poem. It continues with excerpts from interviews with my colleague, of Professor Rhoda Janzen of the Hope College English Department, and two students, Meggie Elliott and Becca Barry, as well as an interview with me regarding my work with an upper level poetry writing class entitled, "Beauty and the Beat: A Study in Versification and Form." The video concludes with the students each reading one of their own poems.

In summary, Professor Janzen's assignments included having pairs of students research and present a lesson on a particular form as a springboard for the class to write poems. The students needed to bring in examples of the form, and background/biographical information on the authors of the particular poems they chose. During a summer workshop in which English department faculty and library faculty met to discuss information literacy in the basic composition course, my colleague and I were assigned to the same small-group discussion; during the discussion the idea for the poetry class collaboration was born. I was invited to come to a class early in the semester prepared to talk about how students might approach their research. Professor Janzen also added, "And, why don't you bring a few of your poems to read; I think that would be great for the students to know that you are a poet as well as a librarian."

Discussion

The following are some of the ideas raised and shared in the post-video discussion at LOEX 2003:

• One participant shared her experience of attending a semester-long Spanish poetry class. She brought some of her own poems (written in Spanish) to the class, and the students enjoyed discussing and analyzing them.

• Another asked, "So, this is one class? How do you connect with others?" I gave examples of other situations in which poetry has served as the connector:

1. Participating in the HopeCollege Visiting Writers' Faculty Poetry Reading.

2. Being asked by a Kinesiology professor to read one of my poems at the beginning of a library session (one of his students had heard me read at the faculty poetry reading). The library session had nothing to do with poetry

or the topic of the poem, but it was a humorous poem that very much engaged the students.

3. I shared a poem I'd written about Madame Tussaud with a French professor who asked if she could include it in her readings for a class that covered the French Revolution. She has invited me to come to class and read the poem and talk about its inspiration.

From the session participants completed surveys, I read aloud answers to the question "If I could give a new instruction librarian one piece of advice for how to connect with classroom faculty, it would be . . ."

• To communicate often.
• Ask them out to coffee; ask them what they're working on currently.
• Know yourself.
• Get out of your office and go find them (in the cafeteria, at campus events . . .)
• Care about your students and what you're teaching, then express that passion.
• Check office hours on their door!
• Consult with them early and at their convenience.
• Ask them about their research (or their dissertation); it gets them talking immediately and usually, at great length!
• Don't be intimidated.
• Take the initiative!
• Show an interest in their research.
• Stop by colleague's offices rather than sending out an email or phoning.

One participant shared how as a result of attending a Psychology Department talk—simply out of personal interest, Psychology is an assigned departments—she inadvertently initiated a strong working relationship with the speaker, who was so appreciative of her attending. This faculty member is now a big fan of hers. We also discussed how various areas of expertise can serve as a starting point for building relationships with individual faculty members and students.

Handouts: Sharing Other Examples of Librarian-Forged Relationships

Towards the end of the session I passed out handouts that gave other examples of how librarians can build relationships with faculty.

Handout #1

A library handout that I created for the poetry class featured in the video. I included it in the presentation to show how I list all of the reference librarians' names, in addition to mine, as possible contacts. I do not want students to think I am the only librarian they should contact for help.

Handout #2

The article, Atkins, Priscilla. "Information Literacy and the Arts: Be There...or Miss It!" *College & Research Libraries News* 62, no. 11 (December 2001): 1086-1088+ describes the time the author spent with arts classes—theater, visual arts, creative writing, the interdisciplinary arts core course "Encounter with the Arts"—during a semester sabbatical and summarizes suggestions for librarians for forging these relationships and capitalizing on them in terms of providing library services to students.

Handout #3

Sample screens from a virtual library display, *Digging Into the Dust*, which portrays the reactions of first-year students to the process of tracking down primary sources for a First Year Seminar assignment.

URL: www.hope.edu/lib/special/fysresearch

Handout #4

Texts of two poems:

Alvarez, Julia. "Why I Am in Love with Librarians." *Library Journal* 128 (January 2003): 58.

Atkins, Priscilla. "82nd Airborne." *Passages North* 18, no. 1 (Summer 1997): 16-17.

YOU MEAN YOU TEACH?
I THOUGHT YOU WERE A LIBRARIAN!
USING TEACHING PORTFOLIOS TO THINK ABOUT AND
IMPROVE INSTRUCTION IN ACADEMIC LIBRARIES

Sandra Hochstein

The preceding conference sessions have explored many creative approaches to teaching and scholarship. We have been encouraged to think about *what* we do and believe in, and *how* we can teach in a way that expresses those thoughts and beliefs. We have also been encouraged to recognize the importance of scholarship, and inspired to participate in the scholarly conversations of our discipline.

In keeping with the LOEX conference theme, *Reflective Teaching: A Bridge to Learning*, this session could easily be re-titled *Teaching Portfolios: A Bridge to Recognition for Librarians*. A teaching portfolio is a way of presenting, in a simple package, all our thoughts about teaching and scholarship, as well as examples illustrating those thoughts transformed into action, in order to get credit for the complex activities we engage in to support student learning.

Building on other presenters' messages, a teaching portfolio allows us to tell our stories, discover our thinking, present our evidence, and make visible our commitment to teaching, learning, and scholarship. In using a model that the academic community is familiar and comfortable with, a teaching portfolio helps us to become more visible players on the academic turf and gain more recognition within the scholarly community.

Hochstein is the Instructional Services Librarian at Douglas College, New Westminster, British Columbia, Canada.

My introduction to the teaching portfolio concept occurred in the early 1990s when Douglas College, a community college located in the suburbs of Vancouver, BC, embarked on a 2-year Portfolio Project. Approximately 75 participants from all walks of college life–classroom faculty, counsellors, librarians, administrators, technical assistants and support staff–met regularly over that period to explore and articulate how we all supported teaching and learning at our institution. Through readings, musings, workshops, guest speakers, retreats, and site visits, we slowly came to appreciate and celebrate each other's contributions to our students' success.

I was the newly-hired Instructional Services Librarian. Having been in the profession for 10 years in a variety of settings, but never having formally taught a day in my life, this Portfolio Project was my first opportunity to formally examine my new role. It was a chance to think about teaching, to talk to others about it, to watch good teachers in action, and to create a plan for my own development as a college instructor.

Over the next hour or so, we will explore in more detail just what a teaching portfolio is and what it includes. Specifically, we will address several questions. What is a teaching portfolio? Who uses it? Why should I? How do I make one? When should I use it? Where will it take me?

Given that my Portfolio Project took 2 years to complete, and that most other workshops on the subject are at least a half-day long, this presentation will be a lot like a bus tour of Europe. We'll move fast, hit the highlights, and you'll go home with ideas for future exploration on your own.

What Is a Teaching Portfolio?

❖ An organized, goal-driven collection of evidence that represents teaching performance.
❖ A comprehensive record of teaching activities and teaching accomplishments drawn up by an instructor.
❖ A way to package our thoughts about teaching and scholarship, including supporting evidence, in an academically acceptable format.

These definitions are drawn mostly from the post-secondary literature and are admittedly jargon-laden, so let's think about them somewhat differently. To put them into a context most of us can relate to, think of an artist's portfolio. An artist's portfolio would be presented in a format (e.g. a folder, video, or website) capable of accommodating the various media in which the artist works. This portfolio would probably contain work samples, favourable reviews of previous shows, and possibly personal statements that provide the back-story of each work, express a philosophy of artistic expression, or demonstrate a connection with cultural traditions. The portfolio could be organized by genre (portraits or landscapes), medium (watercolours or pencil sketches), or time period. The purpose could be to showcase the artist's best, demonstrate growth, illustrate versatility, or present an entire life's work. The portfolio might be shown to prospective clients, gallery owners, academics, or fellow artists. Such a portfolio provides a way to know the artist, what they can do, and what they believe about their art.

A teaching portfolio is like an artist's portfolio, with a twist. It is most commonly text-based and presented in a binder, though electronic portfolios are becoming more popular. It includes representative samples of an instructor's work because our art lies in curriculum design, student interaction and assessment activities. It includes reviews in the form of student evaluations, peer comments on our teaching, and our own personal "back story" behind each work sample. It can be presented chronologically to demonstrate change and maturity; by genre (course or teaching activity) to show versatility, or even by medium (face-to-face instruction compared to distance education). A teaching portfolio may be shown to administrators for tenure or promotion, to prospective employers, or may be a very personal document reserved for professional development purposes only.

Who Uses Teaching Portfolios?

❖ K-12 students and teachers
❖ University professors
❖ Administrators
❖ Librarians?

Our students are probably quite used to using portfolios for assessment, since they were first introduced in the K-12 system in the 1970s. Student portfolios are used because they are very rich documents that are adaptable to a variety of learning styles, reflect critical thinking skills, creativity, works in progress as well as completed accomplishments, and can be used in an individual or group environment. Not surprisingly, practicum and novice K-12 teachers often use portfolios to track their own professional development.

University professors began using teaching portfolios in the 1980s as a way to redefine scholarship so that their teaching activities were given the same emphasis as their research and publishing efforts. The movement began in Canada, supported by the Canadian Association of University Teachers (CAUT), and gained momentum among the faculty at McGill, Guelph, Moncton, and Dalhousie universities. The American Association of Higher Education (AAHE) turned to teaching portfolios in the 1990s for similar reasons, and to answer questions about credibility and public accountability.

University administrators use portfolios mostly for hiring, tenure and promotion decisions. However, in our Project, administrators developed portfolios in order to show how their managerial philosophy and activities supported teaching and learning. Perhaps, after reading your administrator's portfolio, you could better understand why certain proposals were supported and others were rejected.

There is still not much evidence in the literature that academic librarians use portfolios to gain employment, tenure, or promotion. Let's change that.

Why Should I Use a Teaching Portfolio?

❖ To allow our training and habit of documentation to catch up with the reality of our work.
❖ To provide orderly, efficient, and credible documentation of our teaching activities; this is evidence not hearsay.
❖ To give us permission to stop and reflect about what we do and why we do it.

The way academic librarians justify our existence has to change. We are great at keeping statistics. We can tell anyone how many reference questions are posed at any given time of day, and can even divide them into categories. We can talk about gate-count, items circulated, classes taught, and even compare books-to-student ratios among institutions. As wonderful as that sounds, I am reminded of a quotation attributed to Einstein: " Not everything that counts can be counted, and not everything that can be counted counts". If academic librarians are going to be accepted as equals in the scholarly world, we need to stop making our work sound so simplistic. How many tenured history professors achieved this status based solely on the number of students enrolled in their classes? Not many, I'd guess.

Teaching portfolios allow us to provide credible documentation and evidence supporting our activities. The CAUT supported teaching portfolios as a way to emphasize the importance of classroom teaching and student contact, in addition to research and publications. If the importance of teaching is hard to document for professors, how much harder is it to document for those of us who are not traditional teachers, especially when our instructional role is not recognized outside the library? Teaching portfolios give librarians the vehicle to delineate our teaching accomplishments, preparation and goals. They are a way to clearly communicate our teaching successes to those outside our immediate field.

The preparation of a teaching portfolio is also a sanctioned opportunity to think about what we do. If you are like me, you are usually too busy *doing* to stop and think about why you are doing something or how you could do it better. Many people find that the act of writing helps them to clarify what they think. Also, many of us come from task-oriented backgrounds where there is still some kind of guilt associated with reading and thinking, after all, who gets paid to just sit and think? The teaching portfolio imposes a discipline on our thoughts and gives us a framework in which to demonstrate them.

How Do I Make a Teaching Portfolio?

❖ Clarify your responsibilities for teaching and learning.
❖ Describe your approach to teaching.
❖ Select items for your portfolio.
❖ Prepare a statement for each item.
❖ Assemble the portfolio.
❖ Organize the appendices.
❖ Compile backup evidence.

Clarify your Responsibilities for Teaching and Learning

A current job description, if you are fortunate enough to have one, is a good starting point but is not rich enough to articulate all the ways academic librarians support teaching and learning. If you give workshops or teach a course, expand on their calendar descriptions to mention the target performance outcomes, enrollment figures, major topics covered, and types of students who participate. Compare notes with your colleagues to determine how your teaching activities relate to each other. Most importantly, use your daily planner to remind you of all the hidden teaching moments in your day, such as one-to-one teaching at the Reference Desk, advice given online in a Distance Education chat group, or formal and informal discussions with classroom faculty about new resources.

Academic librarians often find it difficult to express the connection between our work and student learning, especially if we are not directly involved in classroom instruction. One of my colleagues at Douglas College, the Collection Development Librarian, used her portfolio to reveal how her purchasing decisions and policies reflected her deep understanding of our curriculum, students' needs, and available resources, as well as her commitment to successful teaching and learning at our institution. A library collection that fails to keep pace with course changes or contains material incomprehensible to its users sabotages the entire educational process.

Once you have articulated all your teaching activities, the final step is to clarify the context and focus of your portfolio. It would be overwhelming, if not impossible, to present a truly thoughtful analysis of every teaching responsibility. A more useful approach is to use your portfolio to highlight one or two activities only. Here are a couple of possible framing statements to indicate portfolio focus:

> *Within the context of the credit course I teach, I am going to focus on my experimental use of reality-based learning activities.*
> *I am going to focus on my use of classroom assessment techniques within the 1- hour workshop format.*

Describe Your Approach to Teaching

This is the heart of a teaching portfolio, and is probably the most difficult section to put together. A statement of teaching goals and philosophy sets the stage for the analysis of the teaching accomplishments (portfolio focus) which follows. The teaching portfolio is shaped by what is written here, and all subsequent sections are a reflection of these beliefs.

The portfolio, then, becomes an ideal vehicle for discovering and articulating what Parker Palmer calls your "authentic self":

- *This is what I believe about teaching* – a personal, reflective statement about teaching philosophy.
- *This is how I developed these beliefs* – references to and thoughtful comments about readings, conferences, classroom observations, mentoring experiences, research etc.
- *This is how I practice these beliefs* – rationale behind your teaching practices, course outlines, assignments, assessment criteria, etc.
- *This is what happens when I practice these beliefs* – student outcomes and comments, peer and self-evaluations, analysis of successes and disappointments, etc.
- *This is what it feels like when I practice them* – emotional engagement of self and others.
- *This is the evidence showing my beliefs in action* – the back up documentation upon which the preceding discussions are based.

A useful beginning exercise is to develop your own metaphor for teaching:

Being a teacher is like being a _____ because…..(fill in the blank with one of the following suggestions Salesperson, Potter, Coach, Gardener, Cook).

As you elaborate on your choice, your beliefs will gradually reveal themselves and you will become aware of attitudes you probably didn't know you possessed. If you then list all your teaching activities and examine them through the lens of these newly-revealed beliefs, do you see a disconnect? Are your beliefs truly reflected in your practice? Until they are, you will not be an authentic teacher.

Select Items for Your Portfolio

The CAUT guide lists 49 possible items in 3 categories: material from oneself, material from others, and the products of good teaching. All items should be relevant to, and illustrative of, the portfolio focus as outlined in the first section and the philosophy articulated in the second section. Here are a few suggestions:

Material from oneself:
- Course/workshop materials prepared for students.
- Description of steps taken to evaluate and improve teaching.

Material from Others:
- From Students: course/workshop evaluations; unsolicited student comments.

- From Colleagues: teaching observations; comments about student preparedness/improvement from classroom faculty.
- From Other Sources: administrator's comments; invitations from outside agencies.

Products of Good Teaching:
- Examples of student work – research projects, workbooks.
- Test scores – before/after tests, final exams.
- Evidence of help given to students in other areas.
- Evidence of help given to colleagues on teaching improvement.

Prepare A Statement for Each Item

This is the chance to articulate the often "invisible" work involved in researching and preparing instructional materials, evaluating assignments, etc. Explain each item (which will be included in the appendices) and how it is related to your portfolio goals, theme, and philosophy.

Assemble The Portfolio

What your portfolio looks like will depend upon your own individual circumstances, as these are intensely personal documents. However, the most successful portfolios follow several guiding principles related to length, organizational structure, and placement of items.

- The narrative section should be 5-10 pages long, with 1-2 pages devoted to the philosophical statement about your approach to teaching.
- The organizational structure should be straightforward–a detailed table of contents, followed by the narrative text and appendices. Use headings and sub-headings throughout the narrative and code the appendices well.
- The placement of items within your portfolio will depend on the activities you want to emphasize and how they relate to each other. It is common practice to begin with the summary of your teaching activities and reflective statement on your teaching philosophy; these establish the context within which the rest of the portfolio will be viewed. Remember not to bury your most important work at the end.

—SANDRA HOCHSTEIN—

Organize the Appendices

This is the place to put the supporting evidence that illustrates the issues discussed in the body of the portfolio. These artifacts can include anything relevant: evolving course outlines, samples of student work, a workshop assignment keyed to ACRL Information Literacy objectives, a summary of student course evaluations, letters of praise, a videotape of a reference interview, etc. Use a release form if you are including samples of student work, and remove any identifying information.

Compile Backup Evidence

A teaching portfolio is a representative, not comprehensive document. Keep copies of all materials referred to or summarized in the portfolio in case they are requested by your intended audience or until your portfolio has served its purpose.

When Should I Use My Portfolio?

❖ Process
❖ Product
❖ Showcase

A *Process* portfolio is a developmental tool that articulates evolution, change, and performance over time. My portfolio showed my "transformation" from a researcher to an instructor. This is best used for personal growth and professional development.

A *Product* portfolio is similar to a project in that it emphasizes work done over a short period of time to meet a specific goal. There is often less personal control over the issues examined and evidence included because of guidelines established by outside forces. For example, a portfolio could be used by all candidates competing for a teaching award, or by the library as a whole to show how it is working within the institution's strategic plan.

A *Showcase* portfolio is a collection of your best work, and is ideal for use in job hunting, performance evaluation, or tenure decisions.

Where Will My Portfolio Take Me?

By now you probably realize that a teaching portfolio is a totally paradoxical document. It is intensely personal, but invites comments from peers and students. It highlights successful teaching activities, but often real growth comes from looking at why something was not successful. It is useful for self-examination, but could be read by others for external evaluation. It can be used to describe a work in progress, warts and all, or target finite projects and portray success stories.

By now you are ready for a new definition that better captures these nuances: A teaching portfolio is a public/private document, presenting personal musings, anecdotes and tangible evidence of our teaching successes and failures, in order to demonstrate professional excellence and creative angst.

A teaching portfolio will take you on an amazing journey of transformation and empowerment. It can change your corporate culture by illuminating unrecognized contributions to teaching and learning, and by making the development of good teachers a priority within your institution. Our faculty development centre was established, and continues to thrive, thanks to the enthusiasm generated by our Portfolio Project.

It is the best, most tangible way for academic librarians to document, improve, and get credit for our teaching and scholarship. It makes us recognizable as faculty to our faculty colleagues, paving the way for team-teaching and other creative initiatives.

I hope you are inspired to begin your own teaching portfolios. Find some like-minded colleagues so you can mentor each other. Start small and use internal resources. To begin the journey, you might start a kind of book club where you discuss journal articles about good teaching, or have a colleague talk about the ideas they gleaned from a book or conference. Invite a drama instructor to conduct a workshop on performance techniques for public speakers. Close your office door for an hour every Friday and record your thoughts about your accomplishments and challenges that week. Start accumulating evidence.

If any of you were wondering about the title of this presentation, it is a direct quote, a comment made to me by a professor at our very first Portfolio Project meeting. He did not mean it as an insult, he had just never thought of librarians in that role. Two years later he had a very different opinion.

Suggested Readings

Bullock, A.A. and P.P. Hawk. *Developing a Teaching Portfolio: A Guide for Preservice and Practicing Teachers*. Columbus OH: Merill Prentice-Hall, 2001.

Campbell, Dorothy M., and others. *Portfolio and Performance Assessment in Teacher Education*. Boston: Allyn & Bacon, 2000.

Edgerton, R., P. Hutchings, and K. Quinlan. *The Teaching Portfolio: Capturing the Scholarship in Teaching*. Washington DC: American Association for Higher Education, 1991.

Erazo, E. and S. Beck. "Teaching Portfolios." *Texas Library Journal* 74, (Fall 1998): 116-117.

Lally, A. and N. Trejo. "Creating the developmental Teaching Portfolio." *C&RL News* 59, (November 1998): 776-778.

O'Neil, C. and A. Wright. *Recording Teaching Accomplishment: A Dalhousie Guide to the Teaching Dossier*. Halifax NS: Dalhousie University, 1996.

Palmer, P. *The Courage to Teach*. San Francisco: Jossey-Bass, 1998.

Seldin, P. *The Teaching Portfolio: A Practical Guide to Improved Performance and Promotion/Tenure Decisions*. Bolton MA: Anker, 1991.

Shore, B., and others. *The CAUT Guide to the Teaching Dossier: Its Preparation and Use*. Ottawa ON: Canadian Association of University Teachers, 1986.

Wittkopf, B. "Teaching Portfolios: How Are We Doing?" *Research Strategies* 10, (1992): 102-103.

—SANDRA HOCHSTEIN—

Light the Fire: Using Experience and Emotion to Ignite Student Learning

Celita DeArmond and Angela Dunnington

Introduction

Student research projects can be divided into three distinct processes: cognitive, physical, and emotional. Librarians tend to spend most of their time attending to the cognitive and physical aspects of these projects. However, educational research shows that there is a significant connection between learning and emotion. Unfortunately, the emotional attachments that many students tend to express towards "library research" include fear, confusion, discomfort, and sometimes, outright hostility. These negative emotions can thwart even the best teacher and leave us wondering, how can we better reach these students?

Instead of ignoring negative emotional attachments and the past experiences that helped to create them, librarians need to find ways to address and validate the feelings of these students. After getting over this "psychological hump," librarians can then further integrate experience and emotion sharing activities into either one-shot or credit courses that can increase our impact as teachers and help students become more positive and reflective in their learning.

The Think, Pair, Share Scenario

Clara, a freshman communications major, is on her way to meet her English class at the library. "I *HATE* the library," she mutters through clenched teeth. ?I already had one of these classes last semester, so why do I need another one?" She clenches her jaw tighter. Clara sees her friend Tom, who's also in the

same English class, making his way up the library steps. As she approaches, Tom comments, "Well this should be boring. Maybe I can get my math homework done." Clara laughs and nods in agreement. Meanwhile, Stephen, the librarian, is busily going over his notes and laying out the handouts for class. He's been looking forward to this particular English class all week. The students are researching urban legends and he's done lots of preparation. "I can't wait to share all these wonderful resources with them!" Stephen says to himself. He smiles, opens the door, and lets the English class in.

Think, Pair, Share Activity

In response to the scenario, participants answered the following questions: Do most students have negative or positive emotional associations with research? Give real life examples. Do these feelings affect your ability to teach and the students? ability to learn? If yes, how? Here are a few participant responses:

Most students have *negative* emotional associations w/ research. They wait until the last minutes—if it were enjoyable, they would not. This also puts added stress on the research situation making it more difficult than it has to be. Yes, these feelings affect my ability to teach & the students' ability to learn. It makes me hesitant.

Occasionally they are negative but overwhelmingly they are indifferent. I was waiting in the midst of a group of students for a classroom to be unlocked when a newly arrived student announced, "this is just going to be boring library stuff." On this occasion I burst out laughing because she didn't realize I was there and the class turned out to be very good.

DeArmond is Reference & Distance Learning Librarian at San Antonio College, San Antonio, TX; *Dunnington* is Reference/Instruction Librarian at Southeastern Louisiana University, Hammond, LA.

Learning and Emotion

There are three principle ways that emotion can influence memory: the emotional content of the memory, the emotional state of the person while the memory is encoding, and the emotional state of the person during retrieval.[1] These three aspects create the "emotion and memory triangle" and must all be present in any act of remembering.[2]

Emotion can be a characteristic of the material that is remembered and also of the psychological state of the person remembering and largely depends on congruent and incongruent learning and recall.[3] For example, if a person feels very sad, and if they read a sad poem, then their mood is congruent with the material they are learning. Getting into a sad mood may enhance this person's recall of the material. Incongruent learning and recall is demonstrated if the person was feeling happy and attempting to learn a sad poem. Learning may take place, but the incongruent emotions may affect recall. Similar to this is how most librarians approach library instruction sessions by trying to assure students that research is indeed easy, fun, and exciting. The librarian's attitude and emotion in class may be well intentioned, but it is incongruent with most student attitudes towards and experiences with research. This incongruence may well have a negative effect on student learning.

Emotion: A Natural Part of Research

In 1989, Carol Kuhlthau studied the information search process of high-, middle-, and low-achieving high school seniors.[4] As she observed students doing research, Kuhlthau noted that students were going through three distinct processes: cognitive, physical, and emotional (affective). It is very important that librarians understand and remember that students' initial emotion towards research is uncertainty, closely followed by doubt, confusion and frustration as their research progresses. It may help to show students Kuhlthau's "Model of the Information Search Process"[5] in order to validate their emotions before attempting to teach information literacy concepts.

Emotionally Sound Instruction

In 2000, Hermann Asleitner published "Designing Emotionally Sound Instruction—an Empirical Validation of the FEASP-Approach" in the *Journal of Instructional Psychology,* in which he outlined how specific instructional strategies can address and reduce negative emotions and create positive emotions in daily instruction. He gave a questionnaire to teachers and students asking "Are emotions important for teachers and students in daily instruction?" 60.4% of students and 38.8% of teachers responded, "Emotions are as important as cognitive and motivational processes."[6] Teachers and students were then asked about the importance of different types of emotions (fear, envy, anger, sympathy, and pleasure) and the use of specific instructional strategies that deal with these emotions in the classroom.[7] One strategy that is relevant to teaching library research is how to reduce fear: "accept mistakes as opportunities for learning" let student talk about their failures, their expectations, the reasons for errors, etc."[8]

Using Experience and Emotion in One-Shots

One of the easiest methods that librarians can use to invite emotion into a one-shot session is to simply ask students at the beginning of a library session, "How many of you *LOVE* to do research?" Invariably, only one or two students will raise their hands. Follow-up on this initial question by asking, "Why do we not like to do research? Why does research create such negative emotions?" This short exercise allows students to express their emotions and helps create the reason for what you are about to teach. Librarians can also show empathy by sharing their own personal research stories. For example, the frustration at attempting to narrow a topic for research, never being able to find the perfect article, or feeling that initial fear over seeing the phrase "research paper required" in a course syllabus.

Another method is to do a five-minute visit with the students before the library session. This visit allows librarians to introduce themselves and mentally prepare students for what the library session will include, dispelling the notion that they will be taking a "library tour." Note cards are passed out and the librarian asks students to list what their previous library experiences have been and what fears, concerns, or questions they have. The librarian compiles these fears, concerns, and questions into a document or web page to share with the students (and their instructor) at the beginning of the library session. This definitely gives the students and their instructors a clear picture of and validates the emotions and experiences that go hand in hand with library research.

One of the more time-intensive methods used to measure the emotions of a class is the comfort level survey. This requires a five-minute visit with the students before the library session where the librarian passes out a survey that asks students to rate their comfort levels with the various research concepts and/or activities. The same survey is then given to students immediately after the library session to assess what impact the librarian's teaching may have had, if

—CELITA DEARMOND AND ANGELA DUNNINGTON—

any, on the students' comfort levels with these concepts/activities. In order to get a more realistic picture of these emotions, the same survey can be given again after students have completed their research projects. Other questions posed to students at the end of the semester include: Do you feel that this end of semester survey of comfort levels also adequately measures your ability to perform each of the research activities listed? What reasons can you give as to why you had an increase, decrease, or no change in your overall comfort level with research?

Using Experience and Emotion in an Eight-Week Credit Course

Library Science (LS) 102: Introductory Research Skills at Southeastern Louisiana University is a one-hour, eight-week credit course. In order to get LS 102 students to express their emotions at the beginning of the eight-week credit course, students are asked to participate in a group exercise titled, "Getting Over the Psychological Hump of Library Research." Each group is asked to answer three questions related to the research process: What fears, concerns, or frustrations do you have about the library, research, or the research process? What are the different kinds of processes we experience during research? Where do librarians fit into the process? Each group is given a large sheet of paper and markers so that they can record and display their answers/emotions to the rest of the class for discussion. To follow up this exercise, each student is given the "Case of Kelly" research process activity.[9] Students evaluate Kelly's search for information and share their knowledge and discover new strategies and sources for finding information. The purpose of this exercise is to help each student identify with and address any fears or frustrations that they have with the research process by discussing more positive and productive ways to approach research.

To further assist students in building their confidence levels with library research, they are asked to participate in a confidence level survey. Very similar to the comfort level survey for one-shot sessions, the pre-survey is given to each student at the beginning of the eight weeks. The survey is designed to measure the students' confidence levels in performing library research. A post-survey is administered at the end of the eight weeks so that students can compare their confidence levels.

One of the most effective ways for students to express emotion and assess what they are learning in the eight-week credit course is through the use of reflection journals. Throughout the course each student is asked to reflect or discuss in writing the experiences they have in the course. Reflecting on one's performances and developing knowledge as well as sharing one's thoughts with others is critical to academic growth. At the end of the eight weeks, students turn in their reflections on a variety of topics covered in four different class sessions. These reflections require students to think as deeply as they can about their own personal feelings concerning what they are learning. A list of reflection questions is provided to each student in preparing their journal entries.[10] Here are a few examples of journal entries from students in the LS 102 course:

Reflections...Library Tour: I was always a little intimidated by the big, gray building. After receiving the necessary information about the library, my fears subsided, as did the size of the building. I can now view the library as an exciting and valuable tool.

Reflections...Search Strategies: The most interesting thing that I found as a result of this activity was that I have been searching databases incorrectly for several years. I realize now the correct way to search for resources on a particular topic and that I probably would not have been so frustrated in doing research in the past if I had known how to create a search strategy.

Conclusion and Reflection Activity

If librarians want to increase their impact as teachers, they should not ignore the emotions that students have towards library research and how strongly those emotions are connected with student learning. Instead, librarians need to create and use methods to address student emotion and ignite the learning process, ultimately helping students build their confidence levels and abilities in positive ways. In closing, we'd like to offer a quote from Claudia Marshall Shelton:

Empowering others is at the heart of great teaching. It requires the ability to inspire and engage, mentor and collaborate. Without self-awareness, and particularly emotional awareness, we are unable to be attentive to our own feelings and, therefore, have little chance of understanding and empowering the feelings and motivations of others.[11]

Reflection Activity

Listed below are statements that assisted participants in reflecting on this presentation. A few participant responses are included underneath each statement.

1. The most interesting thing I found as a result of this presentation is...

"...asking students to express their negative feelings about the library can be turned into a positive."

"...the anxiety level that the students feel regarding research. I had no idea it was so great."

"...the connections between emotions and learning. I had never really considered this before."

"...the idea that we, as teaching librarians, ignore emotions at our own peril."

2. As a result of today's presentation, I have changed my mind about...

"...the value of assessing student's emotional state in approaching library research."

"...asking students for their impressions BEFORE class. I had always hoped my teaching would allay their fears alone but I can see the value of letting them articulate their concerns first."

"...it's going to be okay to take the emotional temperature of each student."

3. I would like to learn more about...

"...the emotion and memory triangle—more examples of how it functions."

"...what makes the students who don't have negative emotions feel that way, and what can be done to help that be a more prevalent attitude."

4. One concept I feel I'll remember most from this presentation is...

"...a reminder that Kuhlthau's work on the research process can inform my instruction planning."

"...another form of assessment. Getting us started on a common ground in addition to my standard of 'here's why you need this...' approach."

More participant responses, student surveys, and other presentation materials are available online at: <http://www.accd.edu/sac/lrc/librns/celita/loex2003.htm>

ENDNOTES

1. W. Gerrod Parrott and Matthew P. Spackman, "Emotion and Memory," in *Handbook of Emotions*, 2nd ed., eds. Michael Lewis and Jeannette M. Haviland-Jones (New York: Guilford, 2000), 477.

2. Parrott and Spackman, 477.

3. Parrott and Spackman, 478.

4. Carol Kuhlthau, *The Information Search Process (ISP): A Search for Meaning Rather than Answers*. New Brunswick, NJ: Rutgers University. Internet online. Available from <http://www. scils. rutgers. edu/~kuhlthau/Search%20Process.htm>. [1 May 2003].

5. Kuhlthau, *The Information Search Process (ISP)*.

6. Hermann Asleitner, "Designing Emotionally Sound Instruction—An Empirical Validation of the FEASP-Approach," *Journal of Instructional Psychology* 28, no. 4 (December 2001): 213.

7. Asleitner, 214.

8. Asleitner, 210.

9. Denise Madland and Carol Hgness, "Case of Kelly," in *Designs for Active Learning; A Sourcebook of Classroom Strategies for Information Education,* ed. Gail Gradowski, Loanne Snavely, and Paula Dempsey (Chicago: Association of College and Research Libraries, 1998), 146-147.

10. Stephen J. Macaluso, "Authentic Assessment in Information Literacy Classes: A Holistic Framework of Student Evaluation," in *Teaching Information Literacy Concepts: Activities and Frameworks from the Field*, eds. Trudi E. Jacobson and Timothy H. Gatti (Pittsburgh: Library Instruction Publications, 2001), 52-53.

11. Claudia Marshall Shelton, "Emotional Awareness: Fundamental to Effective Teaching," *Independent School* 62, no. 3 (June 2003): 64.

BIBLIOGRAPHY

Asleitner, Hermann. "Designing Emotionally Sound Instruction "An Empirical Validation of the FEASP-Approach," *Journal of Instructional Psychology* 28, no. 4 (December 2001): 209-219.

Kuhlthau, Carol. *The Information Search Process (ISP): A Search for Meaning Rather than Answers.* New Brunswick, NJ: Rutgers University. Internet online. Available from <http://www.scils. rutgers.edu/~kuhlthau/Search%20Process.htm>. [1 May 2003].

Macaluso, Stephen J. "Authentic Assessment in Information Literacy Classes: A Holistic Framework of Student Evaluation." In *Teaching Information Literacy Concepts:Activities and Frameworks from the Field*, ed. Trudi E. Jacobson and Timothy H. Gatti, Pittsburgh: Library Instruction Publications, 2001.

Madland, Denise and Carol Hgness. "Case of Kelly." In *Designs for Active Learning; A Sourcebook of Classroom Strategies for Information Education*, ed. Gail Gradowski, Loanne Snavely, and Paula Dempsey, Chicago: Association of College and Research Libraries, 1998.

Parrott, W. Gerrod and Matthew P. Spackman, "Emotion and Memory." In *Handbook of Emotions*, 2nd ed., ed. Michael Lewis and Jeannette M. Haviland Jones, New York: Guilford, 2000.

Shelton, Claudia Marshall. "Emotional Awareness: Fundamental to Effective Teaching," *Independent School* 62, no. 3 (June 2003): 62-64, 66-71.

LOOKING BACK:
DOING END-OF-TERM ASSESSMENTS

Bruce Pencek, Susan Ariew and Penny Burge

Introduction

For nearly two years, Virginia Tech librarians have visited classrooms to conduct end-of-semester interviews with classes in which one or the other of them had previously conducted instruction sessions. These retrospective interviews, ranging in length from 15 minutes to nearly an hour, have had several purposes: to assess our own teaching, and to reinforce and clarify previous instruction in the students' context, with the further hope that the students will better retain what they have been taught.

While it is hazardous to generalize from a relatively small number and somewhat heterogeneous number of cases, it appears that both goals have been realized. Moreover, these retrospective sessions have provided an additional conduit for students to convey their experiences and opinions about the library in general.

In cases marked by strong collaborative relations between professors and librarians, course instructors have noted that their students' comments in "retro" interviews have affected their own teaching: "This project has increased my awareness of how much the well-planned library instruction session can enhance what's happening in the classroom," says one. Says

another: "I feel that I got about as much feedback from listening to the students as you guys did." Retros inform teaching practice and course content for everyone.

Process

It takes two people to do a retro: the person who taught the initial sessions, serving as reporter, and an outside colleague, who conducts the interview. We believe that this is the most practical approach to our goals:

- **Participation**. The interviewer's neutrality should promote less inhibited responses for assessment purposes. Moreover, when an outsider demonstrates interest in the students' views i.e. by taking the trouble to talk on their turf, students seem to enjoy the attention and open up.

- **Perspective**. The interviewer's answers to student questions may give a new—perspective on previously covered material, while the initial instructor, answering from the back of the room, may recapitulate it. The combination raises the likelihood of student understanding.

- **Relevance.** An outsider, less familiar with the students, the previous instruction, and the class overall, may misplace emphases. On the other hand, he or she may be less likely to be sidetracked by conversations with familiar or favored students (or with the instructor).

Pencek is College Librarian for Social Sciences, *Ariew* is College Librarian for Education and Human Development, and *Burge* is Professor of Educational Leadership and Policy Studies at Virginia Polytechnic Institute and State University, Blacksburg, VA.

- **Interpretation**. As the reporter, the initial instructional librarian already has necessary background knowledge to process student comments on the fly—both for his or her own assessment and for compiling a record that can later be compared systematically with other retros or applied to give insight to quantitative data. Moreover, as a practical matter, fast, reflective interpretation is much easier to accomplish than recording or transcribing entire retro sessions: it demands less time and clerical work of librarians, protects the privacy of the interview subjects, and is less restricted by human-subjects research protocols.

Additionally, librarians and professors alike have found it very rewarding when the teaching faculty member participates, encouraging participation in the interview and inquiring about the fit between assignments, library resources and services, and course materials.

A retro interview has three major parts, though for reporting purposes, we make sub-divisions and analyses. (See Appendix A for a sample interview report, built on our standard questions.) Throughout, opportunities arise to seize teachable moments dealing with information resources, research processes, and the ins and outs of our library.

- **The warmup**. After the professor introduces us, we inform the students that our project has been approved as human-subjects research by the university, advising everyone that their response (or silence) is entirely voluntary and will be kept confidential. Our standard first question asks the class what they recall of the library instruction session(s) for that class. This initial invitation for students to reflect serves as an icebreaker more than as a definitive source of information for us. Typically a few students will hesitantly describe skills and resources addressed in the instruction session, and others will join in.

- **The diagnostics**. Most of our questions ask about problems, first with the resources and then with the research process. The slight risk that negative questions will inhibit discussion is more than offset by the likelihood that students will remember better the details of their difficulties and how they dealt with them. It has been consistently difficult for students to keep separate our question about problems with library resources and our question about problems with their research processes. Conversation often turns to shortcomings of the library that the instructional librarians present cannot,

on their own, fix, such as breakdowns in interlibrary loan or circulation/reserve, though we can suggest "work-arounds" to the students and later convey the problems to relevant library departments. We are not satisfied that our current questions adequately get to students' cognitive or conceptual difficulties with research as an activity, beyond the tools.

- **The sendoff**. While we are, after all, trying to identify and resolve problems rather than bask in warm and fuzzy glows, we recognized from the beginning of the project the importance of asking students to talk about their successes. Such stories are instances of peer instruction as well as indicators of the library's ability to satisfy student needs. We then circulate sign-up sheets to identify willing students for brief follow-up questions a semester later. Thus far, using e-mail questionnaires to find out about longer-term retention of library instruction has elicited low response rates and answers too general to be useful. Focus groups and/or more structured, written assessment instruments may be warranted.

Inasmuch as retrospective interviews are driven by the students' opinions, both the interviewer and the reporter must be flexible. While we take the same basic set of questions and reporting forms to every class, the conversations will take turns that may require us instantly to adapt our lines of questioning/answering and our reporting. The questions we take into an interview do not all get equal time nor attention. Lines of discussion will weave across the main questions, which the reporter must unravel and recombine in a record that will be a complete and rich account of every class yet also consistent enough to permit comparison. This requires a good deal of instant analysis while taking notes, which must be fleshed out–as soon as possible–by recollection and discussion while compiling the record of the interview.

Thus, when beginning a project of retrospective interviews, it is important that the interviewer and reporter be compatible, understanding both the project and one another. A team that has done a few retros can comfortably recruit others for one or the other role. We have found that it is better to break in a new colleague as the interviewer rather than as reporter: it requires less background knowledge and preparation (through discussion with the initial library instructor, based on the course profile–see Appendix B–and possibly a review of course assignments). An outsider as reporter will have difficulty sorting out the threads

—BRUCE PENCEK, SUSAN ARIEW AND PENNY BURGE—

of conversation and perhaps less motive to produce quickly a report that adequately represents the tapestry.

The purpose of qualitative research, such as these end-of-semester assessments, is to collect lots of information directed at answering one's research questions, to distill what is really important coming out of that data, and to communicate the findings. Student narratives about the travails of becoming more information literate can be especially helpful in telling the story meaningfully to teaching faculty and other librarians. So the reporter and interviewer must make a particular effort to capture the essence of those stories in each interview. If the thick, rich narrative is not recorded with an eye to subsequent comparison, the value of the interview is diminished: instead of documented qualitative data, one has only recollection and anecdote.

Preliminary revelations

Because retros occur at the end of the semester, librarians and teaching faculty can get a clearer sense of the overall value of the library instruction, how it fits into the course, its relevance to assignments and projects, and to begin to understand what is really taking place with regard to student learning. When library faculty come back to a class, usually near the time when final projects are due, students do appear to reflect on what they have learned. They also try to learn more, using those moments when the librarians are in their classroom to get new information and to reflect on some of the skills that they have learned. They are remarkably unabashed expressing their perplexities, misgivings, complaints, and success stories.

Student observations made in retrospective interviews contextualize and make real—phenomena familiar to teaching librarians (though not necessary to academic faculty), which we have taken into account in subsequent instruction and collaboration, including:

- Different learning styles require a mix of instructional styles and tools, even in an active-learning framework.

- The longer the interval between the instruction session and its application in a course assignment, the worse the retention of the instruction.

- Students want worksheets and library exercises returned (if they must be turned in at all). Such written materials appear to have a mnemonic value to those who filled them out, even if the

librarian had intended them to be only one-time diagnostic tools.

- Students recognize that there is a lot to know, both substantive and procedural, to navigate today's information environment. They often express regret that they had not received information literacy instruction earlier in their careers and note connections among their library instruction sessions. Suggestions that there be more library instruction, perhaps a separate research course, are fairly common, though these appear to be rather abstract suggestions rather than expressions of real preferences for content or sequence in a program.

Even though they require half an hour or so in the most time-stressed part of the semester, retros earn their keep by creating conditions for more effective teaching. Because students in the class interviews tell their own stories about their successes and failures in researching their assignments, their professors can learn more about the variety of learning styles in their classes, the challenges and complexity of the tasks students work through, and what perplexes them even after projects are turned in.

Thus a retro gives librarians and teaching faculty the opportunity to better coordinate assignments, timing of instructional sessions, teaching objectives, and other variables that relate to library instruction. Moreover, as instances of "evidence-based librarianship," the qualitative data accumulated through a retro project may help persuade additional teaching faculty to seek library instruction and eventually join in retros or other assessments.

Conclusion and Invitation

Because this research to date has involved only a few librarians, in a fraction of the courses in which they teach, the project has had a built-in "small-n" problem. That is, there simply have not been enough cases yet to warrant coding interview results for the purpose of analyzing our qualitative data in a fashion that could properly be meshed with other data, including quantitative data, whether compiled at Virginia Tech or across institutional boundaries. To the degree that other librarians pursue retros and share their results, we may hope to improve our techniques, note trends and other patterns that might be useful to instructional librarianship, to our teaching faculty clients, and ultimately to our students.

Appendix A: Sample interview report

End-of-term assessment/instruction interview: sp 2003

PSCI 2024: Political Science Research Methods: 11:15 section	Session date: 28 April 2003: 11:15
Prof. Craig L Brians	Anita Haney (int) / Bruce Pencek (rept)

1) Recollection of library session(s):
   - Jan 29 session (take-home quiz followed by instruction talk):
     - searching index (student said "search engine"[sigh]) for articles
     - remote access
     - too much attention to keyword searching [this might have meant too much attention to identifying alternative terms; on search techniques, instruction session emphasized using descriptors instead of keywords]
     - Not enough copies of the required *Economist* article [NB: library had not received hard-copy of that issue]
     - Confusion about finding that article on reserve: did not know to ask for item under prof's name rather than with citation.
   - March 14 session (database comparisons during lab)
     - Variety of databases
     - Discussion of types of articles [this was actually in first assignment]
     - Application of keyword vs fielded searching
     - Techniques to broaden/widen search
2) Problems using resources discussed in session:
   - Too many/too few hits
   - Journals not where catalog said they were [not clear if this was a current/bound periodical issue, a reserve issue, a missing/misshelved item issue, or misterpretation of holdings record]
   - Worldwide Poli Sci Abstracts crashed frequently in one student's Netscape
3) Problems with research process (if separate from #2):
   - Circulation too picky about worn ID card
   - ILL takes too long for getting cited articles: student gave up instead
4) Dealt with problems:
   - Reference desk,
   - Live Ref;
   - approx 20% of students present said they'd contacted their college librarian
5) Remaining perplexities/misgivings:
   - Not enough library instruction compared instruction in statistical methods and tools
6) Success stories/advice:
   - start early
   - ask for help
   - take more citations that look good than you think you'll actually need, to leave room for missing or irrelevant ones
7) Willing to do followup interview? (sign-up sheet w/emails)
   - XXXXX YYYYYYYYYY <XYYYYYYY@vt.edu>
8) Analysis/observation (of session overall; of this session w/others)
   - Not very lively group. Only 35 students (some scheduled presenters did not show)
   - Prof. active in interview, setting context of the interview, asking questions to inform his design of class beyond library component
   - Approx half of students present said they'd had previous library instruction

Appendix B: Sample class profile

Library Instruction—Class Profile (Spring 2003)

Class Number	PSCI 2004 (CL Brians)	Class Title:	Research Methods
Date(s) of instruction session(s)	Jan 29 in lecture room; March 14 in lab rooms – no sessions in library	**Session evaluation tool**	worksheets
Graduate?	**Undergraduate?** X	**Instruction support tools used:**	
Level	Required course for major: mostly sophomores and juniors; graduating-senior majors blocked.	**Std lib handout**	
Class Size — 2 sections of ~65 **Class Format** — lecture + weekly lab sessions w/TA		**Class-specific handout**	1 – for use in lab sessions: use 1 of 4 assigned databases (WPSA, PAIS, Lexis Nexis, JSTOR) to search for lit. on an assigned concept pair
Student project type(s)		**Class-specific web**	
Indiv. X **Small group** (presentations) **All-class**		**Presentation software**	
Project description		**Other:**	1-- 4 of 5 questions on take-home quiz due on first session date dealt with retrieving different versions of same article
1) Outline due in February: statistical analysis in dataset provided by prof of two variables assigned by prof., with preliminary lit review. By design, variables assigned so that no literature existed on the pairs, though there was abundant literature on each variable separately. 2) Final project due at end of term: refine/revise theory and hypotheses, identify and use intervening variables, in view of stat. analyses and literature. Group presentations of projects performed individually.		**Instructor characterization of student work** Library Research Characterization: "I teach these Research Methods in Political Science classes enrolling a total of more than 100 students each Spring. The courses emphasize marrying a literature review with students' original data analysis. The library instruction is particularly addresses the skills students will need to complete their literature reviews, particularly incorporating scholarly journal articles. Following the two librarian visits this year I have noticed a substantial improvement in student papers; they have been more successful and locating and incorporating academic research into their papers."	

TEACHER'S MIND, BEGINNER'S MIND: WELCOMING THE POSSIBILITIES

Martha C. Smith

This presentation explores the Zen Buddhist concepts of "beginner's mind" and mindfulness. I feel that these concepts have great potential for us as librarians and as teachers, especially in shaping our attitudes towards our library instruction practice, and in opening ourselves to the numerous possibilities that exist in every teaching situation. The presentation also includes practical tips for starting to develop "beginner's mind" and for opening our teaching to new possibilities.

This presentation doesn't provide an overview of Zen Buddhism, nor does it advocate the use of Buddhist practices (e. g., meditation) in library instruction. Nor is this paper the final word on the subject. I regard this as a report from where I happen to be at this point in the journey. Lastly, these are concepts that may or may not work for you as a teacher, and as a librarian. I ask only that you consider them with an open mind. Your mileage may vary.

I became interested in "beginner's mind" as a result of a teaching experience in May 2002. I was preparing for an instruction session with a beginning marketing class, and since I had no formal marketing experience or instruction, I decided to begin the preparation process by reading the reserve material. As I was doing so, I had an "Aha!" moment. I realized that the students and I were both beginners. This was an obvious realization, but I felt that it was important to keep track of, and I did so during the rest

---

Smith is Reference/Instruction and Government Documents Librarian at Elmira College, Elmira, NY.

of my preparation. Eventually I decided that I would use the marketing techniques I'd learned from the reserve material to "market" library information and research strategies to the students.

As I began to consider how I could turn this experience into a conference proposal, the phrase "beginner's mind" popped into my thoughts. In college, I was assigned to read Shunryu Suzuki's book *Zen Mind, Beginner's Mind* for a class on Asian religions. I didn't remember the book's contents, but its title stuck in my mind. I realized after some research (and reading the book) that Suzuki's concept of "beginner's mind" could be relevant to my experience with the marketing class, and to reflective teaching.

Why Zen?

I found during the course of my research for the LOEX presentation that others had written about the potential or actual usefulness of Zen and its concepts in teaching. Some used meditation and other Buddhist practices in the classroom; others adopted Buddhist and Zen principles on an inner level in their personal teaching practice. I concluded that several aspects of Zen would be the most useful: philosophical concepts, such as "beginner's mind" and mindfulness, Zen's emphasis on awareness of the present moment, the use of humor and paradox to help us see different perspectives, and Zen's emphasis on coping with the world as it is, in all its messy reality.

The Zen master Shunryu Suzuki defined "beginner's mind" as a state of mind that is limitless and self-sufficient, "an empty mind and a ready mind." It is also a state of being open to all possibilities, of being completely receptive and spontaneous. "In the beginner's mind there are many possibilities; in the expert's mind there are few" (Suzuki 1999, 21). Suzuki illustrates this by describing the difference between someone reciting a Buddhist scripture for the first time, and someone reciting it for the fourth or fifth time. How do you approach familiar material with the same freshness of mind and spirit as you did when experiencing it for the first time?

I believe that the secret to developing "beginner's mind" lies in the ability to take your knowledge and expertise and set it to one side, while focusing on the situation at hand. Thus, during a library instruction session, I put my teaching and library experience in a mental bundle, and set it to one side in my mind. It will be ready to use if I need it, but since it's not the focus of my awareness during the session, I'm free to perceive and to react spontaneously to what the students are doing, and to adapt the session to meet their needs as they arise.

Zen Buddhism is often perceived as remote from everyday life. In reality, Zen has traditionally focused on the practicalities of life. Its practitioners meditate, but they also do the mundane work of earning a living, preparing meals, and keeping the yard tidy. What binds together both aspects of Zen practice is *mindfulness*. Mindfulness is a state of consciousness in which one is aware of what is happening and of how one is reacting to it. Reactions to events are observed without passing judgment on them. It is also a state of mind described by Suzuki as "to be ready for observing things, and to be ready for thinking" (Suzuki 1999, 115). Zen practitioners are taught to be mindful of all their activities, and to pay attention to them with a focused awareness. No moment is more important than any other; therefore, washing dishes, meditating, and raking leaves can all be valid paths to enlightenment.

Another valuable aspect of Zen for teaching is its use of stories and humor to break through mental and perceptual blocks. Although Zen masters are famous for their "koans", or paradoxical sayings, others have used a more literal "whack on the side of the head" to jolt students out of their perceptual "boxes" and into awareness. Whatever the method, this perceptual shifting is often fun, usually effective, and definitely memorable.

Lastly, Zen doesn't deny that the world can be a messy, chaotic place. It teaches ways to cope with unpredictable reality, and to meet it head-on with calm and balance. This is an exact parallel to the research process that we introduce our students to in the classroom. If our goal is show how to navigate through the vast and ever-changing world of information while remaining focused on our research topic, Zen provides a philosophical model for the journey.

Theory

Although I found much interesting material in the course of my research, four writers were especially relevant: Donald Schon, Ellen Langer, Mihaly Csikszentmihalyi, and Roger von Oech. I will touch on them briefly, for reasons of space.

Donald Schon is an important theorist for reflective practice. Two of his theories are relevant to Zen concepts: "reflection-in-action" and "artistry." **Ellen Langer** writes about mindfulness from a psychological perspective, as well as about mindfulness in relation to learning. **Mihaly Csikszentmihalyi** writes about "flow—the state of being completely focused on an activity, and of feeling intensely alive and "in the zone." Flow is often associated with creative endeavors but not exclusively so. Lastly, **Roger von Oech** is a creativity consultant who has spent over twenty-five years helping people work past blocks and become more creative. He offers practical methods to help shift one's perceptions and get unstuck.

Practical Tips

If you've gotten this far, the next step is to decide whether this is something you want to try. Some things to think about include: getting started; finding the time to do it; getting support to do it; its relevance to you and your teaching situation; and whether it's too different or too strange to be useful for you.

The paradox about "beginner's mind" is that those who are trying to develop it are NOT beginners, but are people with a certain amount of experience. The goal is to recapture the freshness of the beginner's attitude and its limitless possibilities—not just to think outside the box, but to be unaware that there IS a box.

A good way to get started is to use journaling to keep track of your teaching experiences (see Tremmel's article cited in References). This will help you to develop your awareness of what's happening in the classroom and how you're reacting to it. It also supports the growth of reflective practice and mindfulness. As your awareness grows, your self-confidence will grow as well. You can also work with a partner, someone whose judgment and opinions you trust. This person's feedback and support will be very helpful.

I would also suggest that if you haven't developed a good working relationship with your

—MARTHA C. SMITH—

intuition, you should do so. Pay attention to your hunches and see how reliable they are. Good intuition will help you sense your students' moods and needs. It also helps you to improvise with greater assurance.

Improvisation and risk-taking go hand-in-hand. Learn to see opportunities in things that happen unexpectedly, and to work with changes instead of being frustrated by them. Be willing to try something new and run the risk of failure. If you didn't succeed, find out why and learn from the experience.

Play. Shift your perceptions when you're stuck. Vary your routine, or think of different ways to perform a familiar activity. Make your mind work in different ways: play music, do word puzzles, make origami

Be curious. Ask questions. Follow hyperlinks; look up words; learn about something that intrigues you. You never know when or how this information will be useful. Think of it as fuel for future creative projects.

Learn something new. Become a beginning student again; you'll experience many things: new skills, happy accidents, freedom from rules, frustration, even failure. Pay attention to how your instructor teaches the class, and how s/he helps you when you have problems or successes.

Remember to breathe. If you're anxious or stressed, focus on your breathing to help you relax. Also, remember to smile. It improves your mood, and other people tend to smile back at you, thus improving THEIR moods. Laughing helps even more.

REFERENCES

Csikszentmihalyi, Mihaly. Flow: *The Psychology of Optimal Experience*. New York: HarperCollins, 1991.

Endwar and Dave Levin. *The Zen Puzzle Page*. Internet on-line. Available from http://www.phys.psu.edu/~endwar/izen/zpp.html?. [April 2003].

Fluellen, Jerry. *Developing Mindful Learners Model: A 21st Century Ecological Approach*. Washington, DC: World Future Society General Assembly, 1996. ERIC, ED 403020.

Jay, Joelle K. *Untying the Knots: Examining the Complexities of Reflective Practice*. Washington, DC:

American Association of Colleges for Teacher Education, 1999. ERIC, ED 431732.

Langer, Ellen J. *Mindfulness*. Reading, MA: Addison-Wesley, 1989.

_____. *The Power of Mindful Learning*. Reading, MA: Addison-Wesley, 1997.

Langer, Ellen J., and Justin Pugh Brown. "Mindful Learning: a World without Losers." *New Directions forAadult and Continuing Education* 53 (Spring 1992): 11-20.

Mahon, J. Patrick. "The Zen of Teaching." *Educational Leadership* 48, no. 6 (March 1991): 35-36.

Majors, Randall E. *Zen and the Sport of Public Speaking*. San Francisco, CA: Speech Communication Association, 1989. ERIC, ED 313745.

Nhat Hanh, Thich. *Peace Is Every Step: The Path of Mindfulness in Everyday Life*. New York: Bantam Books, 1991.

Reflection Outline. University of Georgia Guide to Collaborative University Induction Programs, 2002. Internet on-line. Available from http://www.usg.edu/p16/induction/mentor/gsu/reflection.phtml. [16 April 2003].

The San Francisco Zen Center. Internet on-line. Available from <http://www.sfzc.com/>. [April 2003].

Schon, Donald. *The Reflective Practitioner: How Professionals Think in Action*. New York: Basic Books, 1983.

_____. *Educating the Reflective Practitioner*. April 1987. Internet on-line. Available from <http://hci.stanford.edu/other/schon87.htm>. [16 April 2003].

_____. *Educating the Reflective Practitioner: Toward a New Design for Teaching and Learning in the Professions*. San Francisco: Jossey-Bass, 1987.

Sheridan, Jean. "The Reflective Librarian: Some Observations on Bibliographic Instruction in the Academic Library." *The Journal of Academic Librarianship* 16 (March 1990): 22-26.

Smith, Brian. *Koans of the Zen Librarian*. 2003. Internet on-line. Available from http://www.laughinglibrarian.com/koans.htm. [April 2003].

Smith, Mark K. "Donald Schön: Learning, Reflection and Change." July 2002. The Encyclopedia of Informal Education. Internet on-line. Available from http://www. infed.org/thinkers/et-schon.htm. [April 2003].

Suzuki, Shunryu. *Zen mind, Beginner's Mind*, rev. ed. New York: Weatherhill, 1999.

Tremmel, Robert. "Zen and the Art of Reflective Practice in Teacher Education." *Harvard Educational Review* 63, no. 1 (Winter 1993): 434-458.

von Oech, Roger. *A Whack on the Side of the Head: How You Can Be More Creative*, 3rd ed. New York: Warner Books, 1998.

—MARTHA C. SMITH—

THE VISION THING: MAKING INFORMATION LITERACY AN ADMINISTRATIVE PRIORITY

Randall Schroeder, Jill Gremmels and James Pence

The Vision's the Thing : James Pence

When I arrived at Wartburg College as the chief academic officer in the fall of 1990, I found an institution primed for significant change. The demographics indicated that a minimum of one-third of the tenured faculty would retire in the coming decade, allowing the dean to build a new intellectual infrastructure with young, well credential faculty. The *Faculty Handbook* was old and out of date, bringing the opportunity to clarify performance expectations and strengthen personnel policies related to teaching and scholarship. The regional accrediting agency was putting pressure on its colleges to assess student learning, thereby providing appropriate means to determine institutional effectiveness. A limited technology program suggested the opportunity to build an electronic network capable of supporting innovation. An ambitious capital construction plan with storing leadership from a "development" president and an awakening board promised a crane on campus for the decade to come. From almost every angle, Wartburg seemed a good fit for my first Chief Administrative Officer (CAO) position.

I came to the college from an associate vice president position in Colorado where I gained tremendous experience in working with libraries and in promoting information literacy. Patricia Senn Brevik, who at the time worked in Colorado, was one

Schroeder is Information Literacy Librarian, *Gremmels* is College Librarian at Wartburg College, Waverly, IA and *Pence* is Provost and Dean of Graduate Studies at Pacific Lutheran University, Tacoma, WA.

of the early adopters of information literacy and a guiding spirit behind the Action Community on Information Literacy of the American Association for Higher Education (AAHE). She taught me the meaning and value of integrating an information perspective into the curriculum. Her book *Information Literacy: Revolution in the Library* (ACE/Macmillan, 1989) provided the theoretical framework for many of the innovations I have encouraged or lead over the years.

Through my connections with Patricia and other librarians in Colorado, I became involved in two significant projects. First, I contributed an essay to one of the volumes in the Jossey-Bass New Directions for Higher Education series, *Information Literacy: Developing Students and Independent Learners* (Summer 1992). In "Transforming Campus Culture Through Resource-Based Learning," I argued that information literacy is a useful tool for the faculty and administration in developing learning communities that support institutional change. Second, I co-edited *Academic Libraries in Service of Faculty Development: A Collection of Essays Commissioned by the Colorado Academic Libraries Committee* (1992). This project put me in touch with several academic librarians in the state and helped me to understand the importance of information literacy to library faculty, who often struggled to find opportunities to connect with their colleagues in traditional academic disciplines.

Coming into administration through a faculty career teaching english, I spent a fair amount of time in libraries, collaborating with librarians to improve students' library skills. The information literacy movement, coinciding with the expansion of computers in libraries and classrooms, provided the opportunity to form new partnerships between the english department and the library. Fortunately for me, a visionary librarian at the college where I taught introduced me, and subsequently my students, to the difference between "add-on" bibliographic instruction and "embedded" information literacy.

So, in my first year as the dean at Wartburg, I brought to the position a deepening appreciation for the role of the academic library as a site for faculty development and a center of campus culture. I imagined the library as the academic heart of the learning community, a place where the community of faculty-student learners gathered to explore, create, and contemplate. The problem I encountered was that I found a library and a staff situated nearly on the opposite end of the spectrum. The words "dowdy," "dilapidated," "tired" and "mediocre" described the situation well. A 1980's-style workhorse approach to library staffing, combined with an under utilized, under funded, and under maintained physical space, created a recruiting eyesore. Hoping for the academic heart, I found the academic armpit. I want to stress that this was not the librarians' fault. Years of benign neglect on the part of the faculty and administration created this problem. The Wartburg Library had become a giant hairball.

The metaphor of the hairball belongs to Gordon MacKenzie, at one time an executive at Hallmark Cards. His book, *Orbiting the Giant Hairball* (Penguin, 1996), helped me to understand what we did at Wartburg to take the library in new directions: we orbited. MacKenzie defines the "hairball" life in organizations as living in the "tangled, impenetrable mass." He argues that hairball organizations suffer from the condition of "corporate gravity," that is, the "gravitational pull a body exerts as the mass of the body increases." It seemed to me that every time we added a book or a journal to the library I felt a kind of corporate gravity pulling the organization down. Hairball organizations, MacKenzie says, spend most of their time "re-synthesizing past successes" and focusing on "policy, procedure, conformity, compliance, rigidity, and submission to the status quo." I had not read *Orbiting* during the Wartburg years, but I realized after the fact that the successes we achieved in improving the library and creating the case statement for a new facility had everything to do with a new vision: a vision characterized by the condition MacKenzie describes as "orbiting": originality, rule-breaking behavior, non-conformity, experimentation, and innovation.

Sadly, and paradoxically, libraries are often viewed by people in my position as institutional hair balls: places governed by rule-bounded, conforming, budget-sucking, status-quo-protecting behavior. On many campuses, a few faculty zealots are the library

geeks; most professors take the library for granted, or don't think about it much at all. Library faculty can be consumed by questions of status (are they "full faculty" or "administrative"), identity (are they "instructional" or "service-oriented"), and procedure (does the institution subscribe to ALA guidelines). These are important issues, to be sure. The problem is that most deans and provosts are less interested in these questions than in the broader questions of curriculum, academic program quality, and educational policy. One of the reasons I have been so supportive of the information literacy movement is that it seems more like orbiting the hairball than being entangled in it.

The story of the transformation of the Wartburg Library is in good measure the story of leadership. When I hired a new college librarian mid-way in my tenure as dean, I hired some one who knew how to orbit the hairball. One of her first actions was to create a book delivery service so that professors who wanted books could have them delivered to their offices. I never knew there was as big a market for delivering Dante as for Domino's. Because she thought about curriculum and not just collections, she made instant inroads with the faculty. She volunteered to be an academic advisor, demonstrating her commitment to student success. She promoted the idea of the learning paradigm, becoming one of the early adopters of the paradigm shift from teaching to learning. More than anything else, she understood the vision thing. That is, she understood the vision's the thing to catch the attention of the king (that is, the president).

My role in today's session is to summarize the conditions leading up to the transformation of the Wartburg Library, which Jill and Randall will discuss in detail. To close my part of the program, I would like to offer suggestions to library faculty about ways to catch the imagination of the provost and the attention of the faculty (and others) in leading change. These are suggestions grounded in the reflections of experience in supervising academic libraries and librarians in four institutions in four states:

Faculty development is the engine that drives change; connecting faculty development to libraries makes good sense. Culture eats planning for lunch; transformation must begin with cultural interpretation, and libraries can be allies in the interpretive act. The role of the CAO is to comfort the afflicted and afflict the comfortable; the library that plays the victim does not need comforting as much as affliction. Academic libraries must be at the center of the institution's academic vision, or they will be on the margin, perpetually.

If the CAO-chief librarian relationship works,

magical things can happen and the hairball can be orbited; if not, one of them needs to go. With a library mission that places learning at the center, the faculty cannot say no to library initiatives; to do so is to deny the core purposes of the University.

The most important complement I can pay to Jill and Randall is to tell the story of the dedication of the new Vogel Library at Wartburg. When I walked into the building, my overwhelming response was that the vision had survived the vicissitudes of budgeting, architects, meddling presidents and deans, and stubborn construction managers. As I reflect on the entire experience, there's no doubt in my mind that the vision was the thing: without it, the library might indeed have perished.

From that inauspicious beginning, several things came together in what Randall likes to call:

The Perfect Storm: Jill Gremmels

Jill was hired as the new director in 1994, with a mandate to build a new library and create and develop an information literacy program. Before that, librarians taught very little, relying on students to develop skills through a self-paced workbook in use since 1980. Once the workbook was discontinued in favor of more concept-oriented, course-integrated instruction, things took off.

A vacant public services librarian position was converted to the first information literacy librarian position in 1995. Each position that came open was revised before being filled. This process allowed the creation of the second information literacy librarian position in 2000. That means that two of the 4.5 librarians on the staff bear this title, a symbolic as well as strategic way of reinforcing the importance of information literacy in the library's mission.

Inspired by the Barr and Tagg article in *Change*[1], Jill and Jim realized that the mission of the entire library enterprise is to produce learning. They wrote the "Learner's Library" document to conceptualize a new library building and give it theoretical frameworks as well as create excitement for a different kind of library. The college mission statement was prominent in the document, pleasing the president, who was very high on it, and showing how the library would contribute to the achievement of larger college goals. One of these goals was distinctiveness. The library was conceived as an architectural symbol of learning to pair with the college's new chapel as a symbol of faith. The document affirmed the uniqueness of the hoped-for new building by claiming, "This library could not be at any other college." Jim took the document and helped to get the president and the Board of Regents

excited about it. The librarian who served on the Board was also very helpful.

The Building

A building program, issued in May 1996 and based on the Learner's Library document, depicted a library expressly designed to promote information literacy learning. Library staff and architects worked to support a variety of learning styles, to create many group and individual learning spaces, to incorporate technology, and to include two classrooms exclusively reserved for information literacy instruction.

Meanwhile, the college began revising its general education curriculum, and librarians were among the faculty members appointed to the task forces working on the new plan. In 1996-1997, a template devised by a committee composed of faculty, administration, and librarian members was not accepted. A subsequent group, also composed of librarian, faculty, and administrative participants, met throughout 1998-1999 to define a suitable plan. Librarians were also extensively involved on design teams that created, among other new courses, the freshman and sophomore seminars. A core of supportive classroom faculty and a very supportive college administration eased the way, and there was probably also an element of luck involved.

The Library and its Mission.: Randall Schroeder

As Jill mentioned, we were fortunate that the general education program (*The Wartburg Plan of Essential Education*: http://www. wartburg.edu/ academics/wartburgplan.html) was ready to be revised at the same time the new library building opened. The new academic dean after Jim left made sure a librarian was on the task forces working on the new curriculum. For those who have had the privilege of hearing Betsy Wilson's presentation, "The Information Literacy IQ (Institutional Quotient) Test," [2] you know that one of the taxonomies of a successful program is whether "librarians are engaged in curriculum planning." This successful experience led to a librarian being elected to the Educational Policies Committee (EPC) for the first time in Wartburg's history.

As coaches tell their athletic teams, good luck comes about because of good planning. While the timing of the new building and the *Wartburg Plan of Essential Education* was good fortune, *The Learner's Library: A Library for the Future* document[3] outlined a plan that meant we were ready to seize an opportunity.

It became apparent that the smartest thing we did was placing the college mission prominently in the library's mission. Robert Vogel, the president of Wartburg at the time, became a booster of the information literacy program. He announced at a faculty meeting that Wartburg's goal with the new library building was to make sure that all students would be information literate upon graduation. If there was any doubt in the faculty's mind about the wisdom of having librarians on the Essential Education Planning Task Force, the president removed it.

In short, a clearly stated library mission in the *Learner's Library* document that captured the dean(s) imagination kept us on task. By keeping the dean and the president on message, the librarians sold many reluctant members of the faculty. In addition, the librarians were and are visible and involved on campus in committee work and advising. Helping with college governance and faculty grunt work gained political points. The librarians demonstrated that they were serious about the college mission.

Yes, but What Have You Done for me Lately?

Wartburg hired yet another new academic dean; this one had a fondness for assessment. Again, with the idea of demonstrating to the college that the library was focused on the college's mission, an assessment plan was developed and implemented. In short, the library became a campus leader in this area. This was not done just for the brownie points. One should assess to learn things, even if it is the brutal truth. Since the college mission was the foundation of the library mission, assessment was always a priority. We just had not gotten to it yet.

Assess What?

The "Information Literacy Across the Curriculum" (ILAC) component of Wartburg's essential education plan was plotted on a curriculum map for faculty consumption. The curriculum map was based on *Information Literacy Competency Standards for Higher Education.*[4] At first, an executive one page summary was provided at a full faculty meeting.[5] Faculty being faculty, some objected that not enough detail had been provided. So, the librarians provided detail with a 22 page document that laid out the entire curriculum map.[6] Faculty, of course, being faculty, some objected that too much detail had been provided. To them, we returned to the one-page summary.

Assessment then became guided by how the curriculum map related to:

1. The College Mission Statement
2. The planning document: *The Learner's Library: A Library for the Future*
3. The Vogel Library Mission Statement
and last, but certainly not least,
4. The Information Literacy Across the Curriculum Mission Statement.

Lest you think that the Vogel Library at Wartburg College is mission statement happy, these document have fulfilled a purpose. It is too easy in the day-to-day business of running a library to lose sight of the library's purpose. So when dealing with the backed-up toilet, the broken photocopy machine, and bugs in the houseplants, the documents keep our eyes on the ball.

Where We Are Now

The following chart illustrates the difference between the library in 1994 and 2003:

	Then	**Now**
	1994-95 unless otherwise indicated	2001-02 unless otherwise indicated
Facility	Engelbrecht Library, 42,000 underutilized	Vogel Library, 71,000 sq.ft. heavily used
Enrollment (FTE)	1347	1652 (2002)
Information Literacy Sessions	20	123
Reference Questions	1804 (1998-99)	4671 (2001-02)
		4156 (2000-01)
		3784 (1999-00)
Circulation	34,052	46,716 (2001-02)
		38,917 (2000-01)
		39,028 (1999-00)
Adult Staffing	5 days a week	7 days a week
Library Staff (FTE)	8.5	8.5

—Randall Schroeder, Jill Gremmels and James Pence—

Lessons

- Figure out why it's in "their" best interest to do what you want them to do, whoever "they" are.
- Put student learning at the center. Show what you can give, not just what you need.
- Recognize opportunities and take advantage of them.

NOTES

1. Robert B. Barr., and John Tagg, "From Learning to Teaching—A New Paradigm for Undergraduate Education," *Change* 27 (November-December 1995): 13-25.

2. Betsy Wilson, "The Information Literacy IQ (Institutional Quotient)" *College & Research Libraries News* 59 (May 1998): 348-349.

3. Robert and Sally Vogel Library. *The Learner's Library: A Library for the Future*. Waverly, IA: Wartburg College. Internet on-line. Available from <http://www.wartburg.edu/library/mission2.html>. [19 May 2003].

4. Association of College and Research Libraries. *Information Literacy Competency Standards for Higher Education*. Chicago, IL: ALA/ACRL. Internet on-line Available from <http://www.ala.org/Content/NavigationMenu/ACRL/Standards_and_Guidelines/standards.pdf>. [20 May 2003].

5. Robert and Sally Vogel Library. *Information Literacy Across the Curriculum (ILAC) Plan*. Waverly, IA: Wartburg College. Internet on-line. Available from <http://www.wartburg.edu/library/infolit/ilac.html>. [20 May 2003].

6. Robert and Sally Vogel Library. *Vogel Library Curriculum Map of the Information Literacy Competency Standards for Higher Education*. Waverly, IA: Wartburg College. Internet on-line. Available from <http://www.wartburg.edu/library/infolit/currmap.html>. [20 May 2003].

ROSTER OF ATTENDEES

Sheryl Adams
Principia College
Elsah, IL 62028
sma@prin.edu

Jeanine Akers
University of Memphis
Memphis, TN 38152-6500
jeanine@cinemapprentice.com

Jaquelina Alvarez
University of Wisconsin-Madison
Madison, WI 53706
jalvarez@library.wisc.edu

Helene Androski
University of Wisconsin-Madison
Madison, WI 53706
handroski@library.wisc.edu

Susan Ariew
Virginia Technological University
Blacksburg, VA 24062-9001
saa@vt.edu

Priscilla Atkins
Hope College
Holland, MI 49422
atkinsp@hope.edu

Margaret Atwater-Singer
University of Evansville
Evansville, IN 47722
m35@evansville.edu

Susan Avery
Millikin University
Decatur, IL 62522
savery@mail.millikin.edu

Randal Baier
Eastern Michigan University
Ypsilanti, MI 48197-2207
rbaier@emich.edu

Betsy Baker
Library Consultant & Educator
Evanston, IL 60202
bbaker@northwestern.edu

Pamela Baker
California State University-
Monterey Bay
Seaside, CA 93955
pam_baker@csumb.edu

Lisa Barnett
Ball State University
Muncie, IN 47306
ljbarnett2@bsu.edu

Mary Ann Barton
University of Nebraska-Kearney
Kearney, NE 68849
bartonm@unk.edu

Dianne Bean
Embry-Riddle University
Prescott, AZ 86301
beand@erau.edu

Lynne Beck
University of Minnesota
Minneapolis, MN 55455
l-beck@umn.edu

Shirley Bennett
Columbia College of Chicago
Chicago, IL 60605
sbennett@popmail.colum.edu

Cheryl Blackwell
Albion College
Albion, MI 49224
cblackwell@albion.edu

Greta Boers
Duke University
Durham, NC 27708
greta.boers@duke.edu

Colleen Boff
Bowling Green State University
Bowling Green, OH 43403
cboff@bgnet.bgsu.edu

Janet Bogenschultz
New York Public Library
New York, NY 10016
jbogenschultz@nypl.org

Mark Bollenback
Valencia Community College
Orlando, FL 32825
mbollenback@vanenciacc.edu

Leslie J. Boyd
Vanderbilt University
Nashville, TN 37203
boyd@library.vanderbilt.edu

Susan Boyd
Santa Clara University
Santa Clara, CA 95053-0500
skboyd@scu.edu

Stephanie Brenenson
Florida International University
Miami, FL 33199
brenenso@fiu.edu

Melinda Brown
Vanderbilt University
Nashville, TN 37240-0007
brown@library.vanderbilt.edu

Melissa Browne
Ball State University
Muncie, IN 47306
mbrowne@bsu.edu

Tim Bryant
University of Northern Iowa
Cedar Falls, IA 50613-3675
tim.bryant@uni.edu

Joe Buenker
Arizona State University West
Glendale, AZ 85306-4908
joe.buenker@asu.edu

Liz Burge
University of New Brunswick
Fredericton, NB Canada E3B
5A3
burge@unb.ca

Robert Burger
University of Illinois-Urbana-
Champaign
Urbana, IL 61801
r-burger@uiuc.edu

Adam Burke
Waubonsee Community College
Sugar Grove, IL 60554
aburke@waubonsee.edu

Paola Ceccarini
New York Public Library
New York, NY 10018
pceccarini@nypl.org

Patricia Clark
Trinity College
Hartford, CT
patricia.clark@trincoll.edu

Patricia Cloud
Roosevelt University
Chicago, IL 60605
pcloud@Roosevelt.edu

Barbara Cockrell
Western Michigan University
Kalamazoo, MI 49008
barbara.cockrell@wmich.edu

Ruth Connell
Valparaiso University
Valparaiso, IN 46383
ruth.connell@valpo.edu

Christopher Cox
Worcester Polytechnic Institute
Worcester, MA
ccox@wpi.edu

Wendy Crist
Arkansas State University
State University, AR 72467
wcrist@astate.edu

Charlotte Cubbage
Northwestern University
Evanston, IL 60208
c-cubbage@northwestern.edu

Celita DeArmond
San Antonio College
San Antonio, TX 78212
cdearmon@accd.edu

Sheila Delecroix
University of Tennessee-
Chattanooga
Chattanooga, TN 37403
sheila-delacroix@utc.edu

Carolyn DeLuna
Edgewood College
Madison, WI 53711
cdeluna@edgewood.edu

Linda Depken
University of Texas-Arlington
Arlington, TX 76013
ldepken@uta.edu

Kristine Derks
Aquinas College
Grand Rapids, MI 49506
derkskri@aquinas.edu

David Dettman
University of Wisconsin-Green
Bay
Green Bay, WI 54304
dettmand@uwgb.edu

Deborah Diller
Madison Area Technical College
Madison, WI 53703
ddiller@matcmadison.edu

Kathy Dobda
Cleveland State University
Cleveland, OH 44115
k.dobda@csuohio.edu

Raeann Dossett
Parkland College
Champaign, IL 61821
rdossett@parkland.edu

Katherine Downton
Gettysburg College
Gettysburg, PA 17325
kdownton@gettysburg.edu

Sally Driscoll
Pennsylvania State University-
Altoona
State College, PA 16801
ssd5@psu.edu

Karen Dunn
University of Wisconsin-Madison
Madison, WI 53706
kdunn@library.wisc.edu

Angela Dunnington
Southeastern Louisiana
University
Hammond, LA 70402
adunnington@selu.edu

Patricia Durisin
MIT
Cambridge, MA
durisin@mit.edu

Tom Durkin
University of Wisconsin-Madison
Madison, WI 53726-0356
tdurkin@library.wisc.edu

Pamela Enrici
University of Minnesota-Duluth
Duluth, MN
penrici@d.umn.edu

Barbara Evans
National-Louis University
Wheaton, IL 60187
bevans@nl.edu

Patricia Farney
Rock Valley College
Rockford, IL 61114
pfarney@ednet.rvc.cc.il.us

Kyzyl Fenno-Smith
California State University-
Hayward
Hayward, CA 94542-3052
kfsmith@csuhayward.edu

Eliot Finkelstein
University of Wisconsin-Madison
Madison, WI 53706
efinkelstein@library.wisc.edu

Marisa Finkey
University of Wisconsin-Oshkosh
Oshkosh, WI 54901
finkey@uwosh.edu

Diana Fitzwater
College of DuPage
Glen Ellyn, IL 60137
fitzwate@cdnet.cod.edu

Brook Freeman
Purdue University
West Lafayette, IN 47906
freemanb@purdue.edu

Steven Frye
University of Wisconsin-Madison
Madison, WI 53706
sfrye@library.wisc.ed

Lora Gault
Purdue University-Calumet
Chicago, IL 60620
gault@calumet.purdue.edu

Anne Giffey
Knox College
Galesburg, IL 61401
agiffey@knox.edu

Kerry Gleason
University of Wisconsin-Madison
Madison, WI 53706
kgleason@library.wisc.edu

Linda Glover
William Rainey Harper College
Palatine, IL 60067
lglover@harpercollege.edu

Jill Gremmels
Wartburg College
Waverly, IA 50677
jill.gremmels@wartburg.edu

Donna Gunter
University of North Carolina-
Charlotte
Charlotte, NC 28223-0001
djgunter@email.uncc.edu

Trudi Bellardo Hahn
University of Maryland
College Park, MD 20742
th90@umail.umd.edu

Elizabeth Hanson
Indiana University
Bloomington, IN 47405
hansone@Indiana.edu

Kathlene Hanson
California State University-
Monterey Bay
Seaside, CA 93955
kathlene_hanson@csumb.edu

Katherine Harris
Ball State University
Muncie, IN 47306
kmharris@bsu.edu

Nathan Hellmers
Sinclair Community College
Dayton, OH 45402
nathan.hellmers@sinclair.edu

Patricia Herrling
University of Wisconsin-Madison
Madison, WI 53706
pherrling@library.wisc.edu

Rebecca Hewitt
Colgate University
Hamilton, NY
rhewitt@mail.colgate.edu

Lisa Hinchliffe
University of Illinois-Urbana-
Champaign
Urbana, IL 61801
ljanicke@uiuc.edu

Sandra Hochstein
Douglas College
New Westminster, BC Canada
V3L 5B2
hochsteins@douglas.bc.ca

Christopher Hollister
State University of New York-
Buffalo
Amherst, NY 14260
cvh2@buffalo.edu

Katherine Holmes
Lesley University
Cambridge, MA
kholmes@mail.Lesley.edu

Karen Hovde
Northern Illinois University
DeKalb, IL 60115
khovde@niu.edu

Rick Huebschman
Moraine Park Technical College
West Bend, WI 53090
rhuebschman@morainepark.edu

Sharon Huge
Ohio University-Lancaster
Lancaster, OH 43130
huge@ohiou.edu

Elizabeth Hutchins
St. Olaf College
Northfield, MN 55057
hutchine@stolaf.edu

Amanda Izenstark
University of Rhode Island
Kingston, RI
aki@etal.uri.edu

Lydia Jackson
Southern Illinois University-
Edwardsville
Edwardsville, IL 62026
ljackso@siue.edu

Elaine Jayne
Western Michigan University
Kalamazoo, MI 49008
elaine.jayne@wmich.edu

Brian Jennings
Pace University
Pleasantville, NY 10570
bjennings@pace.edu

Sarah Jent
University of Louisville
Louisville, KY 40241
sarah.jent@Louisville.edu

Corey Johnson
Washington State University
Pullman, WA 99164-5610
coreyj@wsu.edu

Kristin Johnson
California State University-Chico
Chico, CA 95929-0295
kajohnson@csuchico.edu

Jennifer A. Jones
Emory University
Atlanta, GA 30322
jjone11@emory.edu

Melissa Kalpin
University of Minnesota
Minneapolis, MN 55455
kalpinm@tc.umn.edu

Kevin Keating
University of Alaska-Anchorage
Anchorage, AK 99508
ankmk@uaa.Alaska.edu

Inba Kehoe
University of Victoria
Victoria, BC Canada V8W 3H5
ikehoe@uvic.edu

Emily Keller
University of Washington-
Tacoma
Tacoma, WA 98402-3100
emkeller@u.Washington.edu

Tracy Kemp
Columbus State Community
College
Columbus, OH 43215
tkemp@cscc.edu

Barbara Kenney
Roger Williams University
Bristol, RI
bkenney@rwu.edu

Pam Kessinger
Portland Community College
Portland, OR 97280-0990
pkessing@pcc.edu

Amy Kindschi
University of Wisconsin-Madison
Madison, WI 53706
kindschi@engr.wisc.edu

Jim Kinnie
University of Rhode Island
Kingston, RI
jkinnie@uri.edu

Kristin Kroger
Art Institute of Fort Lauderdale
Ft. Lauderdale, FL 33316
kristinkroger@juno.com

Janice Krueger
University of the Pacific
Stockton, CA 95211
jkrueger@uop.edu

Carrie Kruse
University of Wisconsin-Madison
Madison, WI 53706
ckruse@library.wisc.edu

Kathleen Kurosman
Vassar College
Poughkeepsie, NY 12604-0020
kakurosman@Vassar.edu

Miriam Laskin
Hostos Community College
Bronx, NY 10451
mlaskin@hostos.cuny.edu

Judy Lee
University of California-
Riverside
Riverside, CA 92517-5900
judy.lee@ucr.edu

Kim Leggett
Columbus State Community
College
Columbus, OH 43215
kleggett@cscc.edu

Elizabeth Lindsay
Washington State University
Pullman, WA 99164-5610
elindsay@wsu.edu

Julia Longbrake
Mt. Hood Community College
Gresham, OR 97030
longbraj@mhcc.edu

Abbie Loomis
University of Wisconsin-Madison
Madison, WI 53706
aloomis@library.wisc.edu

Megan Lowe
University of Missouri-Rolla
Rolla, MO 65409
loweme@umr.edu

Mark Luetkehoelter
Madison Area Technical College
Madison, WI 53704
mluetkehoelt@matcmadison.edu

Cynthia Lynch
Milwaukee Institute of Art &
Design
Milwaukee, WI 53202
clynch@miad.edu

Divina Lynch
National University
San Jose, CA 95128-2541
dlynch@nu.edu

Mary Jo Lyons
University of Texas-Arlington
Arlington, TX 76019-0497
mjhandke@uta.edu

Rod Lysenko
Edgewood College
Madison, WI 53711
lysenko@edgewood.edu

Mary MacDonald
University of Rhode Island
Kingston, RI
marymac@uri.edu

Karen McBride
William Rainey Harper College
Palatine, IL 60067
kmcbride@harpercollege.edu

Karen McLaughlin
Davenport University
Grand Rapids, MI 49503
karen.mclaughlin@davenport.edu

Jeanette McVeigh
University of the Sciences-Phila.
Philadelphia, PA 19104
j.mcveig@usip.edu

Jill Markgraf
University of Wisconsin-Eau
Claire
Eau Claire, WI 54702
markgrjs@uwec.edu

Rose Marie Martin
Aquinas College
Grand Rapids, MI 49506
martiros@Aquinas.edu

Annemarie Mascarenhas
Bergen Community College
Paramus, NJ
amascarenhas@Bergen.edu

Molly Mathias
University of Northern Colorado
Greeley, CO 80639-0091
molly.mathias@unco.edu

Brad Matthies
Butler University
Indianapolis, IN 46208-3485
bmatthie@butler.edu

Angela Megaw
Gainesville College
Gainesville, GA 30503
amegaw@gc.peachnet.edu

Bob Menanteaux
Seattle University
Seattle, WA 98406
arobertm@seattleu.edu

Harry Meserve
San Jose State University
Felton, CA 95018
hmeserve@sjsu.edu

Lori Mestre
University of Massachusetts-
Amherst
Amherst, MA
lori.mestre@library.umass.edu

Trisha Mileham
Valparaiso University
Valparaiso, IN 46383
trisha.mileham@valpo.edu

Deborah Moore
Glendale Community College
Los Angeles, CA 90041
dmoore@glendale.edu

Michael Mounce
Delta State University
Cleveland, MS
mmounce@deltastate.edu

Clark Nall
East Carolina University
Greenville, NC 27858
nallh@mail.ecu.edu

Brent Nelson
University of Arkansas-Little
Rock
Little Rock, AR 72204
banelson@ualr.edu

Kerie Nickel
St. Mary's College of Maryland
St. Mary's City, MD 20686
klnickel@smcm.edu

Karen Odato
Dartmouth College
Lebanon, NH
Karen.odato@Dartmouth.edu

Kerri Odess-Harnish
Gettysburg College
Gettysburg, PA 17325
kodessha@Gettysburg.edu

Emily Okada
Indiana University
Bloomington, IN 47405-3907
okada@Indiana.edu

Julie O'Keeffe
Marquette University
Milwaukee, WI 53201
julie.okeeffe@Marquette.edu

Susan Olson
University of Maryland-
University College
Adelphi, MD 20783-8048
smolson@umuc.edu

Teague Orblych
University of Michigan-Dearborn
Dearborn, MI 48128-1491
mtorblyc@umd.umich.edu

Jan Orf
University of St. Thomas
St. Paul, MN 55105
jmorf@stthomas.edu

Beth Orgeron
Loyola University-New Orleans
New Orleans, LA 70118
edorgero@loyno.edu

Beryl Pagan
Point Loma Nazarene University
San Diego, CA 92106
bpagan@ptloma.edu

Russell Palmer
Mercer University
Macon, GA 31207
palmer_rl@mercer.edu

Jim Pence
Pacific Lutheran University
Tacoma, WA
pencejl@plu.edu

Bruce Pencek
Virginia Technological
University
Blacksburg, VA 24062-9001
bpencek@vt.edu

Celia Perez
Harold Washington College
Chicago, IL 60647
cperez2@ccc.edu

Loreen Phillips
University of Texas-Dallas
Richardson, TX 75083-0643
lsp014100@utdallas.edu

Vivienne Piroli
Simmons College
Boston, MA
vivienne.piroli@simmons.edu

Betty Porter
Xavier University
Cincinnati, OH 45207-5211
porter@xavier.edu

Cristine Prucha
University of Wisconsin-La
Crosse
La Crosse, WI 54601
prucha.cris@uwlax.edu

Albert Quattrucci
University of Wisconsin-Madison
Madison, WI 53706
aquattrucci@engr.wisc.edu

Kim Ranger
Grand Valley State University
Allendale, MI 49401
rangerk@gvsu.edu

Robin Rank
Kalamazoo College
Kalamazoo, MI 49006
rrank@kzoo.edu

Billie Reinhart
Cleveland State University
Cleveland, OH 44115
b.reinhart@csuohio.edu

Melanie Remy
University of Southern California
Los Angeles, CA 90089-2571
mremy@usc.edu

Gretchen Revie
Lawrence University
Appleton, WI
gretchen.m.revie@lawrence.edu

Kelly Rhodes
Appalachian State University
Boone, NC 28608
rhodeska@appstate.edu

Sala Rhodes
Emory University
Atlanta, GA 30322
smrhode@emory.edu

Christy Rilette
Loyola University-New Orleans
New Orleans, LA 70118
crilette@loyno.edu

Peggy Roske
College of St. Benedict/St.
Joseph University
St. Joseph, MN 56374
proske@csbsju.edu

Caroline Russom
California State University-
Northridge
Northridge, CA 91330-8327
crussom@csun.edu

Christine E. Ryan
University of Tennessee-
Chattanooga
Chattanooga, TN 37403
chris-ryan@utc.edu

Laurie Sabol
Tufts University
Medford, MA
laurie.sabol@tufts.edu

Randall Schroeder
Wartburg College
Waverly, IA 50677
randall.schroeder@wartburg.edu

Lynn Scott
Calumet College of St. Joseph
Whiting, IN 46394
lscott@ccsj.edu

Priscilla Seaman
University of Tennessee-
Chattanooga
Chattanooga, TN 37403
priscilla-seaman@utc.edu

Joel Seewald
University of Michigan-Dearborn
Dearborn, MI 48128
seewald@umd.umich.edu

Renee Sengele
University of Wisconsin-Oshkosh
Oshkosh, WI 54901
sengele@uwosh.edu

Susan Setterlund
Florida Atlantic University
Boca Raton, FL 33431
setterlu@fau.edu

Jennifer Sharkey
Purdue University
West Lafayette, IN 47907-2058
sharkeyj@purdue.edu

Lynn Sheehan
University of Charleston
Charleston, WV 25304
lsheehan@ucwv.edu

Cynthia Shirkey
University of Illinois-Urbana-
Champaign
Urbana, IL -61801
cshirkey@uiuc.edu

Caroline Smith
Caltech Library System
Pasadena, CA 91125
cline@library.Caltech.edu

Martha C. Smith
Elmira College
Elmira, NY 14901
msmith@elmira.edu

Heather Smith
Oberlin College
Oberlin, OH 44074
heather.smith@oberlin.edu

Keith Stanger
Eastern Michigan University
Ypsilanti, MI 48197-2207
keith@stanger.com

Sarah Statz
Madison Public Library
Madison, WI 53717
theend@merr.com

Eileen Stec
Rutgers University
New Brunswick, NJ
estec@rci.rutgers.edu

Catherine Stephens
University of Wisconsin-Madison
Madison, WI 53706
cstephens@education.wisc.edu

Andrew Stuart
Ohio University
Athens, OH 45701
stuarta@ohiou.edu

Mary Sullivan
Emerson College
Boston, MA 02116
mary_sullivan@emerson.edu

Pauline Swartz
University of California-Los
Angeles
Los Angeles, CA 90095-1450
pswartz@library.ucla.edu

Dorothy A. Terhune
Grand Rapids Community
College
Grand Rapids, MI 49503
dterhune@grcc.edu

Deb Biggs Thomas
LOEX/Eastern Michigan
University
Ypsilanti, MI 48197-2207
dbiggs@emich.edu

Ling Thumin
Fontbonne University
Clayton, MO 63131
lthumin@fontbonne.edu

Monica Tobin
Edmonds Community College
Lynnwood, WA 98036
mtobin@edcc.edu

Michelle Twait
Gustavus Adolphus College
St. Peter, MN 56082
mtwait@gac.edu

Jana Varlejs
Rutgers University
New Brunswick, NJ 08901-
1071
varlejs@scils.rutgers.edu

Jerilyn Veldof
University of Minnesota
Minneapolis, MN 55455
jveldof@umn.edu

Dale Vidmar
Southern Oregon University
Ashland, OR 97520
vidmar@sou.edu

William Vincenti
Montclair State University
Upper Montclair, NJ
vincentiw@montclair.edu

Carolyn Walters
Indiana University
Bloomington, IN 46405
cwalters@Indiana.edu

Leslie Warren
Moraine Valley Community
College
Palos Hills, IL 60465
warren@morainevalley.edu

Kappa Waugh
Vassar College
Poughkeepsie, NY 2604-0020
kawaugh@Vassar.edu

David Weeks
Winthrop University
Rock Hill, SC 29733
weeksd@Winthrop.edu

Leslie Weinberger
Edgewood College
Madison, WI 53711
lweinberger@edgewood.edu

Sally Weston
University of Michigan
Ann Arbor, MI 48109-4811
sweston@umich.edu

Chris Wettstein
Valencia Community College
Orlando, FL 32825
cwettstein@valenciacc.edu

Diana Wheeler
University of Wisconsin-
Madison
Madison, WI 53706
dwheeler@engr.wisc.edu

Susan Barnes Whyte
Linfield College
McMinnville, OR 97128
swhyte@linfield.edu

Kathleen Wiechelman
University of Alaska Southeast
Ketchikan, AK 99901
khkjb@uas.Alaska.edu

Carolyn Willis
East Carolina University
Greenville, NC 27858
willisc@mail.ecu.edu

Amy Witzel
Dartmouth College
Hanover, NH
witzel@Dartmouth.edu

Kristin Woodward
Cardinal Stritch University
Milwaukee, WI 53217
kmwoodward@stritch.edu

Sandra Yaegle
Regent University
Virginia Beach, VA 23464
sandyae@regent.edu

BethAnn Zambella
Wellesley College
Wellesley, MA
bzambell@wellesley.edu

Lucinda Zoe
Hostos Community College
Bronx, NY 10451
lzoe@hostos.cuny.edu

PRESENTERS ADDRESSES

Jeanine Akers
University of Memphis
126 Ned R. McWherter Library
Memphis, TN 38152-6500

Susan Ariew
University Libraries (0434)
Virginia Tech
P.O. Box 9001
Blacksburg, VA 24062-9001

Priscilla Atkins
Hope College
Van Wylen Library
P.O. Box 9012
Holland, MI 49422

Betsy Baker
1236 Judson Ave.
Evanston, IL 60201

Pam Baker
California State University at
Monterey Bay
University Library
100 Campus Center Dr.
Seaside, CA 93955

Lisa Barnett
Ball State University
Bracken Library
Muncie, IN 47306

Melissa Browne
Ball State University
Bracken Library
Muncie, IN 47306

Elizabeth Burge
Faculty of Education
University of New Brunswick
P.O. Box 4400
Fredericton, New Brunswick
E3B 5A3 Canada

Penny Burge
Virginia Tech
314 E. Eggleston (0302)
Blacksburg, VA 24062

Robert Burger
University of Illinois at Urbana-
Champaign
246A University Library
1408 W. Gregory Dr.
Urbana, IL 61801

Ruth Connell
Valparaiso University
Moellering Library
Valparaiso, IN 46383

Wendy L. Crist
Web Services Librarian
Dean B. Ellis Library
Arkansas State University
State University, AR 72467

Charlotte Cubbage
Northwestern University
University Library
1970 Campus Drive
Evanston, IL 60208-2300

Celita DeArmond
San Antonio College Library
1001 Howard St.
San Antonio, TX 78212

Angela Dunnington
Southeastern Louisiana
University
345 Sims Library
Hammond, LA 70402

Pamela Lee Enrici
University of Minnesota, Duluth
416 Library Dr.
Duluth, MN 55812-3001

Kyzyl Fenno-Smith
California State University at
Hayward
University Library
25800 Carlos Bee Blvd.
Hayward, CA 94542-3052

Jill Gremmels
Wartburg College
Vogel Library
100 Wartburg Blvd.
P.O. Box 1003
Waverly, IA 50677

Donna J. Gunter
University of North Carolina,
Charlotte
Atkins Library
9201 University City Blvd.
Charlotte, NC 28223-0001

Kathlene Hanson
California State University at
Monterey Bay
University Library
100 Campus Center Dr.
Seaside, CA 93955

Katherine Harris
Ball State University
Bracken Library
Muncie, IN 47306

Lisa Janicke Hinchliffe
University of Illinois at Urbana-
Champaign
246A University Library
1408 W. Gregory Dr.
Urbana, IL 61801

Sandra Hochstein
Douglas College Library
P.O. Box 2503
New Westminster, BC
V3L 5B2 Canada

Elizabeth O. Hutchins
St. Olaf College
305 Rolvaag Library
Northfield, MN 55057

Amanda Izenstark
University of Rhode Island
University Libraries
15 Lippitt Rd.
Kingston, RI 02881-2011

Melissa Kalpin
University of Minnesota
180 Wilson Library
Minneapolis, MN 55455

Pam Kessinger
Reference Librarian
Rock Creek Library
Portland Community College
PO Box 19000
Portland, OR 97280

Jim Kinnie
University of Rhode Island
University Libraries
15 Lippitt Rd.
Kingston, RI 02881-2011

Janice M. Krueger
University of the Pacific
University Library
3601 Pacific Avenue
Stockton, CA 95211

Carrie Kruse
University of Wisconsin at
Madison
College Library
3219 Helen C. White Hall
600 N. Park St.
Madison, WI 53706

Miriam Laskin
Hostos Community
CollegeLibrary
475 Grand Concourse
Bronx, NY 10451

Abbie Loomis
University of Wisconsin at
Madison
443D Memorial Library
728 State St
Madison, WI 53706

Mary C. MacDonald
University of Rhode Island
University Libraries
15 Lippitt Rd.
Kingston, RI 02881-2011

Jeanette McVeigh
University of the Sciences
in Philadelphia
J.W. England Library
600 South 43rd St.
Philadelphia, PA 19104-4495

Angela Megaw
Gainesville College
Hosch Library
P.O. Box 1358
Gainesville, GA 30503

Trisha Mileham
Valparaiso University
Moellering Library
Valparaiso, IN 46383

James L. Pence
Pacific Lutheran University
Office of the Provost
Tacoma, WA 98447-0003

Bruce Pencek
University Libraries (0434)
Virginia Tech
P.O. Box 9001
Blacksburg, VA 24062-9001

Vivienne Piroli
Reference/Instruction Librarian
Beatley Library
Simmons College
300 The Fenway
Boston, MA 02115

Randall Schroeder
Wartburg College
Vogel Library
100 Wartburg Blvd.
P.O. Box 1003
Waverly, IA 50677

Martha C. Smith
Elmira College
Gannett-Tripp Library
One Park Place
Elmira, NY 14901

Sarah Statz
Madison Public Library
733 N. High Point Rd.
Madison, WI 53717

Eileen M. Stec, MS, MSW
Rutgers University
Mabel Smith Douglass Library
8 Chapel Drive
New Brunswick, NJ 08901

Michelle Twait
Gustavus Adolphus College
Folke Bernadotte Memorial
Library
800 West College Avenue
St. Peter, MN 56082

Jana Varlejs, PhD
Rutgers SCILS
4 Huntington Street
New Brunswick, NJ 08901-
1071

Jerilyn Veldof
Director of Undergraduate
Initiatives
University of Minnesota
Libraries
180 Wilson Library
309 19th Avenue South
Minneapolis, MN 55455

Dale Vidmar
Southern Oregon University
Library
1250 Siskiyou Blvd
Ashland, OR 97520

Sally Weston
Kresge Business Admin. Library
University of Michigan
Ann Arbor, MI 48109-4811

Susan Barnes Whyte
Linfield College
College Libraries
900 SE Baker Street
McMinnville, OR 97128

BethAnn Zambella
Wellesley College
College Library
106 Central Street
Wellesley, MA 02481

Lucinda Zoe
Hostos Community College
Library
475 Grand Concourse
Bronx, NY 10451